Merry

Happy New Year

A. Lincoln

## Abraham Lincoln

From negative No. 2 of the Hesler photograph made
at Chicago in 1860.

There were four negatives made by Hesler in Chicago
in June, 1860, soon after Lincoln was nominated
for the presidency. Numbers three and four
were burnt in the Chicago fire. Number two,
herewith shown, is the most perfect of any photographic representation of Lincoln, and more
satisfactory, to those who knew him intimately
previous to 1861, than any other photograph
ever made of him.

## Abraham Lincoln

From negative No. 2 of the Hesler photograph made
at Chicago in 1860.

There were four negatives made by Hesler in Chicago
in June, 1860, soon after Lincoln was nominated
for the presidency. Numbers three and four
were burnt in the Chicago fire. Number two,
herewith shown, is the most perfect of any photographic representation of Lincoln, and more
satisfactory, to those who knew him intimately
previous to 1861, than any other photograph
ever made of him.

The Lincoln Memorial, Washington, D.C.
Designed by Henry Bacon.

The Lincoln Memorial, Washington, D. C.
Designed by Henry Bacon.

# Abraham Lincoln

# The
# First American

# Personal Recollections of
# Abraham Lincoln

By
### Henry B. Rankin

With an Introduction by
### Joseph Fort Newton
Author of "Lincoln and Herndon," etc.

Youth longs and manhood strives,
But age remembers.

HOLMES : *The Iron Gate*

*With Portraits in Photogravure*

### G. P. Putnam's Sons
New York and London
The Knickerbocker Press
1916

The Knickerbocker Press, New York

# Introduction

He knew to bide his time,
And can his fame abide,
Still patient in his faith sublime,
  Till the wise years decide.
Great captains with their guns and drums,
Disturb our judgment of the hour,
But at last Silence comes;
These are all gone, and, standing like a tower,
Our children shall behold his fame,
The kindly-earnest, brave, foreseeing man,
Sagacious, patient, dreading praise, not blame,
New birth of our new soil, the first American.

JAMES RUSSELL LOWELL.

# INTRODUCTION

LINCOLN lore has become so rich in recent years, and so voluminous withal, that he who would add to it must needs show cause why his book should be read. And yet, in spite of all that has been written, it cannot be said that we yet have a thoroughly satisfactory interpretation of the life and work and character of our First American. A few have had the necessary knowledge and sympathy, but their literary power has not always been adequate. Others have written well, but they have failed of insight and understanding. In the meantime the volume of facts, impressions, and reminiscences increases, and by assembling items from a variety of sources we are coming to a composite conception of our prophet-President that is at once vivid and satisfying.

The present volume unites an intimate knowledge combined with unusual gifts of insight and expression, and is more than justified, not only by the facts which it adds to our information, but also, and much more perhaps, by its portrayal of the background of the life of Lincoln, the atmosphere and environment of his early years, and the development of his unique personality and genius. It is exactly what its title describes, not a biography, still less a history, but a book of reminiscences; a series of musing memories and flash-light pictures, often discursive but always illuminating, recorded by a man who, in the gloaming of his years, would fain add a touch to the portrait of a great Soul whom he revered in youth and whose memory is a precious possession. If time has softened the outlines of the scenes of other years, it has also brought that deeper interpretation which is a reward of the "on-coming evening and the star-crowned night."

For this service the author was singularly fitted, both by opportunity and by temperament. He was one of the "Lincoln boys" who grew up in the valley of the Sangamon, before the sturdy race of pioneers had disappeared, and his pictures of that now vanished time help us to see Lincoln in the setting of his life, amidst the scenery which wrought itself into his mind, and the hardy, wholesome, self-reliant folk who left their impress upon his character and his career. So studied, he is seen as indeed a "new birth of our new soil,"

typical of the best life of the older West; one of the
common people, yet towering above them in his
unconscious greatness—the son of a pioneer whose
story is the history of his nation in its heroic
epoch. Lincoln is hard to know in any event,
the despair of every artist because he was so
unlike any model; nor can we know him at all
unless we see him amid the scenes which these
pages paint with such vivid stroke, reproducing
the very atmosphere which surrounded his early
manhood.

Moreover, the author was for several years a
student in the Lincoln and Herndon law-office,
where he enjoyed the intimate fellowship of two
strong men who were by nature as well as by
political habit gracious to young men and who
were at once his teachers and his friends. Naturally, a lad fresh from college would be a keen
observer of the student-life of the two men with
whose ideals he was in sympathy, and he took
careful note of their methods of work and processes
of thought. He found the deep and quiet mind
of Lincoln contrasting vividly with the swift and
facile intellect of his partner whose conversation
was so picturesque and many-coloured. Lincoln
was a man to know whom was a kind of religion,
and it is not strange that his nobility of character,

his force of intellect, his innate dignity and fineness of nature, his humour and his sadness, and even his moods and habits of life, left a profound impression upon his young student. If, in recording his memories, the art of the author does not equal his opportunity, it is because there was something in Lincoln which no art may ever hope to capture; a blend of power and pathos, of dignity and simplicity, of love and logic and laughter, with much else which all men feel but which no one can describe. A man of exquisite spirituality, he brings to his pages a keen, discriminating insight, joined with a great veneration, and his vision will have to be reckoned with in the final account of a life which, were it not a matter of history, would be regarded as one of the great romances of the world.

About such a man there is a certain mystery, a strange, pervasive appeal to all that is native and noble within us, a sanctity half tragic and half triumphant; and it is no wonder that to a man who felt the spell of his personality, and saw him in his great hours of vision and conquest, all portraits of Lincoln are unsatisfactory. Albeit his pictures show us a face marked with the seams of hard struggle, the light of a high resolve, the touch of an infinite pity; its features written all

over with the hieroglyphics of sorrow, yet having
lines where smiles fell asleep when they were
weary; neither rudely masculine nor softly femi-
nine, but which reminds us always of the mother
and the boy behind the man. · Whoso will study
that face, in the light of the following pages, will
learn not only what America is, what it has cost,
and what it prophesies; but something of what
life means, of what lies hidden in the souls of the
lowliest—aye, something of the cost of all progress
and the majesty of noble human living.

With due regard for the humour of Lincoln,
so rich and often so rollicking, and in no wise
forgetful of the refinements of his sympathies, the
author makes us feel that he was, first of all, a
great thinker. Pledged as he felt himself to be
to the moral verities, his mind was as relentless
in its search for truth as his heart was limitless
in its charity. Into the hard problems of his day
he drilled with patient, pondering, penetrating
thought, and not in vain, though his ultimate
solution was altered by events. His deep musings
on the ways of God, on the souls of men, on the
principles of justice and the laws of liberty, bore
fruit in exalted character and exact insight. Hence
a style of speech remarkable for its lucidity,
directness, and forthright power, with no waste

of words, tinged always by a temperament at once elusive and alluring, which Bryce compares to the forthdarting speech of Bismarck without his harshness, and to the weighty eloquence of Cromwell without his haziness. The scene of the speech at Petersburg in 1856, here rescued from oblivion, is an example alike of his power of words and his mastery of assemblies. No voice speaking in the last century uttered words so much like the mighty words that speak to us out of the old Hebrew centuries, and which still march to and fro in the hearts of men.

All just men, all chivalrous men, will be deeply grateful to the writer of these reminiscences for the gracious and revealing light in which he has portrayed Mary Todd Lincoln, so long misunderstood, so often misrepresented. If she was not a favourite as "the first lady of the land"—lacking that indefinable quality which in her husband so appealed to the popular imagination—surely that was no reason why her less fortunate traits should be magnified to the neglect of others not only more numerous, but lovely and winning. There is nothing in our history more unmanly, more cruel, more devoid of every fine instinct, than the treatment of that noble woman by a prying,

gossiping press, which pursued her even into her
lonesome late years. Here at last is the testimony
of one who knew her, bearing witness to her
worth as a woman, her loyalty as a wife, and
her service to her country, and bespeaking for her
—what will not always be denied—a place beside her husband in the grateful and venerative
memory of the Republic.

Hardly less valuable is the study of what religion meant to Lincoln, about which so much
has been written and so little truth told. No
page in this book of memories is more unforgetable
than that on which the author tells, with such
delicate taste and tenderness, of a quiet talk
between his mother and Lincoln regarding religion
during the campaign of 1847. It brings back
across the years not only the atmosphere of the
evening, and the pensive, half-sad mood of the
man, but something of the spirit of the sweet
woman to whom he confided his perplexities of
faith. That statement, so Lincoln-like in its
spirit and style, is the absolute truth as to
his actual attitude toward the difficulties which
beset every thinking man. Whatever he may
have lacked of the letter which killeth, surely,
if ever of anyone, we may say of Lincoln that he

was ruled by the spirit of the Master, whose he was, and whom he served, equally in private life and public office.

No further word need be added to a book which speaks so well for itself, except to say that its total impression is such a sense of the living Lincoln, of his growth and ripening of character, of his commanding personality and genius, as is to be found hardly anywhere else. As one of the few remaining friends who knew him personally during the early years of his mature manhood, the author has rendered a real service not only to Lincoln, but to the city in which he lived; and his example should bestir the citizens of Springfield to be faithful and care-taking guardians of every place associated with the memory of the greatest man who has lived with us and died among us, whose life is a perpetual legacy of inspiration, and whose character embodied, as no other in our history, the mighty and tender spirit of America.

JOSEPH FORT NEWTON.

CEDAR RAPIDS, IOWA,
January, 1916.

# CONTENTS

# ILLUSTRATIONS

*Henry B. Rankin*

# Personal Mention

O Captain! My Captain! Rise up and hear the
bells;
Rise up—for you the flag is flung—for you the bugle
trills;
For you bouquets and ribbon'd wreaths—for you the
shores a-crowding;
For you they call, the swaying mass, their eager
faces turning;
Hear, Captain! dear Father!
This arm beneath your head;
It is some dream that on the deck
You've fallen cold and dead.

WALT WHITMAN.

# Personal Recollections of Abraham Lincoln

## I

### PERSONAL MENTION

*Some Local Mention*

I MET Abraham Lincoln for the first time in the Menard County Circuit Court, at Petersburg, Illinois. By favour of my father, who was then sheriff of Menard County, I was allowed for several years to stop school during court term and act as messenger boy in the court room during the court's sessions.

Thenceforward, for more than a dozen years, I met Lincoln often. During the four years preceding his election to the Presidency I had close relations with the law-office of Lincoln and Herndon in connection with some of their legal, political, and literary activities. Now in my

3

seventy-ninth year I recall those events with no
little degree of personal pleasure.    Out of my
memories I have been urged to write concerning
some of Lincoln's characteristics; of persons with
whom he associated; and of incidents and scenes of
his life up to the time when he left Springfield
for Washington to occupy so prominent a part in
the making of our Nation's history, and to achieve
for all future ages a world-wide and abiding fame
as the most masterful of men.

Recollections of events and personal affairs
after half a century, though drawn from the most
sensitive memory, and most conscientiously recorded, cannot but be fragmentary.    We cannot
live over again our past with complete fidelity and
harmony as to all details, try we ever so sincerely.
These chapters claim to be nothing more than
an unstudied record of some persons and events
that may give glimpses affording a more correct
revealing of parts of the early history of Abraham
Lincoln.

What I shall relate will be told in the informal
way in which I would talk to a friend who came
from time to time asking me to take him by
memory's light through some of the hours and
days and years of more than half a century ago.

As I pass from one chapter to another, my pen will not be guided by any systematic order of time or coherence of parts. These pages are intended to record some observations, not merely of Lincoln himself, but also of those friends who, like St. Paul's, "were a help," and timely aids in the developing and formation of the unique personality of President Lincoln.

I have tried, when relating incidents gleaned through personal contact, to keep the personal pronoun, as far as possible, out of my paragraphs, wishing the reader to see Lincoln and a few of those friends who "were a help" to him, and not the writer. From this limitation I have departed consciously only when, in my office as reporter, those memory flash-lights necessarily included me in the situations narrated.

The story of those days of the period I write about, that were so fruitfully formative in the character building of this most remarkable man, has already been told over and over; in part wisely and well; in larger part in a manner inaccurate and misleading to the historical research of the future. It is yet too early to expect an adequate biography of Lincoln. We are yet too near to him in time to get the true perspective; to trace the operation of the forces, internal and

external, that contributed to his development,
or to compare him with the rest of earth's im-
mortals. But some day, after all have passed
away who knew Lincoln, and that staging of
peculiar personalities and events, both simple and
tragic, that formed his environment, some master historian will gather the partial and contradictory records left by his contemporaries, purge
them of falsehood and caricature, and from the
material remaining will write upon the unfading
pages of history the true character story of Abraham Lincoln. To contribute in some measure to
this result has been my motive in writing these
pages.

In this connection I wish to further qualify
these musing memories by a foreword of even
more personal and intimate explanation. The
interest and confidence Lincoln favoured me with
in the years of my youth and inexperience, when
I was privileged to be near him, was not because
of my personality or merits. I met his influence
favoured with a family background of many years,
through the active Whig partisanship Lincoln
had with my father. Also, with a much longer
and the more intimate connections of his life at
Salem with my mother and her father's family,
who were settlers there many years before Lincoln.

It was at her home Lincoln met Ann Rutledge. To that home she had come during that acquaintance as a scholar, to pursue the preparatory studies that would enable her to enter the Jacksonville Academy as then planned.

I appreciated at the time that Lincoln became interested in my welfare, as fully as my inexperienced youth then gave me capacity for; that his consideration and confidences thereafter bestowed on me were given, as I have before mentioned, because of my parents' interest in his earlier years of stress and trials at New Salem. More especially so were the associations that had united through so many of those years, my mother's friendship and interests with him, in connection with his acquaintance with the sweet and winsome southern maiden and its ripening through those all too brief months of courtship, into the betrothal that followed; and later through the bitter ones of readjustment he went through, after the death of Ann Rutledge.

It was out of these associations and largely because of the sweet and bitter memories and disciplines in the Salem years of Lincoln's life, that brought me near him and made possible the story it is my privilege to now recall and leave in this record. My personality in what I relate is of no consequence. To have known intimately and to write correctly of Abraham Lincoln, dwarfs my little life. There are, however, certain important parts of his life and of influences that were strong there in the development of the inner and greater Lincoln, that have never all been told. Some of those told are sadly defective. There are slurs and caricatures, luminous with their distortions, that I wish to see removed as excrescences from many of the so-called "accepted historical accounts" of the personality of Lincoln; and other corrections, even more especially due, to the memory of Mrs. Lincoln. My interest and purpose lies in a desire to portray correctly, and understandingly, the humanly quality of them both, differing as widely as they did with each other, so that their strong personalities may be seen in history a little more clearly than now, in the goodness, the charity, and with the clarity of judgment their lives merited.

To return to the first meeting which took place in 1846, ten years after Lincoln had left Salem and had begun the practice of law in Springfield, as the partner of Major John T. Stuart. My recollection of his personal appearance, as I then saw him, forms a picture quite different from that

of 1854 and up to 1860, as shown in photographs
of the later period. At this earlier date he was
in his physical prime. He had the well-developed
muscles and the fresh colour of one leading an
active out-of-door life and overflowing with
physical vigour and health. The angular form,
the long sallow face and swarthy complexion of
later years do not come back to me out of the
sixty-nine years ago of boyhood memory printed
there in 1846. This period was four years after
his marriage to Miss Mary Todd, and he was at
that time, in personal appearance, the best-looking
lawyer attending the Petersburg Circuit Court.

I recall Lincoln's manner towards the people
whom he met in that court room, as being quite
in contrast with that of other visiting attorneys.
His was the manner of one who had come home.
Former friends and neighbours met him with a
cordiality of welcome as one among and of them
still. He was now a rising lawyer and politician
visiting former intimate friends, and they showed
pride in his success by the hearty manner of their
greetings.

Notwithstanding Lincoln's pronounced Whig
principles, and the extreme political prejudices
existing between the Whig and Democratic parties of that time, his personality, wit, humour,

and side-splitting stories held the hearts of the
people of Menard County, irrespective of party
lines, as they had fifteen years before, when he
made his first printed appeal to them on March
9, 1832, as a candidate for the legislature, and
received the entire vote of the Salem-Petersburg
precinct, with only three exceptions.

An easy and approachable bearing toward all
classes was a strong characteristic of Lincoln's
manner.  At the bar, with his lawyer friends, toward the judge, in his considerate examination
of witnesses, or in the selection of jurors, his placid
and even temperament was equally apparent.
These manners were not for the court room only.
His tavern chats with attorney and county friends
showed the same even courtesy to all.

Among these tavern friends in Petersburg at
that time were some men of strong and peculiar
characteristics.  None of these was more striking
than William Engle of Sugar Grove—farmer,
country merchant, Disciples' "Campbellite"
preacher, Democratic politician and member of the
State Legislature—acting in all these capacities
at the same time.  He was a fine conversationalist,
with infinite stores of wit and anecdote.  During
one of the earlier court terms at Petersburg, in

a meeting with Lincoln and their mutual friends at the tavern, they continued a remarkable bout of story-telling and political discussions throughout the entire night, holding all the crowd of mutual friends until breakfast call the next morning.

There was Pantier of Sandridge—the farmer, saw-mill owner, and fortune-teller—a crude forerunner of the Christian Scientist faith-cure healer of later times. There were Godby, Smoot, Rankin, Hill, Harris, the Greens and Armstrongs, with a dozen or two more, similar representatives of those early pioneers, not to omit Menter Graham,—who was always in Petersburg through court weeks,—a typical old-time school-teacher of the best educated class. He it was who introduced Lincoln to Calhoun and Stuart, and this led, first, to Lincoln's surveying experience with the former, and finally to his study of law and entrance into Springfield as a law partner of the latter.

It was Menter Graham who gave Lincoln, while living in Salem, private lessons in surveying, geometry, and English grammar, and who first opened to him the way to an acquaintance with the best English writers; for, though Graham's library was small,—fewer than fifty volumes,—it contained some of the best of English literature, as well as choice translations from the best writers of past literary ages.

In these earlier days of his law practice and as a rising politician, Lincoln was, as I have remarked, the most approachable and magnetic of conversationalists. The individuals mentioned were not typical of Petersburg only, though Lincoln's personal familiarity during earlier acquaintance at Salem made him more easily at home there than elsewhere. He met at all the other county seats within the law circuits over which he travelled, the same early settler's class of folk—in Mason, Tazewell, Peoria, Logan, McLean, Champaign, Christian, and his home county of Sangamon, as well as in his occasional visits into adjoining circuits for special law pleadings or campaign speaking. Association with these common people, of whom Lincoln, later in life, said the Lord certainly thought most of, because he had made so many of them, proved to be a more resourceful training for the peculiar work the future had in store for him, when the days were ripe for service by a master of men, than any scholastic education which he could have acquired in any of the schools. Never did a more receptive scholar attend any school, and his scholarship acquired there remained a life-long asset. Among the common-sense pioneers where his earlier years were spent, he acquired that simple, direct manner of speech and the every-day common-sense philosophy which, in the supreme crisis of our Nation's life, made him the man of the hour,—a most resourceful and masterful leader of men.

# Lincoln's Easy and Friendly Manner

Lincoln was a plain man of the people. He had a face that disarmed suspicion, which inspired confidence, which confirmed good-will. He had a strong sense of duty, which it was easy for him to obey. He had a vast good nature which made him tolerant and accessible to all. This middle-class country had got a middle-class president at last, in manners and sympathies, but not in powers, for his powers were superior. This man grew according to the need; he mastered the problem of the day. In four years— four years of battle days—his endurance, his fertility of resource, his magnanimity, were sorely tried and never found wanting. There by his courage, his humanity, his justice, his even temper, his fertile counsel, he stood,—a heroic figure in the centre of a heroic epoch.

RALPH WALDO EMERSON.

## LINCOLN'S EASY AND FRIENDLY MANNER

DURING one of the sessions of the Menard County Circuit Court of the period mentioned, an incident occurred that furnishes an illustration of Lincoln's easy manner with his former country-folk friends around Salem, even under trying circumstances, and that is worth reciting.

Political "stump speaking" was not then put aside during court terms, but, on the contrary, was promoted by them. A platform had been erected in one corner of the court-house yard, for use during an autumn's session of that Circuit Court, and was being used alternately by Whig and Democratic speakers at the noon recess, or in the afternoons and evenings after adjournment of court.

On the day referred to, the judge announced, at the close of the morning session, that court would not convene again until "about three o'clock." It was understood, without the saying, that this concession was made to give opportunity

for a platform speech. After dinner, the people
from all directions began to assemble in the court-
house yard near the platform. The latter was
a crude affair, yet of generous size and height.
Two rude bench seats, made from slabs, extended its full length at the rear. No table
or board stood on the front of the platform to
hold the "paper-canned" thoughts in manuscript such as some present-day speakers require.
Rude board steps at each end led up to the
platform.

After dinner, on the day referred to, the judge,
lawyers and neighbouring "Squires," and "principal citizens" began filling these seats in anticipation of a speech. Presently, from all sides arose
the cry of "Lincoln!" "Lincoln!"—"Abe Lincoln!" Lincoln, who was never in any haste to
begin a speech, arose leisurely from his seat on
the platform, took off his tall hat, shook down its
contents of letters, papers, and clippings from
newspapers, with which it was always partly
filled, and stooping down, placed it carefully
under the bench on the platform where he
had been sitting, and then turning, faced the
crowd around the platform and began his
speech.

A few minutes later, there appeared in front

of the platform, just beneath where Lincoln was standing, James Pantier, resting his folded arms on the outer edge of the platform. There he stood with face upturned at an angle, so that he could look up the nearly seven feet into the speaker's face. His hat was pushed back to the greatest angle possible, on the back of his head and shoulders; and such a hat! All semblance of rim or crown had been soaked and pressed out of it by rains and snows from without, and by the heat and moisture of the head on which it now rested like a huge funnel-shaped hopper. His clothing would have baffled the descriptive powers of a modern society editor. The hunting shirt was made of home-woven blue jeans, trimmed across the shoulders with buckskin fringe; the sailor collar, wide and overlapping in front, fringed also with long buckskin lacings, most practically designed to fold over the head in storms of wind, rain, and snow; trousers of home-woven, bark-coloured jeans, faced above and below across the knee with buckskin—too short at the ankles by many inches, and showing feet shod with heavy boots foxy-red by long tramps on hunting trips through the wild prairies of blue-stem grasses and timber undergrowths.

Thus clad and poised, for several minutes stood

Jimmie Pantier — hunter, trapper, faith-doctor, saw-mill owner and farmer of Sandridge; one of the oldest settlers there, and among the first of Lincoln's friends to assist him financially when he was sorely pressed by debts at Salem, and at whose home of plenty Lincoln had been often entertained on his surveying tramps, or hunting excursions through Sandridge and Salt Creek bottoms.

At length, failing to attract Lincoln's notice, his clear treble voice piped out, "Howdy Abe! Howdy Abe!" — and yet even the third time, "Howdy Abe!"—before Lincoln, who had ceased speaking, perceived where the call came from. Then looking down, he cordially exclaimed: "Why, how are you, Uncle Jimmie!" and, stooping, clasped Pantier's hand, shaking it heartily, and meantime, half bent, still holding Pantier by the hand, led him slowly along the front edge of the platform to the steps at the end, then up these and across to the seat he had vacated himself a few minutes before, where he seated the old pioneer, and then returning to his former position on the platform, he took up the line of his argument where it had been interrupted, and proceeded as if no pause had been made.

Pantier meanwhile, after being seated, removed

the remarkable hat, twisting it about as if uncertain what to do with it, until, noticing Mr.
Lincoln's hat under the seat, he rolled his up and
thrust the crude bunch into that, and then settling
himself comfortably back in the seat with Judge
Treat on one side and the Hon. B. S. Edwards
on the other, fixed his eyes and attention on
Lincoln as he stood speaking in front of him.

[ But he acted as though ill at ease. There was
something irrepressible in his manner, something
that must come out. He had come to town
that day to see Lincoln and hear him speak,
and he wished to treat him with all possible
courtesy at his former home. He had once before
this visited Springfield to see Lincoln and his
family in their home, where Mrs. Mary Lincoln
had royally entertained and enjoyed the quaint
old character, thus winning this simple-hearted
man's interest and love forever. He now showed
by nervous squirmings about on his seat that
something was unfinished. At length the treble
voice piped out: "Abe! Abe! I forgot to ax
you about how Mary and the babies were!"

Lincoln again stopped, turned half-way around
toward Pantier, and in a low gentle voice replied:
"All well, when I left them at Springfield yester-
day morning, Uncle Jimmie; all very well, thank

you!"—and resumed his speech as if nothing
unusual or private had again interrupted him.

This quality of mind on the part of Lincoln is
illustrated further by an incident that occurred
while he was living at Salem more than ten years
before.  I repeat it as told by one who was
present: Lincoln was on one of his frequent
visits to the home of Armstrong, whose son, years
later, he cleared of the charge of murder in a trial
before the Mason County Circuit Court,—which
incident Edward Eggleston has woven into one
of his novels.  At the dinner, Mrs. Armstrong
had placed by Lincoln's plate a large quart-bowl
of butter-milk, knowing his fondness for that
beverage.  In some way, during the dinner's
progress, Lincoln was unfortunate enough to let
the huge bowl slip from his hand, spilling all the
contents upon the table.

Mrs. Armstrong was quite active in repairing
the damage to the spread caused by this deluge,
but even more concerned to put her guest at his
ease after such a mishap, and very effusively
begged Lincoln to "not mind it the least bit!—
it will be all right in just a minute!"  Lincoln,
having mopped up with the towel brought him
by Mrs. Armstrong that part of the milky overflow

that had reached his personal apparel, leaned back in his chair and stretching the moist towel across both knees said, with one of his most expressive gestures: "Well, Aunt Hannah, if you don't mind it, neither will I."

# Lincoln's Mental Resources and Peculiar Consciousness

The colour of the ground was in him, the red earth;
The smack and tang of elemental things:
The rectitude and patience of the cliff;
The goodwill of the rain that loves all leaves;
The friendly welcome of the wayside well;
The courage of the bird that dares the sea;
The gladness of the wind that shakes the corn;
The mercy of the snow that hides all scars;
The secrecy of streams that make their way
Beneath the mountain and the rifted rock;
The underlying justice of the light
That gives as freely to the shrinking flower
As to the great oak flaring to the wind—
To the grave's low hill as to the Matterhorn
That shoulders out the sky.

EDWIN MARKHAM.

## III

LINCOLN'S MENTAL RESOURCES AND PECULIAR
CONSCIOUSNESS

*Advice to Young Voter*

THE law-office of Lincoln and Herndon at
Springfield was practically the Republican head-
quarters through the Frémont campaign of 1856,
and often presented scenes of sharp discussions
between friends of Frémont and the supporters
of the other two presidential candidates in that
campaign. Lincoln was especially interested in
reaching young men who would cast their first
vote that year.

One of these, with several young friends who
had called at the office, was strenuously advocating
the election of Mr. Fillmore. Particular emphasis
was placed by him in his argument with Mr.
Herndon, and cross-firing with several others
present, on the conservative qualities of Mr.
Fillmore, and especially the "goodness" in that
candidate. Lincoln had been silently writing at
the office table during the conversation, and the

subject had been pretty well threshed out at the time when Lincoln took up his hat to leave the office. He paused a moment beside this young man whom he had known from boyhood, and said:

"You are in favour of the election of Mr. Fillmore because you consider him the best—the 'Good Man' in the canvass—but you concede that his election appears now to be practically improbable, and becoming daily more and more discouraging?"

"Yes, sir, I do, but I shall vote for Mr. Fillmore, the best man, no matter what his prospects of election may be."

"Now, my young friend," replied Lincoln in his bland voice and very deliberately, "I think you are making a mistake in voting for Mr. Fillmore because of his goodness. You can do something so much better. There is One whose goodness and greatness all agree far exceed Mr. Fillmore's and, in fact, all others that could be named. No one will question this; no one doubts it. So on the 6th of next November I advise you to go to the polls and vote for Almighty God for President. He is unquestionably the best being who exists. There is practically as much chance of electing God Almighty President of the United States at this time, as Millard Fillmore!"

Waiting for no reply, and quite hastily, amid
the silence that settled over us all, Lincoln passed
out of the office and down the stairway to the
street.

I may add that several days after, this young
man came again into the office, exclaiming as he
entered: "Mr. Lincoln, I have concluded not to
throw away my first vote on what is not a votable
issue. Neither shall I follow your suggestion of
voting for God. I will vote for John C. Frémont
on the live, practical issues before us at this
election."

## On God's Side

This peculiar power of stating the moral and
practical issues of a subject was often used by
Lincoln in his presidential years with telling force
and effect.

I will give one instance, as it was told me by a
friend present at the time. A delegation called
on Lincoln to represent the ideas prevailing
in their section as to the conduct of the war.
They had read to him a lengthy appeal that
some things be done immediately, and that
certain other policies be discontinued. Lincoln
had answered in a few well-timed and careful
sentences, and had just taken in his hands the

document which the delegates wished him to consider more fully.   One of the delegates came closer to Lincoln, and, in a low voice, said:

"I hope, Mr. Lincoln, that God is on our side!"

To this Lincoln replied, almost abruptly: "That does not concern me!"

The startled delegate responded:—"What!   It does not concern you, Mr. Lincoln, to have God on our side?"

"No, sir," replied Lincoln, with his most positive emphasis: "what concerns me is that we shall be on God's side!"

This was no play of words.   The thought went to the very centre of the great issues of that hour through which Lincoln was then so anxiously and patiently groping his way; the point at which, in the words of his second inaugural, "as God gives us to see the right" he expected to arrive.

At this early period, Lincoln was wholly unconscious of outward eccentricities and I was told by those near him, that he remained so to the end.   The books which he borrowed from the State or Supreme Court Library in Springfield, he carried to his office tied up in a handkerchief and slung over his shoulder, as if the bundle contained game and he was returning from a

backwoods hunt. We are told that, while President, this was his manner of carrying books and
bulky papers back and forth between the White
House and the War Department.

Lincoln had a nameless, native, inner grace
of deportment that rose above all his crude
physical movements, and this with a mind and
emotions completely free from vanity or self-
consciousness. He felt no embarrassment on
many occasions when the ordinary temperament
would have been completely absorbed in the
confusion of personal emotion and self-conscious
chagrin.

He acquired new personal characteristics as
wider and weightier responsibilities in state and
military affairs pressed upon him; but the old,
and first, remained to the end. And had he
wedded Ann Rutledge, or Miss Owen, or some
"Miss Flora McFlimsey, of Madison Square,"
he would have been, at times, the same perplexing
husband, and often as much of a puzzle or sometimes a despair to them in shaping his domestic
and social habits, as he ever was to Mary Todd
Lincoln and many of her friends.

Lincoln's intellect was equally peculiar in most
ways. Most men forget, or at best have but a

hazy abiding consciousness of their experiences, after passing through and beyond them. With very few are they available immediately when needed. Not so with Lincoln. His whole varied past life was with him an active, vivid, present asset upon which he could depend and draw on effectively at any moment when he needed to use those experiences as resources for any present emergency.

Present day psychologists divide life into the conscious and subconscious. If they be correct, Mr. Lincoln's subconsciousness must have been located in the tips of his fingers and tongue, and not hidden away in the silences of the grey matter of any subconscious existence. He was certainly most alertly conscious in every present moment of all that, in the past, had ever existed in his mental or emotional being.

With this rare endowment, with all his varied experience to draw upon, and with his matured and well-poised common sense to enlighten and guide him, the historian will ever have cause to regret Lincoln's untimely death. Had he been spared to serve his second term as President, the mistakes and miseries of the faulty days of reconstruction would surely have been avoided and the re-establishment of peace and harmony between

North and South would have been greatly hastened.

I cannot pass from these incidents, narrated as partially revealing Mr. Lincoln's peculiar consciousness, without quoting a sentence from a private letter of Margaret Fuller Ossoli. It voices yearnings pathetic to read in the light of more than half a century after its writing. This gifted woman's faith, with all her wondrous vision of the time in which she lived, was almost in eclipse in 1843. After making an extended tour of our country, north, south, east, and west, she was writing from Chicago to a friend. Sitting at an open window on Michigan Avenue late at night overlooking the moon-lit undulations of the lake, she likened to those restless, formless waves the unstable condition of public opinion on the great moral issues then before the country, with no leader,—no masterful First American,— to command and control the events then portending. She said:

When will this country have such a man? It is what she needs; no thin idealist, no coarse realist, but a man whose eye reads the heavens, while his feet step firmly on the ground, and his hands are strong and dexterous for use of human implements.

3

Less than two hundred miles from where she
wrote these lines, the man her prophetic pen
called for was preparing,—all unconsciously,—
for the hour and the mission then impending.
With the last of his three law partners he had just
entered upon the close study of those political
problems that were to arouse the national conscience in antagonism to state rights and property
rights in man.   Seventeen years later the hour
had struck, and the greatest event of the century
was ushered in by the nomination of Abraham
Lincoln at the Republican National Convention
held in the same city, and not far from where
Margaret Fuller uttered that cry in the then
darkened wilderness of unshapened national
opinions.   His "eyes read the heavens," and not
as a "thin idealist, or coarse realist," but "while
his feet step firmly on the ground."

On the long roll of the world's great leaders
were there ever "hands so strong and dexterous
for use of human implements?"

# When Lincoln Swapped Horses

Or thus we know, nor doubt it not,
    The boy he must have been
Whose budding heart bloomed with the thought
    All men are kith and kin—
With love-light in his eyes and shade
    Of prescient tears:—Because
Only of such a boy were made
    The loving man he was.

                        JAMES WHITCOMB RILEY.

# IV

## WHEN LINCOLN SWAPPED HORSES

ANOTHER incident in the life of Lincoln at Salem deserves mention as showing his practical way of meeting the emergency of a stranger in sore need of immediate assistance. So far as I am aware, it was the only time Lincoln ever "swapped horses."

In 1830, Dr. Charles Chandler, with his family arrived in what is now Cass County. He became, from the time of his arrival in that vicinity, a valuable professional addition to the settlement, and his practice extended over a wide area of the country bordering the Sangamon and Illinois river-bottoms and prairie-lands adjacent. Like most early settlers of his time, his finances were limited, and what money he brought with him was expended first for labour to build his cabin; for the purchase of two horses and a few domestic animals; and such medical supplies as his increasing practice required his furnishing to all his patients.

The Doctor selected and had located his new home site on the edge of one of the Sangamon

River bottoms bordered by timbered bluffs. This tract of one hundred and sixty acres combined the three essentials of pioneer life, — timber, water, and good land. He proceeded at once to build a log-cabin near the centre of the tract in order to hold a pre-emptor's right to both eighty acres, and intended to secure government title to it at his later convenience.

In those days, gold and silver coin was very scarce, and what little there was brought into the country quickly found its way into the land-office for entry of land; a system of barter supplying its place in all ordinary transaction. The early settlers therefore usually deferred the entry of the tracts of land which they had selected. They built their house and raised one or more crops, before purchasing at two dollars per acre their deed to the land at the United States land office. An unwritten law among them respecting these "squatter" claims made their occupancy as secure as though they held the Government's deed. To violate these rights was to the early settlers the unpardonable sin.

Dr. Chandler received very little pay for his professional services, other than such products as his patrons could spare. These supplied him with provisions for his own family and for hos-

pitable entertainment of those who travelled that
way.  He had been on his claim but a short time
when a stranger named English came with the
professed intention, as he said, of entering land
and settling there.  Later it was found that he
was the agent of a Philadelphia capitalist who
was investing in lands as a speculation.  Dr.
Chandler entertained him and his horse without charge, and exerted himself to accommo-
date and assist him; telling him all he knew
about the country and its prospects in order
to aid him in selecting a suitable location and
becoming a settler.

English looked around awhile, but could find no
land that pleased him as well as the Doctor's
claim did.  Thereupon Dr. Chandler very generously offered to let him enter one of his eighty-acre
tracts, being half of his own claim.  This did not
seem to entirely satisfy him; but he said he would
go to Springfield, after a few days more of prospect-
ing and enter that if he could do no better.  At
his last interview with Dr. Chandler he showed
a map he carried on which he had marked several
other tracts of land, from which he said he might
make his selection.  After his last dinner with the
Doctor, he left, saying he would pass the night
with another settler on the way to Springfield,

and while on his journey he would look at several other tracts of land.

That afternoon Dr. Chandler had several patients to visit and soon rode away toward Beardstown for such purpose. Near sundown another settler, who lived ten miles from Dr. Chandler and on the road leading to Springfield, came hastily riding up to Dr. Chandler's home enquiring for the Doctor who had not yet returned. He said that he must see the Doctor himself and would wait for his return. It was dark before the Doctor returned to his home. The neighbour then informed him that English, when he passed his place, had declared his intention to be in Springfield the next day and to enter not only the eighty acres the Doctor had offered him, but his entire quarter section; and that he had plenty of land-office money on deposit in Springfield to his credit for this and also for entering other tracts he had marked on his map.

The Doctor was more than surprised, and did not relish the prospect of being ousted from his home in such a summary manner. He did not have enough money in specie to pay the government for the land at what was then the fixed price of two dollars per acre. No time was to be lost. None of his near neighbours had the gold and silver, and there was not time to go to Beardstown and get it there. His financial credit was good, but only gold and silver coin could help him in this emergency. In this quandary he mounted his horse and rode away. No one to whom he applied had any money until he came to the cabin of his friend William McCaulley, who happened to have the amount the Doctor needed. When told by the Doctor in what exigency the treacherous "land shark" English had placed him, he cheerfully loaned him the money.

It was midnight when he got back home. After a hurried lunch he changed his saddle and saddle-bags to the horse Mrs. Chandler had fed ready for his night trip to Springfield, forty miles away. His practice as a physician had extended over half that radius. With his knowledge of how to reduce distance by direct cross-country cuts, and taking the stars to guide his course, he started through the woods and prairies in a direct line, to save distance and cut in ahead of English. The undergrowth and tall grass made the route chosen a fatiguing one for the horse to travel over, under the rapid gait he urged him.

As he struck the Springfield road beyond Salem,

his horse was so thoroughly exhausted that the Doctor dismounted and led him, intending to leave him at the first cabin and to try to reach Springfield afoot. He was yet twelve miles from his journey's end, and the sun more than half way to the meridian. In this extremity, he was overtaken by a young man riding a spirited horse. The stranger reined up, and seeing both the jaded condition of the Doctor's horse, and the evident urgency of the journey, enquired the cause. In a few words the Doctor explained who he was, where he was from, and the great need he had for reaching Springfield before that man English.

The Doctor,—in telling the circumstances to my father afterward,—said that the young man, without a word of reply, dismounted and hastily shortened the stirrup straps on his saddle to suit a pair of shorter legs, then thrust the longest pair of arms he had ever seen under the medicine-saddlebags on the Doctor's saddle and swung them across the saddle of his own spirited steed,—saying as he did so:

"There, Doctor, mount my horse and leave me yours, don't let any grass grow under his feet on the way; leave him at Herndon's stables where I will have yours sometime today for another 'horse swap.' I want to get you and your pill-bags and the specie coin in the land-office ahead of that 'shark.' No thanks;—just go."

The Doctor said he never made a mount so quick in his life as that, and as he took up the reins, the young man gave the steed a sharp slap on the rump that started him down the road in a canter which he did not slacken until he rode up to Herndon's stables in Springfield, an hour before English arrived.

The Springfield land-office records show that the first business transacted June 2, 1832, was the entry by Charles Chandler of the lands on which he had built his cabin. Late the same day, Abraham Lincoln walked up to Herndon's stables leading a forlorn-looking horse. The young man had walked the twelve miles and redeemed his promise to "swap back again."

Later in the month, Dr. Chandler, having received remittances from the East, repaid Mr. McCaulley and made a more leisurely trip to Springfield to enter another forty acres adjoining his other land. Having acquired perfect title to all this land, he concluded to have it surveyed to establish accurately its metes and bounds. Making enquiry for a surveyor to do the work, he learned that a young man residing farther up the river,

at a place called Salem, was a competent surveyor
and thoroughly reliable.   He sent word for him to
come and survey the land.   On his arrival Dr.
Chandler was surprised and gratified to find in
the surveyor the young man who had so quickly
solved the apparently hopeless situation involving
the title to his land.   The fresh horse furnished
by Abraham Lincoln to a stranger enabled him to
beat English to the land-office and thus save his
home.

It was this humanly quality of Lincoln that became his most valuable asset during presidential
years.   During the first fifty years of his life he
was brought into such close and sympathetic
contact with the primitive qualities of so many
classes of people, that he became, humanly, a
better educated man than those around him who
prided themselves on their special literary culture.
His career presents a grave problem to the cultural
civilization, which in recent years is endeavouring,
more than ever before, to develop human quality
by educational systems which, as is shown in
practical results, unfortunately tend more and
more to dwarf the human part in character.

Lincoln knew his countrymen far better than
did any of the learned men who were attached

to his civil and military administration. He knew them because he had been so intimate with them. They had seen problems of life as outside observers and students. He had lived close to the people, and lived his life there as one of them. His was not an expert's knowledge. It was something better. His insight came from a deep sympathy growing out of and up with him in his unusual opportunities for studying men during his first fifty years. Those years had brought him into contact with a wider variety of the typical life of mankind than any other public man of his time.

It was this humanly quality of Abraham Lincoln that enabled him to put himself in the position of others and see as they did, that now crowns him as our First American.

# The Bowling Greene Home

Gave resolution to the ruler's pen;
The books he conned beside the open fire
Made strong the brain which battles could not tire;
The law courts with forensic shift and strife
The ax the gaunt youth swung in dale and glen
Prepared him for that tragedy, his life.
He never held his ways from men apart,
Yet kept a sanctuary in his heart
Whence flowed a stream of love and hope, to bless,
Pure as a clear stream in a wilderness.

HARRY H. KEMP.

The mossy marbles rest
On the lips that he has prest
   In their bloom;
And the names he loved to hear,
Have been carved for many a year,
   On the tomb.

OLIVER WENDELL HOLMES.

# V

## THE BOWLING GREENE HOME

SOME confusion exists as to where the Bowling Greene farmhouse was situated. Lincoln's early life was so closely associated with this home that its exact location is a matter of public interest. The records show that Greene entered one eighty-acre tract in 1829 and the other in 1831. The farm was on the west side of the Sangamon, north of Salem and not south, as Herndon and most others locate it. The tract of land included the timbered bluffs on the west and all the prairie bottom on the east, taking in part of the Sangamon River. Greene built his house at the edge of the bluffs, and fronting the level prairie bottom-lands along the river.

The Springfield road ran north and south in front of the house, which was a comfortable and commodious dwelling for that time. Less than a mile south of the house was the old Salem mill and dam with the village of Salem just above the hill to the west. Orchards and garden came up to

4

the yard on both sides, and back of the house
extended to the edge of the timbered bluffs behind
them.

It was to this quaint and hospitable home that
William G. Greene brought Richard Yates during a vacation of Illinois College in Jacksonville,
where both these young men were students.
Greene wished Yates to see his young friend
Lincoln of whom he had often spoken to him.
They walked across from Greene's father's one
afternoon for that purpose. I shall give Yates's
account of how he met Lincoln this first time.
He related it as an introduction to a speech
he delivered in Springfield twenty-four years
later.

This speech by Yates was delivered in 1860,
fifty-five years ago. Lincoln had been nominated
as the Republican candidate for President. Yates
had been nominated by the same party as their
candidate for Governor of Illinois. There was
being held in Springfield the great ratification
mass-meeting to celebrate the event at Lincoln's
home town. More than a hundred thousand
jubilant citizens participated in the occasion.
When the Jacksonville delegation, headed by
Yates, arrived in Springfield, they passed up-
town from the Wabash Station to the Lincoln

home on Eighth Street. The procession halted
there long enough for Lincoln and Yates to ex-
change hand-shaking greetings amid the deafening huzzahs of the thousands who swarmed
around the Lincoln residence. Yates was then
borne along with the "Wide Awake" escort and the
enthusiastic crowd following them to the Capitol
grounds where he was scheduled to deliver the
main speech of the day.

In his first sentences he told of his first and last
meeting with Lincoln in a manner so felicitous
as to call out more enthusiastic cheering than any
other on that jubilant Springfield day when
enthusiasm knew no limits. He told how Greene
and he when college students on a visit at Greene's
father's twenty-four years before, made a trip
across the country to Bowling Greene's to meet a
young man whom his friend had praised most
volubly to his college mates. They found young
Lincoln, he said, spread out all over the inclined
surface of an outside cellar door, reading a big
book which he afterwards noticed was a volume of Blackstone's *Commentaries.* As they approached, Lincoln began straightening himself
out, and up, to greet them. He saw then what an
amazing amount of outcome there was in the
young fellow who had so completely filled the

whole cellar door and whose tip to tip measurement was nearly seven feet.

That first handshake of Lincoln, Yates continued, was the cordial greeting of one of the most self-poised young men he had ever met, and after a couple of hours' conversation, and the bountiful spread to which Mrs. Greene had insisted on their sitting down, they returned to young William Greene's father's. After that meeting he never again doubted "Billy" when he entertained his fellow-students with boastful accounts of young Lincoln's powers of muscle and of wit.

Yates then went on to say that he had just that morning had another and last hand-clasp with Lincoln. This time it was at his own modest home in this city. This time, as he held that great, big, strong hand, he felt every nerve in his body thrilled with the consciousness that he had at that instant the privilege of shaking hands with the next President of the United States. Here his voice was drowned with such deafening applause that he remained silent until it subsided. When he could make himself heard, he resumed, saying: "At the same moment when I was clasping the hand of the next President of the United States, I felt sure that Mr. Lincoln had the privilege of shaking hands with the next Governor of Illinois."

Lincoln's attendance at the Bowling Greene funeral in 1842 brought out some of his characteristics so vividly that I give the scene as I had it from a granddaughter of Greene's, who was less than eight years old; and two of Lincoln's most intimate friends who were at the funeral. Lincoln was then residing in Springfield, and was a law partner of Stephen T. Logan. Word came to him of Greene's serious illness, and a few hours later of his death. Lincoln at once went out to Mrs. Greene's and remained with her until after tne funeral. Greene was a man of considerable local prominence. He had been a Justice of the Peace several years, and was always active in political campaigns. He was a member of the Masonic fraternity, and the first of that order among the early settlers in that neighbourhood who had died. The Masons had charge of his funeral and conducted it according to their ritual.

The granddaughter of Greene said she recalled little else of her grandfather's funeral except the white aprons worn by the Masons; the open Bible carried by the Chaplain; the Tyler with the drawn sword, and some other regalia worn by the Masonic brotherhood, who attended the funeral's procession on its way to the primitive burying-place, and there stood around the grave while the coffin was

lowered into it. She said Lincoln was holding
her hand while her grandmother, on the other
side, rested hers on Lincoln's arm during the
Masonic exercises and while the grave was being
filled.

Both W. G. Greene and Menter Graham gave
me, many years after, this account of the uncon-
trollable grief to which Lincoln gave way before
leaving the Greene home for the graveyard.

The Masons, knowing the long acquaintance
and friendship of Lincoln with the deceased, had
requested him to make some remarks on the
character and life of Greene. He had consented
to do so. The Master of Ceremonies, at the proper
time called Lincoln, who came in and stood at the
head of the casket. He looked down a few moments
at the face of his friend. His whole frame began
trembling with suppressed emotion. He then
turned and faced the friends who filled the room
and crowded the doorways and stood outside
around the open windows. He spoke a few words,
—broken sentences only,—tremulous vibrations of
the thoughts he found it impossible to coherently
articulate. Tears filled his eyes. He vainly
struggled to regain that self-control under which
he had always held his feelings before these friends

on so many occasions. He had no words that could express adequately the thoughts that thronged him as he stood beside the body of his friend whose life had been so near his, and had meant so much to him.

The gratitude, love, and grief expressed in the silence of his emotions, interpreted to all present his depth of feeling better than any words of tribute that could have been offered by him. Abruptly seizing his hat, he buried his face a moment in his handkerchief;—then turned to Mrs. Greene's side, who rose and took his offered arm as he came to her. There, after a short interval, he regained his composure, and with a silent dignity, motioned those in charge to pass out with the casket. The lid was screwed on and the remains borne from the room by the Masons. Lincoln followed, supporting Mrs. Greene on his arm, and, leading the granddaughter, they followed the coffin to the graveyard. This was located on his farm and was only a short distance from the Greene home.

I asked both Menter Graham and W. G. Greene if Lincoln showed embarrassment during, or after, his failure to perform the part assigned him. They both assured me he did not; that he acted with entire indifference to all surroundings, manifested no self-consciousness that confused him; that his signal to proceed with the casket, was given with an authoritative dignity, betraying not the slightest consciousness of his having failed to make the address they had expected.

Lincoln had no boorish or awkward manners. He possessed a nameless grace of deportment that kept him self-poised, self-sustained, in any and all new and unexpected situations. He was master of himself on such occasions, so far as his mental powers were necessary to control his physical movements. He held his nerves in control beyond the possibility of any surprises that might come through his mental sympathetic make up. Under the most unusual and trying circumstances, he showed no embarrassment in his countenance, bodily movements, or deportment, be the occasion a public or private one. He maintained, without visible effort, an even serenity and composure. He was the master of Abraham Lincoln. It is not remarkable, therefore, that in later years he should prove himself so masterful of others.

In a beautiful cemetery at Petersburg, Illinois, amid the oaks and evergreens covering the land-scape, are the graves of the Bowling Greene family.

These are marked by modest headstones inscribed with the legends of their birth and death. A few steps from those graves, on a grassy mound, rests an unpolished boulder-rock that was selected from the banks of a nearby stream. On this glazier-polished stone is carved the name,— ANN RUTLEDGE. This and nothing more appears on her grave to chronicle the birth, life, and death of her whose influence and name will never fade from the annals of our nation's history.

To this secluded repose of death these humble ones of the early Salem life have been brought from their first burial-places, to rest here near each other. It is appropriate that this cemetery should be the resting-place of the Bowling Greene family, and that here also, so near them, should repose that solitary one whose grave bears only a name. Those who visit this secluded locality will recognize the historic surroundings of this cemetery and appreciate the suggestions these graves awaken. In contrast with that solitary grave, and the simple boulder stone, carved with the maiden's name, one thinks of the monumental shaft in Oak Ridge at Springfield and a national memorial at Washington.

These graves, with the modest memorials marking them, are near the Sangamon's slow flowing waters and under skies that once arched above the New Salem life in primitive times amid its scenes of love and joy, as well as those of its pains and griefs. Here beside the grave of her who was the first love of Abraham Lincoln, it is deserved and fitting to pay some tribute of gratitude to the maiden whose charming personality and character, during the brief period of their lover-life, brightened and sweetened and made more lovable the great soul of Abraham Lincoln.

It was her untimely death, with all the bitterness it then brought him, that proved to be for him an event that became the turning-point of his life. Out of her loss arose in his soul inspirations that exalted his manhood more than had any other influence before. Out of this disappointment and its disciplines, with much anguish of spirit, there came to him a poise of character and refined aspirations that never failed to sustain him through his future's greater extremities.

# Ann Rutledge in the Life of Abraham Lincoln

Out of me unworthy and unknown
The vibrations of deathless music;
"With malice toward none, with charity for all."
Out of me the forgiveness of millions toward millions,
And the beneficent face of a nation
Shining with justice and truth.
I am Ann Rutledge who sleep beneath these weeds,
Beloved in life of Abraham Lincoln,
Wedded to him, not through union,
But through separation.
Bloom forever, O Republic,
From the dust of my bosom!

EDGAR LEE MASTERS.

# VI

## ANN RUTLEDGE IN THE LIFE OF ABRAHAM LINCOLN

It is difficult to describe the beginnings of affairs and the personal life of people in Illinois from 1818 to 1850 in such a manner as to represent intelligibly to readers of the present time conditions as they existed then. That period included the larger part of Lincoln's life, and Lincoln's life formed an expressive and important part of that period.

If you would understand Lincoln in the masterfulness of his later life, you must first see him in some of those intimacies of his early manhood and appreciate the associations which, through his careful selection of friends and companions in those primitive times, consistently contributed to his development. To this end there must needs be some mention of people who were near him as friends and, in a few cases, of the women who came nearer to him than friendship, and lastly of her who became his wife and who, despite all her failings, was the strongest and most controlling influence and power of any one who ever came into his life.

Most of what I shall relate in this chapter's medley of memory came to me from the generation before mine, from those who were the first settlers of New Salem and its vicinity and who knew Lincoln while there. They often talked with me of Lincoln's habits and friendships while he lived there, for I sought these conferences and their confidence. Much of what they told me seems worthy of record, for there is no part of Lincoln's life that has been more distorted for sensational effect, or has been told in a more unfortunate manner, than those years he spent at New Salem.

First among the sources of my information, I shall mention my mother, and shall relate what I learned from her about Lincoln's visits at the home of my grandfather, Colonel Matthew Rogers. My mother was next to the youngest in a family of eight children and was sixteen years old when they arrived in Illinois. She lived until nearly ninety.

Matthew Rogers, in the War of 1812 Colonel of the 54th Regiment, New York Militia, resigned his commission in 1818 to remove with his family to Illinois. He sold his farm near Cooperstown, New York, that year and built a large flat boat at Olean Point, from which place he embarked in it with his family and household goods to Pittsburg and thence down the Ohio River in the fall of 1818. He arrived at Shawneetown, Illinois, in December of that year. There he procured teams to transport them to Madison County, east of St. Louis, where he planned to spend the first year in the older settlement, and to raise the supplies, and to procure the necessary implements, teams, and young stock that he would need when he should move north the next spring into what was then called the "Sangamo country."[1] These plans he carried out, visiting the new country in the fall of 1819 and selecting and marking his pre-emption as the law and frontier custom required, before and after Government surveys. He arrived in the spring of 1820 at the claim he had pre-empted, fourteen miles north-west of the site of Springfield, and four miles east of the future New Salem.

Eight years later, Colonel Matthew Rogers was commissioned postmaster of Rogers post office. The establishing of that post office antedates that of Salem by nearly two years, as shown by the

[1] At that early date "Sangamo country" extended from Madison County (east of St. Louis) to Lake Michigan in three parallel strips, respectively named Madison, Bond, and Crawford counties.

following answers to my inquiry of the First Assistant Postmaster:

Post Office Department,<br>
1st Assistant Postmaster General.<br>
Washington, May 21, 1913.

Mr. Henry B. Rankin,
    510 South Second Street.

Sir:

In reply to your letter of the 16th instant, you are informed that according to the records of this office the post office of New Salem, in Sangamon County, Illinois, was established in December 25, 1829, with Samuel Hill as postmaster. He was succeeded by Isaac P. Chrisman, appointed November 24, 1831, who in turn was succeeded by Abraham Lincoln, appointed May 7, 1833. Mr. Lincoln served as postmaster until the discontinuance of the post office on May 30, 1836.

Respectfully,<br>
Daniel C. Roper,<br>
1st Asst. Postmaster General.

Post Office Department,<br>
1st Assistant Postmaster General.<br>
Washington, May 28, 1913.

Mr. Henry B. Rankin,
    510 South Second Street,
        Springfield, Illinois.

Sir:

In reply to your letter of the 24th instant, you are

informed that according to the records of this office
the post office of Rogers, Illinois, was established
January 2, 1828, with Matthew Rogers, as postmaster.
He was succeeded by Henry C. Rogers appointed
February 13, 1829. On November 4, 1831, the name
of that office was changed to Athens and Henry C.
Rogers was reappointed postmaster on that date.
He was succeeded by Jonathan Dunn, appointed
February 6, 1832.

Respectfully,

DANIEL C. ROPER,
*1st Assistant Postmaster General.*

Lincoln had become acquainted with the family
of Matthew Rogers shortly after he arrived in New
Salem on his return from the Blackhawk War, in
1831. He had learned from Menter Graham that
Colonel Matthew Rogers brought with him from
New York a chest of books and among them some
text-books that Rogers's sons had used at Cooperstown. Graham needed these books for Lincoln's
use under his tutoring. This first trip for text-
books was not made, as several sensational chroniclers have asserted, "six miles and barefooted."
He was described to me by one who saw him on
this visit, as clad in the gentlemanly attire suitable for a merchant, which was the business he
was in at Salem. This first visit at the Rogers

5

home made an unusually good impression on the Colonel and family. After this first visit Lincoln often walked across the four miles through the virgin forest that skirted the Sangamon River on the east of Salem, to the prairie's edge where the Rogers farm home was located. These visits became more and more frequent because of the good fellowship of kindred spirits he met there, and Lincoln's interest in the newspapers which the Rogers post office added to those which he had access to in the Salem office.

The two offices were on different post routes, making their delivery of mail on different dates,— one week and sometimes two between trips. The Rogers office east of the Sangamon River was the route from St. Louis via Springfield, Peoria, Chicago, and via the lakes east; the Salem route on the west of the river being via St. Louis, Springfield, Havana, Rock Island, etc. The different days of mail arrivals, and their different destinations, caused Lincoln to come to my grandfather's oftener. He came to bring letters there to mail for going East or to read the eastern papers at the Rogers post office; often bringing with him from the Salem office a St. Louis or New Orleans newspaper or two for the Rogers family to read; and when the carrier was belated,—which often occurred,—staying all night.

Postal patrons were few and lived from five to twenty miles or more from their nearest post office, leaving their mail uncalled for weeks at a time and, with first settlers' generosity, permitting free reading of their papers by any one, while awaiting their call at the post office. Besides this postal and book-borrowing attraction for Lincoln at the Rogers home, there was another. My mother's oldest brother had made several trips down the Mississippi, spending a couple of years in the Gulf states, having invested in Louisiana lands with the intention of permanently settling in the South. Lincoln's two trips down the river inspired a degree of comradeship between them. Also the two other brothers, nearer Lincoln's age, were reading medical books during vacation, under the tutoring of Dr. Gershom Jayne,—father of the present venerable Dr. William Jayne of Springfield,—and attending the medical college in Cincinnati during the fall and winter. The educational advantages these young men had had at Cooperstown, New York, the books their home furnished, and the medical studies they were pursuing appealed to Lincoln's social and intellectual life and made his visits at Colonel Rogers's home mutually agreeable, and much more frequent than they would otherwise have been.  The stalwart young Kentuckian and the three or four Yankee student boys, were mutual revelations and inspirations to each other.

The Rogers and Rutledge families on the arrival of the latter from the South, first at Salem, then on their farm seven miles north-west of Salem, became visiting friends; and although the farm homes were sixteen miles apart, this was then only a neighbourly distance and their cabins became places where church services were held alternately, whenever appointments by itinerant preachers could be procured.  Thus a warm friendship began between Ann Rutledge and my mother, Arminda Rogers.  The latter was nearly ten years older than Miss Rutledge and had taught school several terms before they met. Later she tutored the young girl in Blair's *Rhetoric*, Kirkham's *Grammar* and the elementary studies she was reviewing, preparatory to entering an academy for young ladies that had been opened at Jacksonville, Illinois.

Through this intimacy, and the acquaintance the Rogers household had with both McNeil (later McNamar) and Lincoln, my mother learned

of the engagement of Miss Rutledge to McNamar;
his going East; his protracted silence and long-
continued absence, and the later attraction and
attentions of Lincoln to Ann Rutledge. All these
quite naturally were, more or less, disclosed to my
mother; thus making her all the more interested
in her young friend and scholar up to the time of
Ann Rutledge's death, August 25, 1835.

Of McNamar's personality, I can write from
my own knowledge. I knew him the last ten or
twelve years of his life as intimately as any young
man could know an elderly gentleman of so cold
and unsocial a nature as his. I respected and
admired him both for his ability as an accountant
and as a skillful examiner of land titles, in both of
which I was much interested at the time.

McNamar's marriage the year after his return
to Salem showed he was not inconsolably grieved
by the early death of the good and charming Ann
Rutledge. I did not know his first wife who
afforded such early consolation, but I knew the
second. She was a widow at the time of their
marriage, in all ways a most estimable woman,
and survived McNamar several years. She told
me that in all the years of their married life,
though he was courteous and attentive and a good

provider, there was no more poetry or sentiment in him than in the multiplication table, and that she really never became acquainted with him.

He was frequently at my father's home on political and business matters of mutual interest and often a guest over night. I recall my being inquisitive enough at the time to ask my mother if his cold and unsocial nature in old age was characteristic of him when he was the efficient and successful business partner of Samuel Hill at Salem and had there become engaged to Ann Rutledge. She assured me that age had mellowed and not hardened the man's nature and that his social side had not been chilled by lapse of time or disappointment in love. She was at a loss to understand, when in 1866 she read Herndon's Ann Rutledge lecture, the sentimental moods of McNamar that Herndon therein described; and later, in 1889, reading in his life of Lincoln of the interview he reported having had with McNamar in his home near the spot where Ann Rutledge died, she was even more surprised. McNamar was married to his second wife at the time Herndon had the interview.

As to how the engagement of Miss Rutledge to Lincoln came about, or how long after McNamar's absence and his neglect in writing to her, my

mother's knowledge was indefinite. She said that
in the latter part of 1834, when she saw the two
young people together, there was an increasing
interest between them. This increased from time
to time so that it was apparent to her that Miss
Rutledge was passing out of and above the depression and anxiety she had shown over Mc-
Namar's absence and neglect, and that there was
a new love coming into her life, which found there
a response and called forth attractions she had
never noticed in her while McNamar was the
favoured suitor.

The friends both within and without her own
family, with whom Miss Rutledge had shared her
perplexities, favoured Lincoln's suit for her hand,
and by their expressed opinions contributed to the
indignation that reluctantly she began to feel
toward McNamar. This feeling grew until at
length freely, fully, and without any of those violent neurasthenic agonies that have been sketched
into her life in later years, she unreservedly gave
him up and consented to the suit Abraham Lincoln had for several months pressed with her to
become his wife at some future time, when her
education should be finished and he should become established in his profession. My mother
said she was not told by the young girl, at the

first, of this decision and of her acceptance of
Lincoln, but that she felt assured of it by the
increasing interest she took in her studies through
the spring and summer of 1835, and by the buoy-
ancy of her spirits as she talked about going to
Jacksonville in the early autumn to enter the
ladies' academy there.

In the early summer, having finished the studies
through which my mother had tutored her, she
then fully confided to mother the secret of the
new light that had come into her life, and talked
freely of the absence and neglect of McNamar,
acknowledging that her own judgment and heart
at length approved the advice of both her own
family and the few friends to whom she had confided the perplexities through which she had for
months been passing. My mother said that in the
conversation with her she manifested no regret or
wavering in the choice she had made. On the
contrary, there was a decided spirit of offended
maidenly dignity manifested in all the references
she made to McNamar,—such, my mother said, as
could be expected of a well-bred southern girl under
circumstances showing such unaccountable neglect.

The spring and early summer of 1835, I have
been told, was a time of unusually large rainfall

and high temperature in central Illinois. By July the rains ceased and extreme heat dried up and parched the luxurious vegetation of earlier growth, and chills and fever and what the earlier physicians named "bilious fever" became unusually prevalent. In every home some member was stricken down, and in most homes all the family were ill at the same time. Treatment of these malarial diseases was very crude and drastic at that time. Heroic doses of medicine were administered,—often more fatal than the disease, —killing a person of frail physique instead of effecting a cure. The Rutledge family were among the unfortunate many who suffered. Ann was among the last to be stricken. Lincoln had been a frequent visitor and assistant in nursing at the Rutledge home during their sickness,—going over from Salem with Dr. John Allen, the physician, every day or two. He would stay over night when needed, or return with the Doctor who would stop for him after visiting the other patients in that neighbourhood. At length, toward the end of August, Miss Rutledge's condition passed beyond the help of physicians and nurses and the delirium of her last few days—common in the fatal cases of those malarial fevers—brought an end to her life on August 25, 1835.

For a month or more before, Lincoln himself,—
with all the physical vigour he then possessed and
preserved until that fatal bullet ended his life,—
had been suffering from the chills and fever on
alternate days. He kept up and was helping nurse
others all the while, but was taking heroic doses
of Peruvian bark, boneset tea, jalap and calomel.
Added to the depression of Lincoln from illness in
those days, was that from the death of several of
his personal friends, and the neighbourly aid he
had given unstintingly at the funerals and burials
of those who died. There were no undertakers.
No caskets were kept on hand. Coffins had to be
made after the death; and in a few instances he had
assisted in making them for his friends. In this
environment of distress that he was day and night
helping to relieve, in addition to the poisonous
malaria that had been for weeks alternately chilling and burning his stalwart frame, he was now
to endure the supreme tragedy of his life in the
death of Ann Rutledge.

It is difficult for me to tell in this cold type the
pitiful story, clad in the simple home-life details
in which it came to me from those who knew Ann
Rutledge and Abraham Lincoln both before and
after her death, and who were amid the same sad

afflictions. There is need of no fancy or imagery
to put colour in the environment within, or without
the life of Abraham Lincoln or Ann Rutledge
while the story of the days leading up through
August to its fateful twenty-fifth is told. When
such an experience comes into life,—as this came
into Lincoln's, when the nearest and dearest one
had come with him into the light of mutual love
and joy in the hopeful dawn of life's morning, only
to release the hand of plighted faith and drift away
out on the mysterious sea of death whose pitiless
waves beat so sadly around the world;—when such
an hour comes, it either overwhelms with despair
those who remain, or nerves them to endure and in-
spires with a power to grasp life's higher problems
anew with closer, surer grip than ever before, and
thereafter face with clear vision and high purpose all
the missions and disciplines that open before them.

To Lincoln it brought the dawn of a new and
ennobled manhood. He found no shadows sufficiently gloomy or depressing to darken his life
after that of August 25, 1835. It made a man—
spiritually—of him who, self-satisfied before, had
lived only within the horizon of the present.

The personal influence of Dr. John Allen on
Lincoln and their mutual attraction to each other

at this important period, when he was under such
great physical suffering and mental distress,
makes some mention of the doctor's character
appropriate, before passing on with Lincoln into
the days succeeding Miss Rutledge's death. His
qualifications as a medical practitioner placed
him in the front with such doctors as Gershom
Jayne of Springfield, and Prince of Jacksonville,
with whom he was often called in consultation.
In the practice of his profession he had some
peculiarities. He was a physician of souls as well
as sick bodies. He saw both together. On many
subjects he had a clarity of vision far in advance
of his time. He limited his Sunday visiting to
those patients only whose condition indicated that
his presence was imperatively needed. He considered the patient's needs, not his own ease. He
responded to every new call that came to him
on Sunday; but all Sunday patients, new or old,
that he visited, were listed separately and their
payments applied strictly to church and benevolent
uses. All women working in domestic service, or
dependent upon their own labour, he charged only
for medicine used, and this rule he applied to all
who were financially embarrassed, as not in-
frequently was the case among the new settlers
whose families besides their many privations

often suffered protracted illness. Years after,
some of these became prosperous and insisted
upon paying for those generous professional
services.

He was a devoted member of the Presbyterian
Church, and I recall from the memories of my
boyhood years when I attended the same church
in Petersburg in which the Doctor was an elder,
that if he had not received a professional call
before the meeting began he was punctually in his
seat at the stated hours of service, always with his
large old-style, double-pocketed medicine saddle-
bags with him which he placed at the end of his
pew, ready to respond at once to any call that
might come during church service. He came to
church usually in his gig, or on horseback, so that
he might not be delayed in starting out on any call
to relieve distress. In the skill and thoroughness
of his collections, and in his adaptation to the
peculiar business condition of the country, he was
not less marked and successful. Finding how
scarce money was among the early settlers, and the
absence of a market for nearly all of their products,
he erected a large smoke-house and prepared for
handling pork during the winter months, accept-
ing dressed hogs at market price as payment from
any of his debtors. These he had cut up and

converted into lard and bacon, and, when properly cured, he sent the product by oxen teams to Beardstown to be forwarded by boat to St. Louis and New Orleans.

The most unpopular of the doctor's characteristics were his strong anti-slavery principles and his devotion to the cause of temperance. He also met with no little opposition in establishing the first Sunday-schools in his and other churches. He introduced the first public protest against the general drink habits by promoting in the community the organization of the Washingtonian Society with its pledge of total abstinence. All other peculiarities of Dr. Allen could have been condoned by the great majority of these early settlers more easily than his crusade against the drink habit. One of Dr. Allen's associates in the temperance crusade was the Cumberland Presbyterian preacher, John Berry. It was his son who was Lincoln's partner in the store at Salem and whose unfortunate habit of drinking brought so great a disaster upon the business that it was not until 1850 that Lincoln was able to pay the last debt of the firm.

Menter Graham, the school-teacher, who until then had been a member of what was called the "Hard-shell Baptist Church," joined this reform

movement. For this he was unanimously suspended from that church at a meeting called to
consider the temperance agitation. To preserve
the judicial balance that the church thought proper
on this subject, the same meeting dismissed from
their connection another member who had got
"dead drunk." This led an inquisitive member
who was present to take exception to the proceed-
ings, and to call for some more definite rule for
the guidance of the church members in the future.
He rose from his seat, took from his pocket a
quart bottle that was about half-full, shook its
contents into active sparkling bubbles, and in the
peculiar nasal drawl the Hard-Shell Baptists were
wont to adopt in their meeting-house talks, said:

"Brethering, you have turned one member out
beca'se he would not drink, and another beca'se
he got drunk, and now I want to aks a question:
How much of this 'ere critter does one have to
drink to remain in full fellership in this Church?"

Mentioning Parson Berry in connection with
Dr. Allen's crusade on the drink habit, calls to
mind an event that occurred many years later in
connection with Lincoln and Berry, illustrating
how lasting were the impressions Lincoln ac-
knowledged he had received while at Salem. Years

after Lincoln had left Salem and had attained
eminence in the legal profession, a grog-shop in a
certain community was having a bad influence
upon some married men whose wives consequently
suffered from the evil. These injured women, with
some of their influential lady friends, came together and made a raid on the infamous den,
demolishing the barrels, breaking the decanters
and demijohns and playing havoc with its fur-
nishings generally. The ladies were prosecuted
and Lincoln *volunteered* his services in their defence.
In the midst of his powerful appeals to the jury
in their behalf, and his attack upon the evils of the
traffic and use of intoxicating spirits, the speaker
turned and, pointing his long, bony finger towards
the venerable Parson Berry who was among those
present, exclaimed:

"There stands the man who, years ago, was
instrumental in convincing me of the evils of
trafficking in and using ardent spirits. I am glad
I ever saw him. I am glad I ever heard and heeded
his testimony on this terrible subject."

The reader who has followed me in description
of the character of Dr. John Allen, and has properly
fixed in his mind the real Abraham Lincoln at
Salem,—not the caricature of him there, as so

many have misrepresented him,—will appreciate
the measure of influence that Dr. Allen was able
to exert on Lincoln in the susceptible condition
induced by his physical weakness and mental
distress after the death of Ann Rutledge. No
physician could have been better qualified temperamentally than was Dr. Allen to treat Lincoln's
condition wisely. He saw the two-fold ailment of
the young man. He had a clearness of professional
vision, far in advance of that time, of some things
even beyond what we have seen at present in this
self-confident century. He had the Yankee "faculty" of doing the right thing, at the right time,
and in the right way.

First, he took both professional and personal
charge of Lincoln, who was physically worn out
with overwork and anxiety day and night for so
many anxious weeks. His distress by deaths
among his friends; his own protracted illness from
relapses of the chills and fever that became all the
more difficult to arrest with him because of their
repeated recurrences under neglected medication
and such continuous overwork, all combined, had
made a seriously sick man of him. He prevailed
on Lincoln to go out to the quiet home of Bowling
Greene and remain there under his medical attention and in Mrs. Greene's care to administer the

6

prescribed courses of medicine, until he should
pass three consecutive weeks free from chills.
He knew the motherly care Mrs. Greene would
bestow in the meanwhile, and the quiet of that
farm home at the foot of the oak-timbered bluff
rising abruptly behind the yard and orchards.
This was the rest-cure refuge for body and soul
that Lincoln so greatly needed.   It was cheerfully,
gladly given by both Mr. and Mrs. Greene.

How quiet and refreshing that home, how
motherly and hospitable a welcome Mrs. Greene
gave him and all who came to her home, I know
personally.   I recall the times, years later, when
fishing and nutting excursions, on Saturdays or
school vacations, were made by a half-dozen or
more of us Petersburg boys.  We would trail up
the Sangamon with our fishing rods, until opposite
the Bowling Greene home, where we were always
sure to skip across the river-bottom for Mrs.
Greene's hospitable home welcome, and there we
would fry our fish at the open fireplace on the
kitchen hearth.  Or, when we scampered over the
hills back of old Salem nutting in the fall, we
would come trooping down the bluff behind Mrs.
Bowling Greene's and into her big homey kitchen,
with such voracious appetites for her hot biscuit

smothered in butter and honey, her doughnuts and cookies, buttermilk, apples, and sweet cider! Ah, I know as I look back more than half a century through the fruitful fields of my Salem memories, there could have been no better place this side of the celestial country for Lincoln during those September days of 1835, than the Bowling Greene home.

You worked for the ages, you followed the Master's plan of "doing what you could," oh, wise Dr. Allen! Most motherly of nurses, dearest Mrs. Greene, whose warm welcome and wise silence, as you went quietly about your housework those three weeks, were a blessed balm to body and spirit of the stricken sick man in those hours of healing and of his readjustment to the new sad outlook of his life.

In 1865 a similar climatic condition of malaria prevailed in Illinois, caused by large rainfalls and protracted heat during the latter part of the summer. It was the summer following the assassination of President Lincoln, and many of the residents of that vicinity in 1835 were yet living. They often remarked upon the malarial condition and the type of illness then prevalent as resembling those of thirty years before. It was

their repeated mention of the similarity of malarial
conditions and the fact of Lincoln's death a few
months before, which caused me to inquire into
the details, here recorded, that were so intimately
connected with Lincoln's life at Salem in 1835.

As the word "insanity" has been used as descriptive of Lincoln's life shortly after the death of
Ann Rutledge, I have dwelt with more fulness in
recital of these events of 1835 than I otherwise
would have considered necessary. The assertion
that Miss Rutledge's death was hastened, if not
caused, by perplexing griefs through which she was
passing in consequence of the breaking of her
engagement to McNamar, and the pleading of a
later love and the consent she had given in it to
wed Mr. Lincoln, had no foundation whatever in
fact, and merits none of the fanciful considerations
it has received.

McNamar was a just man. Had he returned
before her death he would have released Miss
Rutledge from her promise to him. He was as
honest and exact as the multiplication table, and
he well knew that his prolonged and unexplained
absence had inflicted a mortal blow upon Miss
Rutledge's confidence and affection for him. She
could never have trusted him again and he would
not have expected her to do so. That her trust and

love for him had died, by his own neglect, none
would have admitted more freely or generously·
than the cold mathematical McNamar.

A greater love had come into her life; and while
its fulness was soon to be denied by death, her
last conscious hours were not those of conflicts
between an old duty and this new love.  They
were lit by her unclouded affection for, and in
the presence of, the great soul who, by her request,
was near her during her last conscious moments.
Their last words at parting,—given to each other
alone—were too sacred for others, and should have
ever remained so.  As though Lincoln's personal
grief were not enough, there has been written since
his death—into certain fictional biography—by
some the implied charge, by others the positive
assertion, that his life was darkened by the shadows of "insanity," following Miss Rutledge's
death.  This is utterly unsupported by any facts
or circumstances transpiring in 1835.

I am sure that neither the memory of this good
and beautiful girl nor of the martyred President,
needs vindication by any words of mine.  The
womanly character and integrity of Ann Rutledge
have been deeply impressed upon me as they were
enshrined in the memory of those who knew her

most intimately. They have told me how they revered her womanly dignity, as well as her beauty in form and feature, and how they knew by hearing from her own lips the unreserved and unclouded love she had given; and that it was as unreservedly sought and accepted by Abraham Lincoln.

Far less is there need to disprove the "three weeks' insanity" charge, made after Lincoln's death. The matchless vigour, poise, and clearness of mind of our First American, lifts him far above the taint of "insanity" at any period of his life, much more in the years of his vigorous young manhood. In later life his well-known capacity for endurance amid disheartening political experiences under the immense strain of those executive and military crises of his Presidential years that were so harassing and so appalling, is the sufficient answer to all these baseless insinuations. Through all his life he maintained a balanced mind and tranquil spirit. In all the annals of time, history does not record a superior, save Him who calmly spake to the wild waves of storm-swept Galilee those words of power,—"Peace, be still," and to the mob,—"Father, forgive, they know not what they do." Justly did Tolstoi speak of him, and his life, as next to that of the Saviour of mankind.

In less than a month—in three weeks—Lincoln
returned to his usual affairs at Salem and resumed
his surveying tramps wherever they were called
for. He used such spare time as his occupations
afforded by reading law with the definite intention of entering that profession. The purposeful
steadfastness maintained by Lincoln throughout
the period spent at Salem in preparation for future
promotion cannot fail to impress all who carefully
trace the records of those years. To a young man
of his vigorous physical strength, with a mind
bubbling over with wit and humour and abounding
animal spirits, in such a community, the tempta-
tions were certainly great. The affairs in which
he was connected required his mixing daily with
the rudest class of frontier men and women on their
own plane and views of life. This he did without
sharing their lower views or becoming at one with
them in joining with their excesses. On the contrary, he maintained his own individuality with
dignity, and secured the respect of all and lasting
love with most of them.

What was even more unusual amid such associations, he himself was always seeking outside his
daily pursuits the better class, and thus enjoyed
at the same time close and lasting friendships with
the best people around Salem. Besides those

mentioned by me elsewhere more particularly, there were others of whom space forbids extended mention. Among these were the Greene, the Graham, the Hill, the Short, and the Godbey families; as well as many later Springfield friends of culture, all of whom were equally attracted to him as he to them, before he made Springfield his home. Among both men and women, in every community in which he lived, he sought and was influenced by the best people; and where circumstances required association with the worst, his character contracted no stain.

Lincoln's closest application to both business and books at Salem was during the two years following Miss Rutledge's death. This was the testimony of those who knew him at that time. His life began reaching out on a larger range. He made frequent trips to Springfield, becoming more interested in the people and life there, and two years later, March, 1837, he was invited by Major John T. Stuart to come to Springfield as his law partner.

When I first thought of putting in writing my recollections of Lincoln, I requested Mrs. Annie M. Fleury, the daughter of William H. Herndon, to look through her father's papers and letters which she had in her possession, to find some of my correspondence with him. I recall my writing often and quite fully to him from time to time, at his request, concerning the general outlines to be adopted in his life of Lincoln, which he had not fully decided on in 1866. At that time I was especially anxious that he should avoid those sensational and debatable features for which afterwards in collaboration with others, he unfortunately became sponsor, in two publications of joint authorship, issued, one in 1872, and the other in 1889.

It is with painful regret and reluctance that I refer to Mr. Herndon's participation in certain portions of those unfortunate publications. If it were possible, I would write in an entirely impersonal manner, so far as he had any connection with the sensational features in those lives of Lincoln. I have given elsewhere in my recollections of the office life of Lincoln and Herndon, from 1850 to 1861, full and hearty recognition of Herndon's influence and helpful services to Lincoln. He was abundantly deserving of all I have written there of his fidelity and efficient service in those years. By temperament, by local prejudices and social antagonisms of long standing in Springfield; by the effects of early habits,—overcome while he was a partner with Lincoln, but resumed after 1870 and with the unfortunate effects of a use of morphine; by pet theories regarding ancestry and heredity, and most especially by his extreme erratic and changing views on theological and religious subjects; Herndon was rendered less competent to write a satisfactory biography of Lincoln. In addition to these prejudices, at times all these would be emphasized by his peculiarly lurid and egotistic rhetoric (pardonable with those who knew him) that rendered him less competent to reflect adequately Mr. Lincoln's life and character with the fair and impartial treatment that the history of so great a life as Abraham Lincoln's demanded. In Herndon's testimony of what he himself saw and knew about Lincoln's life he was generally reliable. With regard to second- and third-hand evidence, when presented by him, he could not refrain from drawing on his imagination for colouring to suit the conclusions already formed.

It was to obtain the situation and views as presented by me to Mr. Herndon at the time immediately preceding his writing Lincoln's life, that I wished to get my letters, written to Mr. Herndon in the years following Lincoln's death. Mrs. Fleury, as I have said, went through all her father's papers and letters that she had not parted with, but found only one of mine left among them. She kindly returned it to me. This letter was written by me to Mr. Herndon forty-nine years ago, just after I had for the first time read his lecture on Lincoln and Ann Rutledge. I greatly regret that I kept no copies of my correspondence at that time, nor preserved those written to me. With what I have already written in these pages, this letter, which I give in full, will show that my forebodings of so many years ago were not groundless. When this letter was penned I had not given the Ann Rutledge period in Lincoln's life the extensive inquiry I did afterwards, with the results reproduced here. My letter was as follows:

ATHENS, MENARD CO., ILLS.,
Dec. 24, 1866.

FRIEND HERNDON:—

You told father, when we were last in Springfield, you wanted me to call up if only for five minutes. He did not see me until we were starting home. I promised previously to write to you. I will do so now.

When I got home I carefully read your lecture— reading then as I have since tried to weigh it,—*not* as a baby of W. H. H.'s, but as a part of what I, with all other men, desire it should be,—a part of *the* portraiture of Lincoln to appear in your forthcoming work. Of course I do not look on it as a "lecture" but, as you told me, a fragment from Mr. Lincoln's life.

When I read the lecture I thought that the rules of criticism would deal rather harshly with considerable of your "dressing" of the ideas, but I was hardly prepared to anticipate what I saw a week later in an eastern paper, (*Springfield*, Mass. *Republican*) the surmise that you yourself were one of Miss Rutledge's suitors.   Your fancy has far overshot the facts.

To one like myself, whose life has not led them into criticism and whose mind is not moulded by loving contemplation of those fair symmetries in style, which the skeleton of ideas fleshes itself with, it is not my province to criticize, even were I capable, which I *know* I am not.   Yet the interest I have in your present work, and friendliness for you, leads me to say all I can that by any means could draw your mind to care and revision.

The point in the lecture that lacks, chiefly, is that,— at the death of Miss Rutledge,—when, apparently, Mr. Lincoln's mind gives away.   You do not claim for Lincoln "insanity" in your statement of the facts, yet in attendant circumstances you insinuate it, and in the words you put into Mr. Lincoln's mouth there is positive insanity.   The phrase, "insanity of Lincoln," is a shock to all who did not know of the facts.

I learn through my mother—who, personally, was acquainted with Miss Rutledge,—that Mr. Lincoln's grief, not "insanity,"—was well known.   This charge is something so entirely new—you being the first to publish the story, and for so long his law partner,—

the world is asking you stern questions, and it will consider that you have overdrawn the picture from the fact of his sudden recovery.

The biographer must use the elements that contributed to form the character of his subject as the artist does his pigments, the colours must melt one into the other with no beginning, no ending.

To me the picture of Lincoln's early life shows variously, about this way:—The boy Lincoln in the log cabin: Wielding the ax: Studying: Loving: Then death comes with its icy rush over his warm life throbs, blackening with temporary despair the once love-lit future, sobering him with sickening, rebellious thoughts, and flinging his soul back on itself, there finding himself and his God, and so changing the rollicking life to the calm, deep reasoning soul that made a philosopher of a jovial hail-fellow-well-met citizen of Salem. Here is where Mr. Lincoln first *began to be a man.*

This is the great transition my mother tells me she saw in the mind and character of Mr. Lincoln while in, and through, and after Ann Rutledge came into his life.

Mr. Lincoln was born of and amid what I choose to term the Great World; *i.e.*, the class of merely *existing* people whose heaven is sensation, or highest enjoyment of the sensuous universe. He passed, at Salem, into the next class,—*In the World*—that class on the surface of the present, to whom life is only one vast *Now.* Here he lived and joyed, held high holiday over his every last pulsation, until he met his first love in the sweet and winsome personality of Ann Rutledge.

Then came an incident,—shall I call it only such?—Death! that flings his nature away from all his old moorings, and he was lost for a brief period until he entered a life—rare in this world of ours—of silence, as you and I have often seen in him; "Out of The World," his mind soaring above all mere sensuous, or "Today," existences and fluttering around the very throne of the Father of All.

His jovial "Great World," and the not less wondering "In The World" people he had so intimately been an active part with and of, stared, queried,—wagged their heads with knowing import,—"crazy!"

Mr. Lincoln, at that time, doubtless, reveled and explored this hitherto untrodden universe,—"Out of The World,"—heedless of his surroundings for some time, and then, when out at Bowling Greene's, adapted his outer self to surroundings; but his mind, the inner Lincoln, never left in all after time the elevation to which it arose.

His manner was strange to old associates, but, therefrom came his fine capacity to dwell in thought-life in one high realm and yet grasp the passer-by with a friendly clasp on the plane of every-day life we both well know. But enough of this.

Of any change of Mr. Lincoln's peculiar religious

views held at Salem, I am unprepared to believe either way in a historical sense. His state papers, his tranquil life, his Christly poise in great emergencies, convince *me* he did change. *My faith* is one way, but history is a tissue of *facts*, not faiths. I hope you have heard from Drs. Smith, Chapin, and Beecher by this time. On this point bring every resource to bear, and move with caution. Remember you have prejudices and some preconceived opinions to guard against, while writing Lincoln's Life. Once more reflect.

I've written more than I intended. I began writing to say only what I *think* of this lecture, and found I could not help but make some suggestions. Write me when you feel like it.

Your friend,

HENRY B. RANKIN.

# Lincoln's First Law Partners: Stuart and Logan

The learning rule for a lawyer, as for the man of every other calling, is diligence. Leave nothing for tomorrow which can be done today.

Extemporaneous speaking should be practised and cultivated. It is the lawyer's avenue to the public. And yet there is not a more fatal error to young lawyers than relying too much on speech-making.

Discourage litigation. Persuade your neighbours to compromise whenever you can. Point out to them how the nominal winner is often a real loser— in fees, expenses, and waste of time. As a peace-maker the lawyer has a superior opportunity of being a good man. There will still be business enough.

Never stir up litigation. A worse man can scarcely be found than one who does this. . . . A moral tone ought to be infused into the profession which should drive such men out of it.

There is a vague popular belief that lawyers are necessarily dishonest. . . . Let no young man choosing the law for a calling for a moment yield to the popular belief. Resolve to be honest at all events; and if in your own judgment you cannot be an honest lawyer, resolve to be honest without being a lawyer.

Note for a Law Lecture, by LINCOLN.

# VII

## LINCOLN'S FIRST LAW PARTNERS: STUART AND LOGAN

### From Salem and After

THE cross currents and aimless wanderings of Abraham Lincoln's life may be said to have nearly, or quite, ended with his settling down at New Salem. Everything before that formed a background for his life portrait that then began slowly to take on the features and character-tinting that was ever after so remarkable, so unusual in all ways. A young man of less virile physical or mental make-up would never have survived the breaking-in, and the character strain, that Lincoln patiently endured at New Salem. Even after all this, a less ambitious man would have settled down there, a village or a country squire for life.

His seven years among the peculiar and original characters at New Salem may be called his Freshman term in the University of Life with the common people as professors. They sifted him, tried him out thoroughly, and put everything

God had given him possibilities for, up to that time, to the fullest test. He came out of it with such a wide and varied development and manhood as only such a youth as Abraham Lincoln was capable of attaining. The Clary's Grove boys, the wilder Wolf Creek contingent, and the Sandridge rowdy roysterers had their coarse rustic innings with him, and gave him such genuine athletic polishings and tumblings about as no college coach, even in our time, could offer a young man. There was no neglect of muscular training for young men in that primitive community. Young Lincoln took cheerfully all that came in his way and became physical master of the best of them.

Then came the personal instruction of Menter Graham, aided by the sundry volumes in his library of choice English literature and translations of ancient classics. Nor should we forget the stray volumes of Blackstone which even in those immature years the young clerk picked out of the barrel of rubbish in the country store warehouse, and which, as he told me many years later, he literally devoured long before he took up the systematic study of law under John T. Stuart. All these influences were a fuel to the fire already kindled in those latent mental faculties which, as yet so unconsciously, he possessed.

He spoke of this to office students who were reading Blackstone for the first time, and said he caught
his first inspiration in the art of defining words and
stating principles from this master.  Sometimes in
the office he would take up a volume of Blackstone
and read pages aloud, occasionally commenting on
the author's judicial acuteness as he went along.

It was while Lincoln lived at Salem that he
formed his first Springfield acquaintance worth
mentioning.  Menter Graham introduced him to
Calhoun, the County Surveyor, and at his suggestion, Lincoln took up the study of surveying.
Later, he became Calhoun's deputy, and the fees
thus earned became for a time his principal
source of livelihood.  This required many trips to
Springfield, where new friends became more and
more attractive to him.  Thus the circle of his
mental horizon enlarged.  He met men of keen
intellect and trained mind, and began acquiring
a new vigour of thought from their personality.
It was in the midst of this stimulating environment that he began the study of law, getting
books and personal directions from John T. Stuart.  Finding his village student so capable and
promising, in 1837, Mr. Stuart invited Lincoln to
come to Springfield and enter into partnership with
him in the practice of law.

It would reveal and illuminate an important
period of Lincoln's life, and at the same time be a
pleasing task, for one who knew John T. Stuart,
Stephen T. Logan, and William H. Herndon—
not only as lawyers, but also as individuals with
their strong though widely different characteristics
—to describe fully the part contributed by them
individually and collectively, through a series of
remarkable years, to the character-building and
mental development of Abraham Lincoln.  In all
the biographies of Lincoln the vital influence of
these personal factors upon his life during the formative years from 1838 to 1860 has been either
wholly neglected, or passed over all too hastily.

Would Major Stuart have invited Lincoln into partnership with him had the latter when he
left Salem and came to Springfield been the crude
country bumpkin described by some biographers?
No one who knew Stuart would say so.  To
those who knew Lincoln, then, this description
is an absurd caricature.  The invitation was a
recognition and a measure of Lincoln's merits and
personality at that time, to be understood fully
only by those who knew Major John T. Stuart
personally.  His education and manners were
those of a polished gentleman of the olden school,
at its very best.  In ability as a politician at that

time he had no superior in Illinois, and his sagacity and ability to judge men accurately were superior. His own professional preparation had been liberal for that period, and his law practice was then well established in Springfield. Here, and in the surrounding judicial districts whose courts he attended, his cases and clients were equal, if not superior, to those of any other attorney connected with the Springfield bar. His political friends and foes alike had complimented him with the political name of "Jerry Sly," because of the unusual ability and shrewdness with which he had managed the political affairs of the Whig party in his Congressional district.

John T. Stuart was a gentleman not likely to make a mistake in selecting a law partner. If, at the time when he left Salem, Lincoln had not been a man of well established, refined character, and of mental abilities forecasting a promising future, John T. Stuart would never have suggested the partnership. Lincoln brought his own spurs with him into the office. He did not need to look up any cast-off pair of Major Stuart's when the latter was elected to Congress, and Lincoln during Mr. Stuart's absence took charge of all the legal work of the office and no small part in political activities at home.

Those who study Lincoln's biography in the three or four years of this law partnership will learn how ably the senior partner by his courteous manners assisted the junior in his first legal work in the courts and in political strategy, and how well the junior profited by this partnership's influence on him. Its close did not sever their personal friendship, which continued on through later years, even though they were finally aligned on different sides of the very definite issues which divided the political parties.

The entrance of Lincoln into partnership with Stephen T. Logan marks another epoch, and gives evidence of an enlarged estimate of his standing as a lawyer at the termination of his partnership with Stuart. On the strict lines of law and business affairs, it was a promotion for Lincoln. As Judge Logan has never had a superior at the Springfield bar in all the mental qualities that go to form the ideal lawyer, it is quite impossible to sketch his character within a few lines. I shall, therefore, not attempt it within these narrow limits. It is another story. It is, however, at least partially told in the addresses on Judge Logan, delivered after his decease before the Illinois Supreme Court in memory of the man and his services. These were published at the time, and a copy may be found in our State Historical Library.

In this new firm of Logan & Lincoln the junior partner found himself measured up daily, in office and court work, with a partner whose mind was alert, keen, and at the same time as profound and analytical as that of Edmund Burke, whom he in many ways resembled. This ever-toiling, "haste not, rest not," tireless law partner, as well as most strict and exact business man, gave to Lincoln the pace of his life up to that time. Lincoln became aroused by Judge Logan to greater legal ambitions than had ever inspired him before. His mental development had come to a point where he was fully equal to taking this training.

Passing so briefly from mention of Lincoln's first two partners, I cannot forbear a further word of tribute to the high character and noble ideals characteristic of both John T. Stuart and Stephen T. Logan. They lived long, useful, and notable lives in the city of Springfield. It becomes us all to keep their memory green and aspire toward their excellences. In all of moral and mental stamina that makes good citizenship, they were the peers of each other. In mental

characteristics and business methods, in their
social manners and religious views, they differed
widely; and the passing of Lincoln from one
firm to another brought him into connection with
such sharp contrasts that they could almost be
said to have introduced as great a change into his
mental drill as his passing from Salem and country
life to Major Stuart's law office in Springfield did
in the first event.

Each in his separate way left a lasting impress
on the future President. He profited profoundly
by them both, as few minds are capable of profiting
by close contact with others. In later years,
as President, amid vast problems of political and
diplomatic issues, as well as of military strategy,
the influence—even some word selections and
sentence moulding methods in state papers—
of these two former partners was occasionally
discernible by those familiar with the courteous,
suave skill of the one, and the keen, dagger-like
thrusts of logic of the other.

How fortunate it is to the memory of these two
eminent gentlemen to have had so apt and original
a student and partner as Abraham Lincoln, and
that they discerned his worth and assisted him
through those years. The highest excellence is
capacity to be taught, to grasp opportunities in

occasions and personalities as they come and go. Lincoln was singularly well endowed with this trait. All his life he lived with mind and soul all open to the four winds of heaven and earth. This was a chief source of power in his eventful life.

# William H. Herndon: The Last Law Partner

There by the window in the old house
Perched on the bluff, overlooking miles of valley,
My days of labour closed, sitting out life's decline,
Day by day did I look in my memory,
As one who gazes in an enchantress' crystal globe,
And I saw the figures of the past,
As if in a pageant glassed by a shining dream,
Move through the incredible sphere of time.
And I saw a man arise from the soil like a fabled giant
And throw himself over a deathless destiny,
Master of great armies, head of the republic,
Bringing together into a dithyramb of recreative song
The epic hopes of a people;
At the same time vulcan of sovereign fires,
Where imperishable shields and swords were beaten
      out
From spirits tempered in heaven.
Look in the crystal!   See how he hastens on
To the place where his path comes up to the path
Of a child of Plutarch and Shakespeare.
O Lincoln, actor indeed, playing well your part,
And Booth, who strode in a mimic play within the play,
Often and often I saw you,
As the cawing crows winged their way to the wood
Over my house-top at solemn sunsets,
There by my window,
Alone.

                              EDGAR LEE MASTERS.

# VIII

## WILLIAM H. HERNDON: THE LAST LAW PARTNER

Now followed the last, the longest, and probably the most influential of all of Lincoln's law partnerships. Lincoln selected this one, the others invited him. There was a difference of nearly ten years in their ages. Temperamentally, there was more than twice what those ten years stood for. Few partners ever differed more widely in fixed characteristics when they entered upon their partnership, and yet maintained these to the extreme without change and with no break or jar in any hour of their partnership to its close.

The senior partner was deficient in three very common elements in the character of most men who arrive at eminence. These deficiencies largely contributed to partnership harmony, and, it may be added, promoted his fortunes in his future public and political life as well. Usually the things we possess are the ones expected to add to the credit side of character. But character has a very desirable debit side, as well. The advantageous

deficiencies that made Lincoln stronger were that
he was a man who had few settled prejudices; that
he was free, to a large degree, from obstinacy; and
that in him there was no petty egotism. With
these threefold deficiencies cancelled out of his
character credits, it is not remarkable that he
was the most adaptable and considerate of partners; and that at last, in larger relations and
responsibilities, he became such a master, even
when associated, as he was, with most masterful
men.

Lincoln met Herndon for the first time, to
become interested in him, at Speed's dry-goods
store, over which Lincoln roomed with Mr. Speed
when he first came to Springfield to enter into
partnership with Major Stuart in law practice.
Part of that time Mr. Herndon also shared that
upper room with both his employer and his future
law partner. Friendly relations began there which
were destined to continue and deepen through
future years. Some little mention of the moulding
influences around the life of William H. Herndon,
previous to this and on up to the time this partnership began, seems desirable for several reasons
before considering him in his relation as partner
of Lincoln.

Unlike Lincoln, Mr. Herndon had been reared
in a home of wealth, with the best opportunities
for early instruction which the schools of Springfield then afforded.   He had never felt the privations and grinds of poverty amid squalid rural
surroundings on the frontier, as had Lincoln.
Through childhood he had been the favourite
son, and his father's plans for his education were
liberal.   Having finished the courses offered by
the schools of Springfield, his father sent him to
Illinois College at Jacksonville.

This college was then under the control of the
Yale band of professors who had come west to
establish, if possible, a new Yale College, plus
greater liberality of thought in both religion and
politics.   In this college, under the personal instruction of such professors as Beecher, Sturte-
vant, Turner, Adams, Post, Dr. Jones, and others,
young Herndon began his college life.   He has
told me in private conversations of these most
enjoyable years in his life; of the wider world
opened to him by his advanced text-books; of
the inspiration and ambition aroused in him by
the excellent college library; and especially of the
personality of his professors, and the deep, abiding impress which their scholarship and political
principles made on his life.   The time spent there

8

was, as he said, a perpetual romance; but its
ending, so unexpected and sudden in its coming,
made those years seem a dreamland when he
looked back to them.  A boy's will may be as
unstable as the wind; but the thoughts and principles implanted in young manhood are destined
to abide.  In young Herndon's case they did abide,
were passed on, and, in some degree, helped to
mould the character of a nation's executive.

Young Herndon was more than half-way through
college when on November 7, 1837, the Alton riot
occurred, resulting in the throwing of the Abolition
newspaper press and material into the Mississippi
River, and the murder of its editor, Lovejoy.  Great
excitement was aroused throughout the country.
This brought the Illinois College professors and a
number of the student body and a few citizens of
Jacksonville to the front with the war-cry of the
Revolution on their lips.  Jacksonville was then
one of the active stations on the Abolition Un-
derground Railway that secretly passed runaway
slaves on to Canada.  A public meeting on the
campus was announced at chapel, to be held that
afternoon.  The college bell chimed the call on
time, and a crowd assembled.  Several professors
and citizens addressed the assembly in short im-

promptu speeches. The people, mostly Southern
in their political ties, were turbulent; and outside
the college influences, they sympathized with, or
condoned, the actions of the Alton mob. The
meeting seemed likely to end in a row. At this
critical moment the young student, Herndon, made
his way towards the front and took the platform.
The student body caught the excitement, and seeing Herndon speaking privately with President
Beecher, on the platform, they raised the college
yell, and shouts for "Herndon," "Herndon"—
"The son of a Democrat. Let us hear what this
'son of a gun' can say!" Beecher, already appalled by the noisy crowd on the campus, without
finding exactly what the young student proposed
to say, in his perplexity told young Herndon to
speak if he chose.

How long Herndon held the crowd I never
could learn—no one noted the time. But several
who were there agree in the account narrated in
later years of the remarkable speech he made,
and the degree of quiet with which the assembly
received it. His appeal was surprisingly moderate,—for a free press on free soil at least; and was
voiced decidedly, yet so skillfully as to gain the
attention of an adverse audience to the principles
of freedom taught by the Illinois professors and

claiming that they should be maintained in all free states and territories. The student body began cheering; hisses and catcalls became fewer; and as he closed he was picked up by his college mates and borne off the campus on the shoulders of his fellow-students, and the whole affair came to an end as a sort of College Hill pyrotechnic display.

A local paper had a short but witty write-up of the event from the college student standpoint; and by some means this and a fuller verbal account of young Herndon's part in this "anti-slavery" meeting, as it was called, came to the notice of his father at Springfield, the Hon. A. G. Herndon, who, with Lincoln, was of the "long nine" members in the Illinois Legislature who secured the State Capitol for Springfield. He saw at once that his favourite son William had imbibed the horrible political heresies of Professors Beecher, Turner, and their associates—in plain words, that he had become what these professors called a "Free Soiler," but what the fond parent called "Abolitionist"—not to add here the abundant and expressive epithets which the Hon. Archie G. Herndon was so competent to prefix under the excitement of warm political discussion.

Young William got peremptory orders by the
first mail to pack his goods, pay all bills, and
return home. This he promptly did, and on ar-
riving, the fond but indignant parent informed
the youthful student that he would have none of
this in his house and name; that unless he re-
nounced his horrid abolitionism and all his d—d
abolition associates and came back to the fold of
the true and undefiled Democratic party for good,
he would have no more of him in college or out of
college; nor should he ever have any financial
assistance from him thenceforward. The father
was too late. Father and son were of the same
unbending, independent, and impulsive temperament, and discussions of political principles and
parties only widened the breach between them.
The seeds of liberty had been well planted. The
free-soil principles had taken too deep root in the
warm young heart of the enthusiastic son. He
was immovable. Ever after, on all occasions,
through good and evil report, every throb of his
heart, and all the energy and force of his active
temperament, kept time with the advance of free-
soil sentiment throughout the nation until the final
consummation was reached.

Young Herndon left home, bereft of all ties
there save his mother, on whom it became his

habit to call daily, or salute as he passed by the
home. To meet his first expenses, he began clerk-
ing in Speed's store. In the back part of this
store-room was a huge fireplace. This, after business and office hours, became a meeting place for
circles of local business and professional men of
the city, both old and young, where all manner
of business, professional, and political subjects
were discussed, often until the small hours of
morning. Mingling with such company, the young
clerk did not drift from his studious habits nor
long remain a dry-goods clerk. He was soon
reading in a law-office, and became a more zealous
student there than he had ever been at college.
He was admitted to the bar in due time, and
settled down to office work and court practice for
such clients as began to recognize his merits.

Thus William H. Herndon had worked up to
a day when, to his great surprise, Lincoln—who
had just withdrawn from his partnership with
Judge Logan,—walked into his office and proffered
him a partnership in their law practice. To Mr.
Herndon's modest but sincere objection, in view
of his youth and lack of experience in the law,
Lincoln would not listen, but closed all discussion by saying: "If you can trust me, Billy, I

can trust you!" That was their partnership pact.
They had then been intimately acquainted for
five years. For nearly seventeen years thereafter,
this trust was mutually kept sacred in loyalty to
each other, mutual and untarnished.

Lincoln's readings during his partnerships with
Stuart and Logan were principally confined to
law, with only an occasional diversion in history
or essays by English writers of the Queen Anne
period that were favourites with Major Stuart.
None of the latter strongly appealed to Lincoln.
Thus it happened that, during these two partnerships, aside from consulting authorities and
precedents connected with their clients' cases, Mr.
Lincoln did scarcely any reading, and his leisure
hours were usually spent in conversational enjoy-
ments where his friends were accustomed most to
congregate. Professional engagements were less
exacting at that period than now; and offices,
banks, and stores were meeting places in a social
way of congenial friends during the day and
evenings to an extent quite different from the
custom of the present day. In this respect,
Lincoln's habits began to change after his partnership with Mr. Herndon began. The latter had
become a regular reader of State Library books,

and this he had supplemented by purchases of many of the best books written in later years. At the time of which I write, Herndon's chief extravagance was buying books. I was told by the principal bookseller in Springfield, sometime before the Frémont campaign, that in addition to all his professional reading, Mr. Herndon read every year more new books in history, pedagogy, medicine, theology, and general literature, than all the teachers, doctors, and ministers in Springfield put together; a statement which was probably correct.

Another marked characteristic of Mr. Herndon's —aside from his ability as a lawyer—was the rapidity with which he could go through a book and master its essentials, and, after laying it aside, could thereafter, on a few moments' reflection, give a digest or rehearsal of its contents, admirably condensed, and sometimes more interesting than the book itself. He had cultivated this faculty for years and, at this period, it had become a habit with him, and one he greatly enjoyed when with congenial friends.

This way of acquainting himself with the contents of books suited Lincoln much better than his own reading of most books. No public man since Socrates ever enjoyed more thoroughly, or used more successfully, the art of getting from question-asking conversations most of the information he desired on any subject that was interesting him. There has been no little discussion, in later years, about some one's absurd affirmation "That Lincoln never read any book through himself!" and Herndon's off-hand statement, intended only to emphasize Lincoln's ability as a thinker, viz.: "Abraham Lincoln read less and thought more than any other man in his generation." Superlatives and extreme generalizations were never more faulty than when used to define the characteristics and mental make-up of so unusual and original a man as Lincoln. These statements in some degee have colouring from this habit acquired after he and Mr. Herndon became partners. Before that, Lincoln had read, and read most thoroughly, quite a variety and no small number of the best books. He said as much in regard to many books which he mentioned, and referred to and spoke of having read them before he came to, Springfield.

His marriage,—it may be remarked here,—was another most controlling circumstance in the literary and intellectual life of Lincoln. Mrs. Lincoln, while a resident of Springfield before and after her marriage, impressed all who were ac-

quainted with her with the excellent and accu-
rate literary taste she had acquired by education
and general reading, especially in history, poetry,
and fiction.  She stimulated Lincoln's ambition
politically; and at the same time by her brilliancy
as a conversationalist, and her appreciation of all
that was best in literature, and in the books which
they mutually enjoyed in their home, was a forceful stimulus to Lincoln's intellectual life.  She was
a good writer of terse, strong sentences, and an
excellent critic to correct anything submitted to
her revision.  She delighted to entertain her family and friends by reading aloud evenings.  Above
all, she had the most constant and enduring faith
in Lincoln's political future, and tried by every
means in the range of her unusually inspiring and
vigorous personality to assist her husband in season, and—as some friends thought—out of season,
when she saw Lincoln's own ambition beginning
to fail.  By some who were less intimate and knew
less of her character and of the real home life of
Mr. and Mrs. Lincoln, this solicitude on her part
was often misconstrued as officiousness.

Mr. Herndon's books and his constant addi-
tions to them became of increasing interest to
Lincoln.  They first opened to him the new, wide,
modern world of science, political history and

philosophy, as well as of literature. Then the
growing State Library also became an attraction
to him.   There he met many kindred spirits
whose conversational interests became almost a
daily pastime with him.   It was a new atmosphere
that mingled politics with science and literature.
This State Library attraction was greatly increased
by the charming personality of Hon. Newton
Bateman.   He was then State Superintendent of
Public Instruction and his office adjoined the law-
office of Lincoln and Herndon.   Here Lincoln
was to be found nearly as often as at his own
office.   In those important years, these intimacies
harmoniously continued, with literary and political
friends coming and going, meeting at the State
Library and privately at the office, with literary
and political discussions between friends and partners.   Not that Lincoln cared equally for all the
literary selections his friends and the junior partner found in their readings, or which Mrs. Lincoln
shared with him at their home.   The partner, at
least, soon saw what kind of books would interest
his senior, and these he brought forth as Lincoln's
request or mood called for them.   Often at the end
of an office day he would remark: "Billy, what
book have you worth while to take home tonight?" or he would already have one, procured

at the State Library during the day, and stowed in or on his hat, so that he would be sure not to forget it when starting for home.

No part of Lincoln's life has suffered more in history from false colouring and belittling sensationalism than that of the earlier years he lived in Springfield; and especially is this true in respect to his mental and literary activities of that period. While I knew Lincoln in office life then every new book that appeared on the table had his attention, and was taken up by him on entering to glance through more or less thoroughly. I can say the same of the books in Bateman's office adjoining the law-office. Walt Whitman's *Leaves of Grass*, then just published, I recall as one of the few new books of poetry that interested him, and which, after reading aloud a dozen or more pages in his amusing way, he took home with him. He brought it back the next morning, laying it on Bateman's table and remarking in a grim way that he "had barely saved it from being purified in fire by the women."

Readers of this day hardly comprehend the shock Whitman's first book gave the public. Lincoln, from the first, appreciated Whitman's peculiar poetic genius, but he lamented his rude, coarse naturalness. It may be worth while to relate the office scene when Lincoln first read Whitman's poetry. It was exceptional for Lincoln to read aloud in the office anything but a newspaper extract. Only books that had a peculiar and unusual charm for him in their ideas, or form of expression, tempted him to read aloud while in the office,—and this only when the office family were alone present. It was quite usual and expected by us at such times, when he would become absorbed in reading some favourite author, as Burns's poems, or one of Shakespeare's plays, for him to begin reading aloud, if some choice character or principle had appealed to him, and he would then continue on to the end of the act, and sometimes to the end of the play or poem.

When Walt Whitman's *Leaves of Grass* was first published it was placed on the office table by Herndon. It had been read by several of us and, one day, discussions hot and extreme had sprung up between office students and Mr. Herndon concerning its poetic merit, in which Dr. Bateman engaged with us, having entered from his adjoining office. Later, quite a surprise occurred when we found that the Whitman poetry and our discussions had been engaging Lincoln's silent attention. After the rest of us had finished our criticism of some peculiar verses and of Whitman in general, as well as of each other's literary taste and morals in particular, and had resumed our usual duties or had departed, Lincoln, who during the criticisms had been apparently in the unapproachable depths of one of his glum moods of meditative silence,—referred to elsewhere,—took up *Leaves of Grass* for his first reading of it. After half an hour or more devoted to it he turned back to the first pages, and to our general surprise, began to read aloud. Other office work was discontinued by us all while he read with sympathetic emphasis verse after verse. His rendering revealed a charm of new life in Whitman's versification. Save for a few comments on some broad allusions that Lincoln suggested could have been veiled, or left out, he commended the new poet's verses for their virility, freshness, unconventional sentiments, and unique forms of expression, and claimed that Whitman gave promise of a new school of poetry.

At his request, the book was left by Herndon on the office table. Time and again when Lincoln came in, or was leaving, he would pick it up as if to glance at it for only a moment, but instead he would often settle down in a chair and never stop without reading aloud such verses or pages as he fancied. His estimate of the poetry differed from any brought out in the office discussions. He foretold correctly the place the future would assign to Whitman's poems, and that *Leaves of Grass* would be followed by other and greater work. A few years later, immediately following the tragedy of Lincoln's assassination, Whitman wrote that immortal elegy, "O Captain! My Captain!" which became the nation's—aye, the world's—funeral dirge of our First American. When I first read this requiem its thrilling lines revived in my memory that quiet afternoon in the Springfield law-office, and Lincoln's first reading and comments on *Leaves of Grass*. That scene was so vividly recalled then as to become more firmly fixed in my memory than any other of the incidents at the Lincoln and Herndon office, and this is my apology for giving space for rehearsing it so fully here.

Lincoln's manner as a reader differed greatly from his public speaking. He read very slowly, with strong stress and emphasis at times, to bring out any peculiar meaning that strongly impressed him in what he was reading. I cannot fix this in the mind of my reader better than by giving the letter he wrote to James C. Conkling, enclosing the fuller open letter or appeal he had addressed to the "Unconditional Union Meeting" to be held September 3, 1863, at Springfield, Ills., and to be read there by Mr. Conkling.

WAR DEPARTMENT,
Washington City, D. C., Aug. 27, 1863.

MY DEAR CONKLING:

I cannot leave here now. Herewith is a letter instead. You are one of the best public readers,— I have but one suggestion,—read it very slowly.

And now God bless you, and all good Union men.

Yours as ever,

A. LINCOLN.

Mr. Conkling read this shorter note first, before reading Lincoln's lengthy letter at the "Unconditional Union Meeting." The letters were read by Mr. Conkling at several other union rallies held that month in adjoining counties for enlisting volunteers.

James C. Conkling was a near and valued friend of Lincoln. He was a man of refined culture, with the deserved reputation of great stability of character. His personal appearance was commanding, and Lincoln could have selected none at his former home better fitted to deliver his letter. Conkling had an unusually clear-toned, far-reaching voice for out-of-door speaking. He was by far the best elocutionist of the Springfield bar, and the "reading slowly," as requested by Lincoln, was complied with in the delivery of every sentence. The serious attention of those who heard the original manuscript so impressively delivered, or read it after publication in the press throughout the country, recognized it, even in the intense tension the nation was under through those weeks, as the most apt and inspiring of Lincoln's presidential appeals to his fellow-countrymen up to the close of 1863.

Enough has been said of the life at Lincoln and Herndon's office to show Lincoln's interest in books and literary friends during that period of his life. Professor Bateman's office, adjoining the law-office, was an educational centre for publishers and their agents, as well as for teachers and college men. As mentioned elsewhere, Lincoln was as often to be found there as in his own office. Most of the school-books with which publishers so liberally supplied Superintendent Bateman were examined and discussed there by him and Lincoln with as much interest as if the latter were an educator.

Emerson and Carlyle were greatly admired by Herndon, but Lincoln cared little for either. He

9

enjoyed particularly Holmes, Theodore Parker, Beecher, Whittier, Lowell, the elder Abbott, and Hawthorne. He cared little for fiction, though Mrs. Stowe's *Uncle Tom's Cabin* moved him deeply while reading it. His literary taste was keen and delicate, and his zest for the best in current literature was unerring to recognize and appreciate beauty of style and strength of personality in a writer's method of expressing thought. He was deeply moved only by such writing. His likes and dislikes in literature were quick, strong, and positive, a few brief glances, a sentence read here and there, a hasty turning of leaves, sufficed with him for a decision to toss the book aside, or to make it his own as he found leisure to read it. Lincoln was an earnest seeker of the best thought and form in literature.

Lincoln when with Herndon, his last law partner, and the office family,—with Bateman and his educational friends, at the State Library with book lovers he met there,—was entirely different from the Lincoln that was known in Court circles, or among the hale-fellow friends at taverns on the rounds of the Eighth circuit, or amid the rush of political conventions and noisy huzzahs of stump-speaking campaigns. He could and he did meet in closest companionship the widest variety of men, at home with all of them. He could be comrade and friend in full fellowship with all conditions of men, because he had lived a life of the widest companionship. Some who thus met him thought they had measured all there was in the man; and as they and their friends thought they saw all there was in him, so some few have written him down in history. A sad and wearisome mistake! No friend or foe, none of all the many men who were near him, should ever claim to have clearly seen, to have thoroughly understood, or to be competent to interpret, all in the life of Abraham Lincoln.

Of all the men who have sat in the White House, he was the one who had lived nearest, and most understandingly nearest, to *all* the people. His life was nourished and enriched by that rare and difficult culture to be gleaned only from close associations with all the people; until in his country's hour of supremest need, he was found to be the one so thoroughly prepared that he was competent to stand forth as The First American; victoriously to live and die for all the people; "that this nation, under God, should have a new birth of freedom; and that government of the people, by the people, and for the people, shall not perish from the earth."

In my library is a little morocco-bound book, five by seven inches, and less than an inch thick. On its front cover, in large gilt lettering, faded and worn like the leather, is inscribed, "AUTO-GRAPHS." Opening it, I copy a page, first giving some mention connected with its writing, as an appropriate leaf of these incidents in the office life at Lincoln & Herndon's. Coming into the office with this book (just from the bindery) in my hand, it attracted Lincoln's attention. Taking it from me, and finding the pages blank, he asked what it was to be used for. I explained that I meant to procure from time to time autographs of friends, and I had brought it with me then to get his signature for the first page of the book. As I spoke, he was caressingly stroking with his strong hands the soft new leather. He opened it, playing the gilt-edged leaves through his fingers for a brief moment; placed it, open at the first page, on the table before him, took his pen and wrote:

To-day, Feb. 23, 1858, the owner honored me with the privilege of writing the first name in this book—

A. LINCOLN—

Handing the open book back to me he said: "Henry, that is the first book for such a purpose

To. day. Feb. 23 1858, the owner
honored me with the previ-
lege of writing the first name
in this book —
                        A. Lincoln —

_____

The Struggles of this age and
succeeding ages for God &
man — Religion — Humanity, &
Liberty with all their Complex
and grand relations — may
they triumph and Conquer
forever, is my ardent wish
and most fervent Soul-prayer

Feby 23ᵈ 1858          Wᵐ H. Herndon

I ever saw, and of course the only one I have ever written my name in." I placed the book next before Mr. Herndon, and requested him to write on the same page. He read Lincoln's lines, paused, as if considering what he would write, then took his pen and rapidly wrote:

The struggles of this age and succeeding ages for God and man—Religion—Humanity and *Liberty*—with all their complex and grand relations—may they triumph and conquer forever, is my ardent wish and most fervent soul-prayer.

WM. H. HERNDON.

Feb. 23rd, 1858.

When the reader will recall that this book was a souvenir for a youth just past twenty—immature as most young men were, turned out at that age in the primitive West—the tolerant, gentle-spirited thought which Lincoln traced to satisfy a youth (and this only a few months before his celebrated debates with Mr. Douglas), says in and between its lines more than any words of mine now could of his genial, gentlemanly manner toward all who approached him. I never knew a man whom I would have been more willing to send to heaven on his own merits, nor one who would be less willing to go there on such a recommendation.

The junior partner's more extended lines reveal their marked difference in temperament, and in a flashlight disclose the virility and high ideals that then inspired Herndon in those strenuous years. The word *"Liberty"* was underscored by him, and that scored line means to those who lived through the fifties and sixties of the nineteenth century much more than will be appreciated now. It was the mistake of Mr. Herndon's life that he did not become a college professor rather than a lawyer.

From the beginning of the Herndon partnership, the chief interest of both partners,—after the discharge of strictly law duties to their clients,—was in national politics. Mr. Herndon was not an aspirant for office, and only once was a candidate, when he was elected Mayor of Springfield for a single term. This was without his solicitation, and against his personal wish. It would have been better for him and his country had he possessed more personal and political ambitions. He needed that steadying process which, under public official responsibility and criticism, can give stability to character.

With Lincoln, political interests were personal. He was more ambitious to deal publicly with problems in national politics than persistent for office.   Mrs. Lincoln was always an inspiration, and sometimes a prodding one, to her husband's ambition, because of her personal belief that high national preferment awaited him politically, if she, with others, could only keep him steadfastly aspiring thereto.   More than most men of his exceptional ability, Lincoln needed this prod.   For this service there is a large, and as yet unrecognized debt of gratitude due from the American people to Mary Todd Lincoln.   This is another story, yet one of such importance that the history of those years cannot be fully understood and is only partly told, if her intense and loyal devotion to her husband's political interests and ambition be left out.   Later, when the stress of public discussion rose to more than fever heat in 1858, and thence on to the fiercer white heat of 1860 and succeeding years, Lincoln was in the current's full pressure and momentum, and these held him to ambitions with a steadiness that in former years he had often lacked.   Fortunately, his wife and other judicious friends were then inspiring influences.

As before said, the study of national politics was pursued with unusual interest by both Mr.

Lincoln and his partner.    Besides the full use of all
the *Illinois State Journal's* exchanges, they took
regularly at the office, up to the closing of Southern
mails by the Confederate States in 1861, the
*Charleston Mercury*, the *Richmond Enquirer*, and
the *Louisville Journal*, also the *Southern Literary
Messenger*, an able monthly political and literary
magazine, formerly edited by Edgar A. Poe, and
later by Hon. J. R. Thompson.  This was a
periodical of unusual ability, published at Richmond, Virginia, and Lincoln gave no other periodical that came to the office the attention he gave
to this.  He had preserved an accumulation of
these *Southern Literary Messengers* on top of one
of the office presses, and he directed my attention
to them a few weeks before setting out for Washington, while sorting up odds and ends about the
office, saying that he wished me to take charge
of them and to have them bound and kept for him
until he should return to the office life again, a
purpose which he often spoke of as being his
intention.  This I did, and they are now in my
library.  They comprise no one year's numbers
complete, but the broken set is highly valued, for
with it are associated the memory of Lincoln, and
his wish to have them put into preservable shape
for his future use.

The *State Journal's* editorial rooms began to have more alluring attractions for Lincoln than the Springfield court room. He contributed political editorials for the *Journal*, more or less regularly; and Mr. Herndon did more often. The latter had several correspondents among prominent Abolitionists of Ohio and New England, and he read and discussed their letters, as well as his replies, with Lincoln. The most remarkable circumstance that now impresses me, as I look back over daily intimacies with this law firm from 1856 to 1861, was the student-like way in which they both steadfastly kept the average political affairs of the whole nation under attention; using all sources and, in their private conferences and discussions with each other, reviewing and sifting all conflicting opinions on national questions that came to their office table from North and South, East and West. Had they foreseen the political and executive battles before Lincoln, his preparation could not have been more thorough, exact, and comprehensive to fit him for his duties as President in 1861–65. It was his wish that led to their subscribing for Southern papers and periodicals, and he was a more diligent reader of these than his partner. The latter had first supplied the office table with the leading Abolitionist papers of the North. It was their first discussions on the extreme opinions which Northern papers presented which brought the Southern views, represented in Southern papers to the office table. This was Lincoln's suggestion and choice, for, as he then expressed it: "Let us have both sides on our table; each is entitled to its 'day in court.'"

I do not say that Lincoln's change of opinion leading up to the marked change about 1854, depended upon, or was brought about, by this or that special person or environment. He was not a man of ordinary mould. He cannot be measured by any conventional yardstick. He reacted so slowly from and to the mental stimulus of printed pages, or of his personal surroundings, that it is hard properly to estimate the power or extent of the influence these had with him. But most assuredly he was impressible and did react. Yet it must be said with emphasis that one could never anticipate what effect a thought or argument brought to his attention would have to influence him, or what his retort or answer would be, or how long afterward it would be made. His mental character was one of unusual depth and poise. Part of a sentence from one of Theodore Parker's political sermons, read aloud in 1857 by Herndon

in his office, and to which Lincoln listened attentively, discussing the political and rhetorical peculiarities of it with Herndon and two young friends
then present, years afterwards flashed into the
Gettysburg speech as part of one of its immortal
sentences, viz., "of the people, by the people, for
the people." This peculiarity was often shown by
him in the apt and pertinent biblical quotations
in his writings and speeches, throughout his presidential years.

While giving due credit to all other influences
surrounding him, it must be conceded that the
deepest influence that entered into Lincoln's character during this last partnership was the strength
of Herndon's anti-slavery views, and the political
literature in the study of which they had been
united for so many years. At the same time, Mr.
Herndon was turned aside from his former extreme Abolitionist views, by Lincoln's wider and
more practical vision of the political situation at
that time. Lincoln's influence over Herndon was
not limited to political affairs, though these have
naturally received more special consideration.
From the day in 1837 when Lincoln, after looking
at Speed's room upstairs and leaving his saddle-
bags, and, on returning, told Speed that he had
moved, these two occupied with Speed the same

room over his store.   Thenceforth until Lincoln's
departure for Washington in 1861, his influence
over Herndon was a controlling one.   It was a
quaint, peculiar power that Lincoln exerted; silent,
steady, masterful.   No father or brother ever exerted a more complete control over his own kin
than did this senior partner over his junior.   It
was not a changeful influence only occasionally
exercised, but one constantly maintained throughout the period of their close personal relations.   On
the other hand, aside from political subjects, Herndon had little, if any influence, over Lincoln.   Their
habits of thought and methods of composition
were as wide apart as the poles.   The poetry of
Bailey's *Festus*, the writings of Carlyle and Im-
manuel Kant charmed Herndon, while it was Whitman, Burns, and Shakespeare of whom Lincoln
became more and more fond.   The authors mentioned indicate the wide difference of their literary
tastes.

This strong personal influence of the senior partner did not cease while Lincoln resided in Washington.   During those years of separation Herndon
spurned all approaches by reporters desiring to
secure his opinion of Lincoln's policies and views
as already revealed, or his forecast of the President's future course in the discharge of his execu-

tive duties at Washington. His loyalty to Lincoln was such as to render him extremely careful in expressing his own opinions on vital national questions in advance of definite information as to the President's position. Herndon is entitled to great credit for his discreet reticence regarding President Lincoln's official actions, for he was not naturally a secretive or prudent man; and at that time many things were going entirely too slowly to suit his impetuous temperament and radical views.

After the spring of 1858 there is little to narrate concerning legal and literary matters transpiring in the office of Lincoln and Herndon. The time and energy of the firm became actively engaged in the exciting political affairs of the State and Nation. As mentioned elsewhere, Lincoln, in the early months of 1858 devoted himself almost exclusively to the preparation and revising of his great speech to be delivered June 16, 1858, following his nomination by the Republican State Convention as their candidate for United States Senator in opposition to Senator Douglas. After that, until the great debates with Douglas began, he was busied in preparation for that remarkable series of speeches. From that time on Lincoln

gave scarcely any personal attention to clients
in the routine of the office practice.

Herndon, with the clerical assistance of the
office students, attended to this practice, depend-
ing upon Lincoln to appear only in the most
important cases where clients insisted on his
personal presence at the trial.  It was wonderful
to us young men how quickly the chief grasped
everything in the cases thus prepared and presented for his consideration.  Such summary of
evidence and decisions pertinent to these cases
were usually brought to his attention just before
the trial, in night meetings at the office.  His
days were full of other affairs.  His capacity
and power for intense mental concentration at
such conferences enabled him to master, in a very
brief time, the important points involved in the
suits into which he was called by Mr. Herndon.
So thorough was this mastery that he usually
took the principal part in conducting these cases,
whether the trial was before juries or the judge.
Some of the most important suits in which he
ever appeared were tried during these last two
years of his active legal practice.  The strength
and control of his mental powers, as shown by this
faculty of concentration, stood out more promi-
nently before the students in the office than at

any previous time.   Herndon himself on several
occasions expressed his surprise that Lincoln could
be so occupied in political affairs and yet at the
same time could so fully grasp and retain the complicated details of lawsuits, never blundering as to
either the facts of the evidence or the points of
law while in the stress of the court trials.

The work he could accomplish in the way of
preparing briefs for presenting before the Supreme
Court, during the few hours after the rest of us
had left the office and gone home, was a surprise
the next morning to us all who had participated
in the details of their preparation up to the night
before, preparatory to Lincoln's arrangement and
final statements.   He desired to be left alone after
having once gone over these cases.   It irritated
him, he said, to thresh over straw a second time.
Any young man in the office whose zeal for a
client's case led him into any restatement of
evidence would be sure to get some quaint reproof
that we all were careful not to merit again.

Musing upon these memories of the office life
in the early and later part of 1858, I recall how
little we were then conscious of the serious changes
in the life of the firm which were even then imminent.   I have related elsewhere something of

Lincoln's preparations for his debates with Douglas in the senatorial canvass of that year, and also for the Cooper Institute speech. There is little to say further of the life in the office than has been already stated on the subject in connection with other chapters.

The closing hour of Lincoln's presence there came on the evening of February 10, 1861, when he and Mr. Herndon passed down the stairway for the last time. Lincoln had just before requested Mr. Herndon to let the office sign remain and conduct business in the firm's name as it had been, until he should return to Springfield when, he said, they would resume their legal practice the same "as if nothing had happened."

The departure of Abraham Lincoln from Springfield measured a larger loss to our city than that of any other citizen who ever left us. During the five years following his departure, the little swinging sign,—"Lincoln and Herndon,"—was a reminder and assurance that some day the senior partner would return and go in and out as of yore, brightening our city by his presence and genial personality as none other ever had done. Lincoln had no foes among us other than political, and even these when they came near enough to him, forgot their partisanship and learned to love him. The little sign had hung outside the narrow stairway entrance to the office, with its inviting welcome to friend and foe alike, for twenty-one years. None of us were prepared for the startling shock that came when black drapery covered it and darkened the familiar stairway and office front on the terrible morning following America's darkest night of April 14, 1865. The end had come. The sign was removed only when the bullet of the pro-slavery assassin Booth dissolved the firm, and the senior partner passed beyond his strange, strenuous, sacrificial life here below. That day, after martyrdom closed this law firm, was the saddest that ever came to Springfield, the darkest one recorded in the nation's history; for in the hour of our supremest need, we had lost our First American.

Lincoln's death was in many ways the severest stroke that ever came into the personal life of Herndon. He had come under his influence in the wild and reckless years of student life. Thereafter, for twenty-eight years he had depended upon and had the strength and masterful poise of Lincoln's influence to steady his life. The last

five of those years, though Lincoln was so far
away, he had exercised a no less active restraint
over Herndon. Lincoln was to return. Life
with the partners was again to be resumed "as
if nothing had happened." This expectation
had braced Herndon up for meeting and deserving
that anticipated future. It had warmed and
strengthened him during the waiting years.

After Lincoln's death it became Herndon's ambition to write a great life of Abraham Lincoln.
Hindrances hedged him about in many ways and
prevented his doing this as he had first planned.
He lost his first wife who, with their children,
had given him domestic quiet and happiness.
A second marriage was less fortunate. Then his
father's death brought him a considerable estate
that came under his management at an unfortunate time of general financial depression. Debts
accumulated, and false friends took advantage
of his confiding nature until his part of the estate
was greatly reduced, and his last days were so
filled with bread-winning tasks that they became
drudgery to him. He had never had any aptitude
or experience to fit him for the life of a business
man. The anxieties that necessarily fill such a
life were hardships too severe for one of his na-

ture to master. They ground the book lover and
idealist in a way that was pitiful to those who
knew him intimately.

It was amid such untoward circumstances as
these that he had been forced to find all the time
which he could devote to contribute to those
manuscripts which, in collaboration with others,
he prepared for the press. He honoured the
memory of Lincoln sincerely and was full of good
intentions to do justice to his great life by telling
all the truth, as he understood it. He was, however, over-confident in the opinion that he knew
Lincoln, as he expressed it, "better than Lincoln
knew himself." How many others, with much
less reason to say so, have made this mistake?
God alone knew the man He had sent and prepared for the task. An hundred years more may
elapse before this life can find a historian large
and clear visioned enough to write into the pages
of history the full and correct proportions of
Abraham Lincoln's life and services.

The great confidence Herndon had in himself,
his assurance that he had exhausted all the facts
that ever could be reached, misled him. Then the
intensity of his emotions and the aggressive,
restless vehemence of his vocabulary led him

at times still further astray.    In so far as he failed
it was not for lack of honesty or purity of purpose.
He wished to deal fairly with the material he had
collected, but his collation was incomplete, and
his interpretations were found to be not always
correct; besides, his own personal peculiarities
and some preconceived opinions hampered him
with limitations he could not always overcome.
Perhaps more than all else, he was peculiarly sensitive and responsive to the sensational stimulus
of the collaborators and publishers with whom he
was associated in bringing out the several biographies of our great President with which his
name is connected.    These facts sufficiently account for his incomplete and unsatisfactory treat-
mont of oome portions of the Lincoln biographies
which he was sponsor to.    Howbeit, we should
not allow these imperfections and his shortcomings to obscure or lessen, in any measure, the substantial obligations history will be under for the
valuable contributions Herndon has made by his
revelations of so much that he was intimate with
in the life of Lincoln, and whose personality he
has, by his vivid imagination and forceful rhetoric,
projected into history for the future better understanding of our great President's remarkable
life.

For some time after that fateful day of April 14, 1865, the old office of Lincoln and Herndon was left most desolate. The young men who were there from 1858 to 1861 had all left and no others had filled their places. The junior partner remained but he was never the same "Billy" Herndon again. One partner after another took the vacant chair, but none ever filled to him his senior's place, or steadied and strengthened him in so many ways as his first partner had done. He missed Lincoln every hour. Wearied with law and politics and the unresting throngs about him, and oppressed by many cares history needs not to mention, he left the office at length and sought quiet and rest in the work and solitude of his farm. He found that even these good nurses could not long give solace to his restless life. Earth could never give him the rest he sought.

He was now an old man, bent and aged beyond his years. He was still fond of outdoor life, and communings with forest and field. He loved nature with a love akin to the mother-love of a dutiful son. He was a great walker and was often seen early in the morning, or returning in the late afternoon, walking back and forth over the five miles between his farm and the city where

his active years had been spent; but now his only
mission there was to see his children, meet a few
friends, get his mail, and carry back and forth
some of the books he still loved so sincerely. He
was no recluse; he was companionable and lovable
to the last. But he was a shattered man. The
assassin's bullet that paralysed his senior partner's
heart reached also the vital forces of the life of the
junior. His once brave heart beat slower and less
steadily; no longer did it drive those currents
throbbing through his veins, filling his life as in
earlier years with an energy and abounding vigor
such as few mortals ever possessed.

Life had once been, through its every day, a
thrilling joy to Herndon. I never have known a
friend who could live so much in a day, or inspire
with more energy those about him. This was all
changed. It had become his lot to linger on
through years which to him meant little; the saddest, loneliest one of all the intimate friends my
life has ever been close to. He said to a friend
on meeting him for the last time: "If you see
my good friend Death, tell him I am ready and
am very weary waiting for him and wish he
would come soon." It was not long he waited.
The delayed guest arrived suddenly at the last.
Those ultimate problems of man's origin and

destiny that had engrossed him so intensely and honestly through speculative studies during all his years, were now to be faced for his personal solution. Death found in him the welcome of a weary soul glad to pass Beyond. No longer would

> His way be hid.  He could not see
> By human lights, where he would be;
> But when this midnight bell did toll,
> The Gates were opened for his soul,
>     In that blessed land;
> In which the burden and the mystery,
> In which the heavy and the weary weight
> Of all this unintelligible world
>     Is lightened.

I wish to borrow from my friend Joseph Fort Newton the words of appreciation he gave in his excellent book, *Lincoln and Herndon*, as expressive of my own sentiments, a last word of estimate and farewell to William H. Herndon.

Mr. Herndon died on March 14, 1891, at his humble home on his farm five miles from Springfield, his last words being: "I have received my summons; I am an overripe sheaf; but I will take the weaker one with me,"—referring to his son who died the same

day.  So passed an ardent, impetuous man of great
native ability, radical of mind but lovable of soul;
a strong man whose zeal often exceeded his wisdom,
but whose charity was unfailing; a man of noble
integrity as a citizen, a lawyer, and a friend; unwilling
to compromise truth, yet eager to give every man his
due.  He has been cruelly misjudged, if not foully
belied, but all this may be forgotten, for he has
passed

"To where, beyond these voices, there is peace."

# The Springfield Life of
# Mary Todd Lincoln

To him she bore four children; with him she sat by the death-bed, and stood by the graves, of two of them. She rejoiced with him in his successes, she condoled with him in his defeats; and whenever she saw an opportunity for his advancement, she stimulated his ambition to compete for it. They were *en rapport* in all the higher objects of being; when he was nominated for President his first act was to go home in person to break the glad tidings to her. That the nation is largely indebted to Mary Todd Lincoln for its autonomy, I do not doubt, as to the full measure thereof, only God can know.

HENRY C. WHITNEY.

# IX

## THE SPRINGFIELD LIFE OF MARY TODD LINCOLN

In 1837 Miss Mary Todd visited her sister, Mrs. Ninian Edwards, at Springfield, Illinois, and remained three months before returning to her father's home at Lexington, Kentucky. She was then nineteen years of age. This first visit was made very pleasant by her sister and the many friends of the Edwards family, and two years later she returned to make this city her home. I wish the reader to get a correct impression of her life while she resided in Springfield. There were some things in her life here,—something in her character, her personality, and her influence,—that deserve recognition and appreciation by all who would know Abraham Lincoln.

It was said of her by her friends in Lexington, that while as a young lady there, she mingled freely in society, but never manifested any desire for attention from young men. Her home was one of refinement and her life had been free from care and anxiety up to the time she left. She

had spent the last four years of her school life in a
select French school, kept by a Mrs. Martelli.
Nothing but French was spoken, and Mary
acquired a thorough knowledge of that language.
She always kept it up, reading in the original the
latest French literature and the best old French
authors. An incident illustrating her familiarity
with the language and her appreciation and interest in French literature is worth relating.

In 1856, while sorting over magazines and
pamphlets in the Lincoln and Herndon office,
I found among them in the *Southern Literary
Messenger* for September, 1851, a letter of their
Paris correspondent giving full translation of
Victor Hugo's address on capital punishment,
delivered in connection with certain court pro-
ceedings. Knowing Mrs. Lincoln's fondness for
French literature,—Victor Hugo's writings especially,—and being delighted with the oration,
I called at the Lincoln home with the magazine
that she might read it. She had not seen it before
and was as delighted in reading it as any school-
girl would have been.

This address was really part of a speech delivered
by Victor Hugo before a French court in defence
of his son, who was on trial for "conspiring against

public order" by publishing in a Paris newspaper the description of a most gruesome scene and terrible struggle connected with the execution of a criminal. The condemned man resisted the officers in a terrific and bloody hand-to-hand struggle for his life, fighting them fiercely for three-quarters of an hour before they accomplished his execution. The elder Hugo's defence was one of his most brilliant oratorical efforts, and resulted in the acquittal of his son.

The translation by the Paris correspondent did not entirely satisfy Mrs. Lincoln. She insisted that a copy of the speech in French should be procured, the better to show the strength of Hugo's oratory and the difficulty of translating into English a French oration of such intense feeling so as to preserve the true Hugo fire and force. It was two months before the French copy came. I took it at once to her, taking with me also the Paris correspondent's translation in the *Southern Literary Messenger*, so that I might follow the thought while she read the speech as delivered in French. I hoped that she would read it aloud, which she did, stopping often to compare the translation with the original. She read with such clearness and dramatic fervour, and translated with such sympathy that, instead

of following the English translation, I could only
sit entranced by the force and effect of her tones
as she translated or, at times, read Hugo's inspiring
oration in his native language. She was an
excellent reader, and her sympathy with French
was perfect. This incident occurred fourteen
years after her marriage, and indicates how well
Mrs. Lincoln kept up her school-girl interests.

In personal appearance Mrs. Lincoln was not
strikingly commanding, nor was she considéred
handsome. On seeing her for the first time,
one would be drawn to closer inspection by something in her features which, though not of a strictly
regular or beautiful type, were yet pretty when
viewed in connection with her complexion, her
soft brown hair, and her clear blue eyes that
seemed to penetrate the very soul as she fixed them
steadily upon you while speaking. Her husband
and she were alike in one particular. Having
once met and conversed with either, one would
never forget the impression made on one. Neither
was of a conventional type.

She had a plump rounded figure, and was
rather short in stature. Physically, mentally,
emotionally, she was the extreme opposite of
Mr. Lincoln. She was exceedingly sensitive. Her

impulsiveness of thought and speech had no need of restraint, because her face was always an unerring index and reflection of her passing emotions, even if she had not expressed them in words. She thought quickly, spoke rapidly; and the expression of her face was always in harmony with her words. Without intending to wound, she sometimes indulged in sarcastic or witty remarks. At times of deep feeling, her words might bring keen pain to persons toward whom she felt kindly. It was remarked to me by one who had known Mrs. Lincoln long and very intimately, that her frank and spirited manner, her candour of speech and independence of thought, often gave offence where none was meant.

She was never ungracious towards strangers nor did she ever intentionally wound a friend. She loved children with the real all-mother love; and when death took her own children, it was as though part of her own life had gone away with them. Always and everywhere she showed her refinement and dignity of character, entirely free from affectation or the putting on of manners for special occasions. Those who were not close to her, or who had not found her pliant to their wishes, might greatly misjudge Mrs. Lincoln. If not her friend, it required sometimes an effort

not to be her critic; or, with those having similar
impulsive peculiarities, her enemy. This was
the sad and unfortunate relation between her
and Mr. Herndon; he being markedly similar to
her in his impulsive antagonisms and equally
unforgiving. They began their acquaintance
wrong and they maintained that attitude ever
after so consistently that neither could see the
sterling qualities of the other.

The first time they met was at a dance at
the residence of Col. Robert Allen in Springfield.
Herndon had engaged her for a waltz, and as
they glided through it Herndon said that he had
never before danced with a young lady who
moved with such grace and ease. A few moments
later, as they were promenading through the hall,
Herndon, to compliment her, said she seemed to
glide through the waltz with the ease of a serpent.
She halted for a moment, drew back, and her
eyes flashed as she retorted: "Mr. Herndon,
comparisons are odious, yours of a serpent is
rather severe irony, especially to a newcomer."
With a recoil from him,—part bow and part
courtesy,—she passed from his side. They were
never friends in all the years afterward. There
seemed to be nothing they could unite on, to work
together for, in a common interest between them.

I shall not in this writing seek for or endeavour to set forth all the sources, or motives, nor follow the trail of either the personality, or criticisms, of Mrs. Lincoln's foes; much less shall I try to account for their animosity. But this significant fact faces future historians who will winnow the records of these years of the trash and caricatures heaped on the memory of Mr. and Mrs. Lincoln, and they cannot ignore its significance:— That the writers who have exhausted the resources of both gossip and fiction to write Mr. Lincoln's early life down in a way calculated to coarsen and cheapen those years with as much vulgarity as possible, are the same writers from whom have come the attacks on Mrs. Lincoln in even worse caricatures, when they have attempted to portray her life as maiden, wife, and mother.

Lapse of time, and an accumulation of criticisms with which Mrs. Lincoln has been assailed since the death of her illustrious husband, has furnished the occasion, as well as the justification, for a statement calling attention to the good traits and merits of her character, and a recognition of the excellent influence Mrs. Lincoln exerted for good on Lincoln. No fair and candid statement of the interrelation and inspiration she had in

her husband's life while in Springfield, or of the
influence of her personality as the real inspiration
of those formative years, has been honestly given.
Most gladly would I prefer to pass in silence the
cruel aspersions against her, if by so doing it would
contribute to the oblivion those slanders deserve.
The silence of her friends has been misconstrued.
Death, which, with most all others, silences the
voice of calumny, in her case stimulated it.
Since this woman's life ceased and her mortal
remains were placed at rest in the tomb beside
her illustrious husband, an increasing accumulation
of odium has been heaped upon her memory.   In
many respects, during her later years, she was the
most unfortunate of all the widows and mothers,
either North or South, that the Civil War made
desolate.   She deserved a better fate, and history should give her more just and considerate
treatment.

I ask you to hear something about her life in
Springfield as I knew it.  To this I will add,
compositely, something of the appreciation she
inspired in many others who knew her intimately.

The reported failure to meet a marriage date on
the "fatal January 1, 1840," has been so fully

disproved in later biographies, and by such un-
questionable testimony, as to render it unnecessary
here to give that story any attention other than
some slight references to its falsehood and absurdity. There was no licence issued, no wedding
party, no expectant bride, and no distracted
bridegroom wandering far away in deep despair.
That the engagement between Miss Todd and
Lincoln was suspended in the early days of 1840,
is no doubt true. My own opinion, formed from
conversations I have had with mutual friends
since 1872, is that the words "deferred engagement" would more truly describe the situation.

Those writers who tell of "a marriage company
and supper without a groom," and of a dis-
consolate maiden "toying her head-dress in
nervous agitation," are guilty of a cruel fiction.
Had such an event happened in a town the size of
Springfield, the story could not have been kept
locked up in the memory of a few, and they
unfriendly and not social intimates of Miss Todd
or her Springfield relatives. It would have been
scattered widely, a notorious piece of delightful
gossip to be published from the circles of five
hundred homes. Social gossip was never more
active or long-lived than in Western communities
of that period. Love and matrimony were its

staples, and a broken marriage date and feast would have been the sweetest of morsels to the tongue of Madam Grundy.

A visit made by Lincoln in company with Joshua Speed to Louisville, Kentucky, was coincident with Speed's leaving Springfield and returning permanently to Louisville. Lincoln went in response to Speed's invitation. At the time he was in one of his periods of depression from ill health, or as he termed it, "attack of hypo," aggravated, probably, by the opposition of Miss Todd's relatives to their marriage and to the breaking off, for the time, of the engagement. Lincoln was sensitive to the reflections of Miss Todd's family on his humble parentage and poverty as a barrier to their marriage. In view of this, he felt it to be his duty to all parties concerned at that time to release her from her promise. This he had done.

An engagement between a couple with such strongly marked mental, emotional, and educational differences,—to say nothing of their contrasting characteristics, could not be expected to progress smoothly at all times, especially in view of the opposition of relatives, in such a community as Springfield was in the early forties, and amid such active social attractions as were among Miss

Todd's relatives and friends. Her guardian and near friends planned for her a marriage of wealth and distinction. She was, by all odds, the reigning belle of the little city. Lincoln was ten years older than she. Pique and jealousy and temperamental misunderstandings among their friends had plenty of edges to cut and mar their courtship, as can easily be seen when we look back upon the condition in which they lived. There is no need to call up the pipe-dream shadows of a Salem story, and invoke the uncanny word "insanity," to account for the temporary estrangement of Lincoln and Miss Todd in 1840, and his extended visit with the Speeds at Louisville.

I quote now from Mrs. Emily Todd Helm,—a half-sister of Mrs. Lincoln,—a statement written by her regarding this subject:

There has been so much written and printed upon the subject of Mrs. Lincoln's marriage, that I will only say that Mrs. Lincoln's family had no knowledge of any want of faith or honour on Mr. Lincoln's part. Mrs. Dr. Wallace, Mrs. Lincoln's sister, positively asserted that there was never but one wedding arranged between Mary Todd and Mr. Lincoln, and that was the one that occurred. Mr. Herndon says that it was a large wedding, and that Mrs. Lincoln

was married in a white silk dress.  This is an error,
and he must have confused Mrs. Lincoln's wedding
with that of her sister, Mrs. Wallace, who was married
a little before.  Mrs. Lincoln, by preference, had a
quiet marriage.  Mrs. Wallace says that on a Sunday
morning Mr. Lincoln and Mary Todd called Mrs.
Edwards to where they were sitting, and told her
they had decided to be married that evening.  Mrs.
Wallace was sent for, and she says that she never
worked harder in her life than on that day.  Only a
few people were present.  Mr. Dresser, the minister,
held a short service in his church, and afterward
went up to Mr. Edwards's house, where the marriage took place.  There were present Mr. and
Mrs. Benjamin Edwards, Major and Mrs. John
Todd Stuart, Dr. John Todd and family, Dr. and
Mrs. Wallace, and Mr. and Mrs. Ninian W. Edwards.  The bride was clad in a simple white muslin
dress.

Dismissing the fictitious wedding picture, we
find Lincoln, immediately on his return from
Louisville, writing back to his friends there that
he is made very happy by hearing that Miss
Todd, who had gone with a train load of merry
young folks on a trip to Jacksonville, was reported
to him as being cheerful and happy.  This letter,
with events soon to follow, clearly enough shows
that Lincoln had not lost his affection for Miss

Todd, and that her happiness was still a chief concern in his life.

It was not long until they met by a purposeful "accident," arranged by Mrs. Simeon Francis, a veritable adept in reconciling differences, and, as I can personally vouch, the most social of all the society-loving merry dames of Springfield at that time. She was a close friend of all the best society people, and was inferior to none as a leader in all the good things among Springfield's social affairs. She held to a very strict observance of all the courtesies and obligations due in social life. Had Lincoln been guilty of failing to keep his wedding date, she would never have recognized him again, much less invited him to meet Miss Todd socially in her home, and afterwards made her home their trysting-place until the marriage was arranged. Results justify our saying that even this first meeting was mutually enjoyed, since it led to another date at the Francis home, and so on there, frequently, until the wedding.

Miss Todd, influenced, no doubt, by the mature social wisdom of Mrs. Francis, this time determined that the event should not be deferred, lest it come to the attention of several of her captious and opposing relatives, who might again interpose objections leading to delay and possibly

to another breach of the engagement and a new
series of misunderstandings.

It must be remembered that the two parties
here most interested were not children. Miss
Todd had met Lincoln three years before. She
had known him two years intimately, and one
year more as her accepted *fiancé*. She was
twenty-four years old and was unusually well
endowed by nature, by education, and by experience to select with wisdom and discretion a
husband from her admirers, all of whom had been
gentlemen of the best social standing. She had
arrived at the full maturity of womanhood when
she accepted Lincoln's proposal of marriage, and
she did so in the face of opposing relatives, preferring
him before all others of her many suitors she had
been acquainted with among whom were some
very prominent gentlemen who had sought her
hand in marriage. To say, as some biographers
have said, that Mary Todd accepted Lincoln and
"married him in a spirit of pique and petty spite
to wreak vengeance on him through wedded life,"
is beyond reasonable conjecture. It is absolutely
inconsistent with all womanliness, and it will not
stand up under any light you can place it in against
a lady of Miss Todd's culture and character.

The statement does violence to our exalted ideal of womanhood, and discredits the historian who made it, and, unfortunately, impairs confidence in much else he has written so clearly and accurately concerning Lincoln's personality and characteristics.

As has been said, Lincoln was ten years her senior. He had passed the "susceptible age" when marriages are contracted on impulse, and repentance comes afterwards with plenty of time for meditation. He had had other and unusual experiences qualifying him for contemplating the seriousness of marriage. For two years at least he had studied Miss Todd with that serious thoughtfulness with which any mature and balanced man, such as he was, studies the woman whom he thinks of asking to become his wife. The statement that Lincoln deliberately gave himself up to this lady as a "willing sacrifice," and with no love for her, is only a little less improbable than the one of pique charged as the motive of Miss Todd.

I saw Mr. and Mrs. Lincoln in many and widely differing situations during their married life at their home; saw them leaving home; saw them

separating for more or less length of absence for
business or pleasure; saw them again when calling at the law office, during busy hours, in hurried
consultation between each other on family, social,
or business affairs; saw them in their carriage
together, driving out on our city streets and
country roads; saw them at parties; saw them
regularly attending church together every Sunday,
when both were at home; I saw them often in
crowded assemblies of all sorts and conditions of
public affairs; often again in both pleasant and
trying circumstances with their children; with
their friends, their political foes, and later with
huzzahing party admirers filling their modest
home and sometimes overflowing the streets around
their residence on Eighth Street with embarrassing
familiarity.  In none of these situations did I
ever detect in Mrs. Lincoln aught but the most
wifely and matronly proprieties and respect toward
her husband, her family, and her friends.  She
adapted herself cheerfully to all those exacting
functions at their home required of Lincoln in
his public life.

Lincoln had Chatterton engrave on the wedding
ring, which he placed on Mary Todd's finger the
evening of their marriage,—"Love is Eternal."

I did not know, in the years I saw that ring on Mrs. Lincoln's hand, the marriage legend it bore so securely within its circle. But now as I write these lines, the memory of the years during which I knew Mr. and Mrs. Lincoln's wedded life brings with it no shadows that darken or doubts to discredit the sacred pledge which Lincoln then gave his bride and which she accepted with fullest maidenly confidence. He was a sincere man; she was a loving and loyal wife.

There were moods of inner solitude into which Lincoln sometimes lapsed, when his silences were mysteries to all his friends. I have referred fully to this mood elsewhere, as one of his personal peculiarities. None should be so rash and unjust as to interpret them as shadows cast by Mrs. Lincoln over his married life. That would be false and more than cruel. They were characteristic of him long before he met her; they remained inseparable from his remarkable personality all his life. Mrs. Lincoln, on the contrary, so far from being a cause of this mood, was his greatest solace in those inner solitudes. Her sprightliness of spirit, her keenness of wit, the brightness of her versatile mind, lit up many times,—as I personally know,—the gloom and self-centred

moodiness of his spells of melancholy that, as
Herndon aptly said, "at times dripped from
him." She, of all who were near him, was the only
one who had the skill and tact to shorten their
duration; the only one privileged to attempt it.
I revere her memory for this most gracious service,
as much as for others that speak more loudly.

She was the animating cause, I am glad to say,
of Lincoln's absence on tours out in the Eighth
District to extend his law practice and help swell
their slim finances, as well as to promote his
political influence by more extensive acquaintance. But his going on those long trips was not
to escape his home, as some historians have
intimated. That was a cruel, bitter, false charge.
His wife was at home attending to its every interest
and discharging willingly, faithfully, gladly, every
duty that Lincoln's absence added to her usual
cares. The stories about the crackers and cheese
luncheon at the law office; about the long moody
walks when Lincoln was at home, and so many
other of the petty matters of gossip that have
lodged in what purports to be history—all these
could be taken up, one by one, and shown to be
independent of any and all relation to Mrs.
Lincoln. For example, the sound of Lincoln's
axe heard from his wood-shed at one o'clock at

night, was interpreted by a gossiping neighbour and put into more than one history, as evidence that he stole back home at that late hour and was "preparing to get his lonely supper." The fact was, that Lincoln often remained at his office into the small hours engaged in legal or political work when he could be free of all callers; that he always retained and enjoyed his Salem-grocer munching habit and provided frugal lunches of cheese and crackers then and at various other times in his office; and that on his return home in the evening, early or late, it was his custom to go by his wood-shed and split the kindling with which to build the morning fire.

Mrs. Lincoln had forebodings about her husband's health. This was the cause of her watchful interest with all details about his clothing and diet. She had been advised by her brother-in-law, Dr. Wallace, that Lincoln had tendencies to ailments that without prudent attention to his nutrition might be serious. This opinion was confirmed by other physicians she had consulted, without her husband's knowledge. Several of Lincoln's friends—Herndon, John T. Stuart, B. F. Edwards, and his two brothers-in-law Dr. Wallace and C. M. Smith among them—I recall as speaking of Lincoln's inherited tendency to consumption.

None of these opinions were ever mentioned to Lincoln. It was remarked between friends who had these forebodings, that Lincoln's best physical safety was in his not being aware he had any liability to consumption. This view was probably the correct one to be taken for his good, at any rate it was the opinion and motive they acted upon.

Connected with Mrs. Lincoln's attention to her husband's clothing, she was always most concerned about the regularity with which he partook of his meals and the quality of his food. Without her supervision he would have given little or no attention to any of these matters. He was prone to indulge in "browsing around," as he called his irregular habit of partaking of any food that was handy, at any hour and any place. If left to himself, when he was very busy, he would skip several meals and not be aware of it. This did not suit Mrs. Lincoln's ideas of the well-ordered life she wished him to have, and she insisted that he should be punctual at the appointed time for all meals, and partake leisurely of a bountiful and varied amount of food.

This watchful interest in her husband's welfare and care for his health was one of common knowledge among those near Lincoln, or intimate with their well-ordered home in Springfield. It was more difficult for her to enforce this regularity with the President, amid the stress of his official life, than when at Springfield. Washington officialdom, and the political crowd that thronged the White House, resented this and misinterpreted the wife's interference with what they considered their exclusive claims on him at any and all times. But Mrs. Lincoln in those strenuous years relaxed none of her insistence that Lincoln be punctual to respond to the call from the dining-room. No matter how closely he might be engaged with official business, or persistent politicians applying for office, or discussing party matters in their localities, she could tolerate no delay without manifesting her displeasure and if possible enforcing her calls for him at meal-times.

I will illustrate this care of Mrs. Lincoln's by relating an extreme incident that occurred at the Executive Mansion in the latter part of Lincoln's first term. One of the chief assistants in the Treasury Department had come to see Lincoln on a matter of such serious importance that it must be acted on immediately. So important was the subject that the department's head having the matter to decide did not feel at liberty to do so without consulting the President, and the papers connected with it were brought by his assistant for Lincoln's examination and final direction. While both were closely engaged over the documents in the President's private office, the butler appeared at the door and announced that dinner was served. Lincoln paid no attention to this, and the conference continued as before. In a short time Lincoln's younger son came with a message from his mother that all were at the table awaiting Lincoln's joining them. Still the President continued the examination as before. The little fellow became very insistent by pulling and tugging at his father's coat and hand to pull him away with him. His father firmly disengaged himself and dismissed the boy both by his manner indirectly, as did his words, saying, "Yes, yes; directly." The little fellow at last withdrew reluctantly, and returned slowly to the dining-room. A few minutes later Mrs. Lincoln appeared at the office door and in her emphatic tones of command, so characteristic of her when she was displeased, informed Lincoln of the repeated calls he had had and that they were awaiting his presence at the dinner table. At this, Lincoln, without the slightest show of displeasure, laid aside the documents his attention had been engrossed with and quietly arose and passed across the room to Mrs. Lincoln who had paused after advancing several paces into the room. As Lincoln approached her she partly turned as if intending to leave the room with her husband. On reaching her side Lincoln took hold of both Mrs. Lincoln's arms just above the elbows and slowly moved forward, gently pushing her before him, until she was through the door. He there released her arms and stepping back, closed the door between them and, locking it, quietly returned to his seat at the table without a word of reference to the incident, or the slightest indication of being ruffled by the interruption and its decisive conclusion. He then went on with the business as if no pause had been made. The episode was ended.

Mrs. Lincoln's motive behind this scene was a proper one and, in the busy later years of Lincoln at Springfield, as well as through his official ones at Washington, it was often the case that only by some such persistent insistence that Mrs. Lincoln could secure the President's conforming to habits that would safeguard his health. Mrs. Lincoln's watchful care about her husband's personal welfare was no small part in contributing to the maintenance of his strength and promoting his efficiency through the exacting labours he was required to pass.

In all these affairs, as well as in so many others that have been distorted and misinterpreted, they understood each other's peculiarities and motives quite well, and the limits to which their insistence for conformity to each other's wishes could be successfully carried. This understanding was one of mutual and respectful recognition between them. Usually, in all domestic matters, Lincoln yielded his own preferences to those of his wife; but there were times, as in the incident related, when he acted adversely to Mrs. Lincoln's wishes, and then he had a peculiarly balanced manner of deciding and disposing of the situation in the way he considered to be necessary. He usually did so, as in this affair, by actions, not by words. At these times Mrs. Lincoln recognized that she had reached her limits of influence, and with rare exceptions she graciously accepted and conformed by silence to Lincoln's stronger will, as she did on this occasion.

I beg pardon of my reader for trailing my pen through such trivial scandals. I have done it in the briefest possible way and will inflict you with no other. This brief mention is made to show the injustice and cruelty of much of the false insinuations against Mrs. Lincoln that have found their way into history. The few I have mentioned show how distorted many simple acts and incidents may be made to appear when taken apart from their relation to other facts with which they were connected.

Without Mary Todd for his wife, Abraham Lincoln would never have been President. Without Abraham Lincoln for her husband, Mary Todd would, probably, never have been a President's wife. From the day of their marriage they supplemented each other in many unusual times and ways through those remarkable years. Out of many instances in which she shaped his course in public affairs, I will cite two which were perhaps of chief importance in their far-reaching results.

President Fillmore offered Lincoln the governorship of Oregon. John T. Stuart and other influential friends insisted that he take it, saying that Oregon would soon be a State, and he one of the Senators. Lincoln was inclined to accept the offer, but qualified assent by saying "if my wife approves the plan." Mrs. Lincoln, with that quick, instinctive, deciding wisdom which she usually showed in practical affairs as well as in politics, "refused her consent," Lincoln reported, and the matter was dropped.

Again in 1855 she showed her ability as a political forecaster of events. During Lincoln's absence from Springfield his friends took the liberty to announce his name together with Judge Logan's, in the *State Journal*, as a candidate for election to the House of Representatives of the Illinois Legislature. The morning she saw the notice in the *Journal*, Mrs. Lincoln drove down to the office, went upstairs to the editor, Simeon Francis, and ordered Lincoln's name out of the list of candidates. The name was taken out. In a day or two it was inserted once more. Again she drove down to the *Journal* office and not only ordered Lincoln's name withdrawn, but secured a promise from Editor Francis that it should be left out until Lincoln's return home. On Lincoln's return, Dr. William Jayne, who it seemed was responsible for putting both Logan's and Lincoln's announcements in the *Journal*, went to see him. Jayne reports: "I went to see him in order to get his consent to run. This was at his own house. He was the saddest man I ever saw, the gloomiest. He walked up and down the floor almost crying. To all persuasion to let his name stand in the paper, he said: 'No, I can't. You don't know one half and that's enough.'"

Jayne, or some other party, did go, however, in Lincoln's absence, and again had his name reinstated in the *Journal* a few days before the election. Both Logan and Lincoln were elected by about six hundred majority. But, after all, Mrs. Lincoln's forecast of the state election was right, and Lincoln's, Jayne's, and their friends' wrong. The state had elected an anti-Nebraska Legislature, as Mrs. Lincoln had felt positive it would. Lincoln became a candidate, as Mrs. Lincoln had planned, for United States Senator to succeed Shields. He and his friends then thought it a necessary preliminary for him to resign his seat in the Legislature. This he did, and in his stead, at a called election, there was elected a Nebraska-Democrat. This would not have been the case if Lincoln had been kept out of the candidacy in the first place, leaving the field open for some other anti-Nebraska Republican candidate with Judge Logan's popularity and influence to pull both through. This caused considerable criticism among Lincoln's friends at home and in the Legislature, and was one of the minor causes of Lyman Trumbull's election to the United States Senate instead of Lincoln, by uniting on the former the votes of the anti-Nebraska Democrats in the Legislature.

Mrs. Lincoln in her attention to political movements did not in any degree neglect her household or her domestic and social duties. At the same time she did not allow them to monopolize her life, or obscure the hope she ever kept in view, inspired by her girlhood dream that she "was to be a President's wife." None other ever had such faith in Lincoln as her's. He had less faith and hope in himself than she. This vision of the Presidency was no fancy or joke with Mrs. Lincoln, as some supposed. No denial was too severe, or service too hazardous, if it promised the goal she had in view for Lincoln. She was more aggressively ambitious than her husband. She steadfastly inspired and kept him aiming higher. Until 1858 he needed influences outside himself to push him to the political front and hold him there. She gave him this unstintingly. Some misunderstood, regarding her officious in this, and said cruel, harsh things about her for it. This annoyed her greatly, and her replies were equally stinging, creating life-long enemies.

Through that strenuous campaign of Lincoln and Douglas for the United States Senate, she had an important part. In the privacy of their home she insisted on his going out, and staying out, with Douglas to the end of that celebrated debate. With the children and household affairs and Lincoln's personal wants to be provided for, she was the managing partner who kept the expense accounts within the limits which their moderate income placed at her disposal.

Again, from 1856 to 1860 she accomplished a task in family affairs such as the wife of no politician had ever accomplished before in a struggle for the nation's highest office. Lincoln himself accorded her both before and after the Douglas debates unstinted appreciation for her efficiency in all home and financial affairs, as well as in forecasting the progress of political events.

Only a limited few knew the intense spirit of her who remained behind at the home to inspire his going forth, to welcome his return, to rejoice at any good news, to stimulate him to renew the struggle when disappointment had to be met. Lincoln was despondent at times during those high-strung days. The stress and turmoil and tumult went hard with him. Not so with her. She had a spirit that never tired on the battle line. She was less pleasant on a retreat, and could stand almost anything better than a political dead calm.

Lincoln could be at entire ease on the retreat, or in a calm, for he then went into one of his moods of meditative silence that was at such times exasperatingly unintelligible to her, and to so many of his friends. To whom would this mood not have been a trial? Yet she always found a way of getting him out of it and back on the firing line again.

I will here quote a few sentences from Emily Todd Helm, a younger sister of Mrs. Lincoln's. They throw direct rays of light from one who knew their home life into the false, gossipy fog that has been floating around the Lincoln home life at Springfield:

It has been said that Mr. and Mrs. Lincoln were not happy. Mrs. Wallace (her sister) denies this emphatically, and the present writer's knowledge bears out Mrs. Wallace's assertion. They understood each other thoroughly, and Mr. Lincoln looked beyond the impulsive words and manner, and knew that his wife was devoted to him and to his interests. They lived in a quiet unostentatious manner.

She was very fond of reading, and interested herself greatly in her husband's political views and aspirations. She was fond of home, and made nearly all her own clothes. She was a cheerful woman, a delightful conversationalist, and well-informed on all subjects of the day.

The present writer saw Mr. and Mrs. Lincoln together some part of every day for six months at one time, but saw nothing of the unhappiness which is so often referred to. Many of Mr. Lincoln's ways, such as going to answer the door bell, annoyed her, and upon one occasion a member of the family said, "Mary, if I had a husband with such a mind as yours has, I wouldn't care what he did." This pleased her very much and she replied: "It is foolish,—it is a small thing to complain of."

Another event in the life of Mr. and Mrs. Lincoln at Springfield presents a scene that illustrates how utterly unbelievable, how absolutely unthinkable, is the story of their unhappy married life. It was "to the little woman over on Eighth Street" that he first thought to communicate the news, when he received the telegram announcing the third ballot of the Republican Convention in Chicago. It was about nine o'clock on the morning of May 18, 1860, when Lincoln came into his law office. J. H. Littlefield, a student, Lewis Rosette, a lawyer, the writer, and one or two others were present. His first words were: "Well, boys, what do you know?" Mr. Littlefield told what he had last heard. Lincoln then said that Dr.

Wallace had come down from Chicago that morning, and had said that he thought Seward showed great strength.

In a few minutes, Edward L. Baker, one of the editors of the *Illinois State Journal*, came in with two telegrams. The first told of the delegates coming into the Convention hall. The other told that the names of the candidates for nomination had been placed before the Convention, and that Lincoln's name had received by far the greatest applause. Baker then went out, but returned hurriedly in a short time with a telegram showing the votes on the first ballot. Lincoln took the dispatch in his hand and looked at it with no expression of word or manner. His face was a blank. Again Baker went out. Lincoln remained silent for several minutes, then got up, saying: "The dispatches appear to be coming to the *Journal* office, by arrangement, I presume; we had better go over there." On our way to the *Journal* office, as we were passing the telegraph office, Lincoln said: "Let us go up. It is about time for the second ballot to come." All but Littlefield and I went upstairs to the telegraph office, while we went on direct to the *Journal* office. Baker and Bailhache, the editors, and a few others were present when we arrived.

A few minutes later the second ballot came in, showing a gain of seventy-nine votes for Lincoln while Seward had only gained eleven votes. Just then Lincoln and several others came into the editorial rooms. The dispatch was handed to him. No one spoke a word. I can never forget the look that came on his face as he read it. At that moment he believed he would be nominated. It was only a short time by the watch,—but it seemed long to the expectant friends in the *Journal* office,—before the third ballot was handed in, and it was shouted: "Lincoln's nominated," and there followed a call for three rousing cheers. But the desire to hear the vote as reported in the dispatch cut them short. "Read the dispatch," was the call. It was read aloud and handed to Lincoln who, after glancing at it, said, "I felt sure this would come when I saw the second ballot." There was a hearty hand-shake of congratulations all round, followed by three rousing and prolonged cheers. No one but the nominee was able to control the joy the nomination had brought. He sat erect, rigid, and his face wore the firm-set stern lines I had seen in it when he spoke at Petersburg in 1856.

A merchant from Boston, Mass., who happened to be present and standing by Lincoln, suggested that Lincoln's life be written at once,—a remark so characteristically Bostonese that Littlefield and I, in our boyishness, exchanged glances that came near convulsing us, had it not been for the serious look with which Lincoln turned to the merchant, as he gravely said: "My friend, I do not see much in my life as yet to write about."

After a little further talk Lincoln made his way slowly through the company and down the stairs. He paused for a moment as he reached the sidewalk fronting Sixth Street. He still looked very serious, but in a brief moment remarked, rather gravely, yet with the peculiar mellow emphasis he had when speaking with great sincerity: "There is a lady over yonder on Eighth Street who is deeply interested in this news; I will carry it to her"; and he walked rapidly south on South Sixth Street, across Washington Street, and as he came in front of the old Marine Bank building, which then stood well back from the street walk, Robert Irwin, the cashier, seeing Lincoln passing by, and having heard about the third ballot, came out to the sidewalk to congratulate him. He was a heavy, short, lion-faced man—and Lincoln so tall. They clasped hands in silence only a moment. Their friendship had been of long standing. Their manner expressed more than words. Leaving him, Lincoln started on again at a rapid pace, but was stopped before he reached the middle of the block by the messenger from the telegraph office, who handed him a message for which he receipted and, opening the envelope, read it, then hurried on with rapid strides, holding the message in that large right hand as he hastened to her who had in vision expected that news for him through all their wedded life. No one saw their meeting. His thoughts were first of her to whom he gave the pledge: "Love is eternal."

Most biographers state that this dispatch handed to him on the street was his first notification of his nomination; but the telegram announcing his nomination on the third ballot had been in his hands twenty-five minutes, and he had been congratulated by a number of people before this last telegram was delivered. This was due to the fact that there was direct communication between the Convention hall and some newspapers. A private dispatch from the superintendent of the telegraph company was sent, after all changes in the ballots had been made, and this was the telegram which was actually handed to Lincoln on the street, and which he carried home to Mrs. Lincoln.

No wife of a presidential nominee ever received news of her husband's nomination with greater joy than did Mrs. Lincoln. It was the most gratifying moment of her life. To Lincoln it was one of the gravest days he ever had passed through. It was only the exuberance of his fellow-townsmen, and their constant thronging around him with congratulations, that kept him out of a mood of meditative silence into which he would have lapsed. No citizen of Springfield, probably no citizen of the nation, knew better than Abraham Lincoln did that day what were the tasks and problems before him. For years he had been making the political situation of the country a careful study. Mrs. Lincoln was oppressed by no such weight of forebodings. She was radiant with joy, and faced the future without the shadow of a fear to darken that one most perfect and brightest day of her life. She, in common with most other Springfieldians, never closed her eyes for sleep that night. The shouting and blazing of bonfires made the whole night luminous and hideous. Thousands of "Wide Awakes," clad in capes and bearing torches, marched the streets most of the night singing campaign songs. None of us then had the slightest doubt but that Lincoln's nomination was tantamount to his election;

neither did we realize the national tragedy fore-shadowed by the event which we were celebrating.

Thrills of excitement from that 18th of May, 1860, throb in my every nerve as my pen writes about its full and exultant minutes. The fires then kindled on Springfield's streets have not been extinguished or even chilled in my memory, though they are viewed across half a century's winters since then, whose frosts have whitened all my hairs. There was not a full tar barrel, nor an empty one, nor a loose box left in Spring-field the next morning, and few old fences or loose gates.

Next morning's train brought home from the Convention the Springfield delegates and citizens —hoarse, dusty, exhausted, but hilariously joyful. Some of the home-staying celebrants, after a sleepless night, in the "cold grey dawn of the morning after," had begun to feel as though they had been prematurely jubilant. Lincoln expressed it next morning to some of them, saying: "We are not out of the woods yet. Be careful you don't trip up on it." We were in the fray, but the greatest presidential campaign ever known in our history had opened, and its mysterious out-

13

come no human vision could or then even tried to penetrate.

But our enthusiasm was justified beyond all criticism, we thought, when we heard how wildly jubilant the staid, cool-blooded Judge Stephen T. Logan had been in Chicago. He had gone there to head the Illinois delegation, clad in the finest new suit he had ever worn, and his head crowned with a tall new shining silk hat, the best that our Springfield "Adams, Hatter" had ever made. He came back with his suit a sight to behold, dusty and wrinkled beyond all recognition, for he had not been out of it since he had left Springfield. He came back wearing a little Scotch cap, the glossy tall silk hat having been left somewhere in the debris of the Wigwam, near Lake Michigan, after Logan had beaten it into shapeless ruin over the heads and shoulders of his fellow-delegates upon announcement of the third ballot. No one would credit this report at first, but everybody who had been there said it was true—except the Judge. And he was silent! How we boys loved the grim Judge for his firmness, grit, and nerves of steel before he went up to the Chicago Convention in May, 1860. Ever after that event we worshipped him for the big-souled loyalty and love he had shown for

Lincoln at Chicago, which burned and throbbed in his veins with every heart-beat of this truest and noblest Roman of all the old Tenth Legion that was there. He took both my father's hands in his own when they met on his return, and, in a whisper,—for he had shouted away all the voice he had in Chicago,—said: "Rankin, I'm even with Lincoln now. He made me drop him and vote for Trumbull for United States Senator in 1856, to keep Matteson out. I cried then like a baby with vexation and wrath. Now I've had my revenge. He will be President"; and the two grey Kentuckians,—old Whig veterans of the Henry Clay campaigns,—clasped each other, crying for joy like children. I did not understand it then. I do now, for I am seventy-nine.

I now give a few extracts from letters Mrs. Lincoln wrote to Emily Todd Helm, giving the dates. The letters show Mrs. Lincoln in her active years; and Mrs. Helm's words are more revealing of Mrs. Lincoln's life in her last days than anything I should be able to say:

SPRINGFIELD, Febry. 3, 1856.
Mr. Lincoln has just entered and announced that a Speaker has been elected at Washington, that Mr. Banks is the happy man. They have had great trouble in the political world.

SPRINGFIELD, November 23, 1856.

Your husband, like some of the rest of ours, has a great taste for politics and has taken much interest in the late contest which has resulted very much as I expected, not hoped.

Although Mr. Lincoln is, or was, a Frémont man, you must not include him with so many of those who belong to that party,—an abolitionist. In principle he is far from it. All he desires is that slavery shall not be extended,— Let it remain where it is. . . . The Democrats have been defeated in our State in their governor, so there is a crumb of comfort for each and all. What day is so dark that there is no ray of sunshine to penetrate the gloom? . . . Now sit down, and write one of your agreeable missives, and do not wait for a return of each from a staid matron, the mother of three noisy boys.

SPRINGFIELD, February 16, 1857.

Within the last three weeks there has been a party almost every night, and some two or three grand fêtes are coming off this week. I may surprise you when I mention that I am recovering from the slight fatigue of a very large and, I really believe, a very handsome and agreeable entertainment, at least our friends flatter us by saying so. About five hundred were invited; yet owing to an unlucky rain, three hundred only favored us by their presence. And the same evening in Jacksonville, Colonel

Warren gave a bridal party to his son, which occasion robbed us of some of our friends. You will think we have enlarged our borders since you were here.

SPRINGFIELD, September 20, 1857.

The summer has strangely and rapidly passed away. Some portion of it was spent most pleasantly in traveling East. We visited Niagara, Canada, New York, and other points of interest. When I saw the large steamers at the New York landing, ready for their European voyage, I felt in my heart inclined to sigh that poverty was my portion. I often laugh and tell Mr. Lincoln that I am determined my next husband shall be rich.

I will add a few paragraphs written by Mrs. Helm about the last sad and lonely years of Mrs. Lincoln's life:

Mrs. Lincoln was devoted to her children, and their loss was a distracting grief to her. Willie's death at Washington was a sorrow too deep for the President or Mrs. Lincoln to refer to. Mrs. Lincoln regularly attended the Presbyterian Church, and it was her request to be buried from the church where she had professed her faith. Her wedding ring had engraved within it, "Love is eternal." The last words President Lincoln said to his wife were, "There is no city I desire so much to see as Jerusalem." With these words half-spoken, the fatal bullet entered his brain and struck him down by her side.

What wonder that such a shock was followed by great nervous prostration! Mrs. Lincoln went abroad to divert her mind.

Mr. Paul Shipman, of Edgewater Park, New Jersey, who saw much of her during her sojourn in London and on the Continent, says: "Her residence was in sight of Bedford Square, and her life subservient to the welfare of Tad (her son) who was pursuing his studies under a tutor. She shunned, rather than courted, attention, and desired peace and retirement above all things. I found her sympathetic, cordial, sensible, with that *bonhomie* so fascinating, with no trace of eccentricity in conduct or manner. She was simply a bright, wholesome, attractive woman; and I could not for the life of me recognize the Mrs. Lincoln I saw." A letter written by Mrs. Lincoln to Mrs. Shipman says: "I hope we will meet whilst we are abroad—you with your life so filled with love and happiness, whilst I, alas, am a weary exile. Without my beloved husband's presence the world is filled with gloom and dreariness for me."

In 1871 Mrs. Lincoln's son Tad died in Chicago, at the age of eighteen. "Ah, my dear friend," she said to one who knew her well, "you will rejoice when you know that I have gone to my husband and children." She was done with life. After years of failing health, in quiet seclusion from the world, shrinking from all publicity, and sensitive to every misrepresentation; sustaining the dignity of widowhood by perfectly appropriate behavior, she awaited release from her sufferings. She died at the home of her sister, Mrs. Ninian W. Edwards, July 16, 1882. Three days later she was laid to rest by the side of her illustrious husband.

The Rev. John A. Reid of Springfield expressed the feeling of many when he said: "The taller and the stronger one died, and the weaker is now dead. Growing and struggling together, one could not live without the other. Years ago Abraham Lincoln placed upon the finger of Mary Todd a ring bearing the inscription "Love is eternal." Side by side they walked until the demon of tragedy separated them. When the nation was shocked at the sad and dire event, how much more must she have been shocked who had years before become a part of his life. It cannot be any disrespect to her memory to say, that the bullet that sped its way and took her husband from earth took her too

The time will be brief until the last of those who knew President Lincoln and Mrs. Lincoln shall have passed away. In coming years, now near, another generation of citizens will often stand before the monument erected at Springfield over the remains of Abraham Lincoln; or before

the national memorial at Washington commemor-
ating President Lincoln's illustrious life and services. They will be drawn to both by their
reverent gratitude for the preservation of the
Union of the States for which we are so largely
indebted to him. His noble spirit and unfailing
faithfulness will forever be an inspiration to
those who view those monuments and recall the
purpose of their erection.

But there is another whose life and personality
deserve the tribute of being recalled by our
citizens while standing before those monuments.
In their silence these shafts are vocal of more
than one life. I would have my countrymen give
some moments while there to thoughts of her who
lies beside him in the one; and who was associated
in personal devotion and services with him in all
the great achievements commemorated by the
other. At both these shrines erected by a grateful
nation, let us recall, as a part to be associated in
Abraham Lincoln's memory, the strong personality, unfailing faith, and devotion of the wife who
was so loyally with him, and an inspiration to him
during all his strenuous years. Well did she earn
such recognition.

Think kindly, gratefully of her who, at last,—

after that fatal bullet stilled in martyrdom her husband's generous heart,—was left to the loneliest life of all the wives widowed by the Civil War. Give, even though so late, that justice which the harassed, stricken nation unwittingly denied Mary Todd Lincoln in the busy generation through which she lived. She was allowed to go on through the last years of her life, so solitary until their sad end, amid chilling neglect and misrepresentation. During the bitter years following her bereavement it was her lot to suffer the daily martyrdom of her great sorrow under so many shadows, until released by death.

The Pen of History, in the long lapse of years, is a discriminating, diamond pointed one that engraves in the crystal pages of Immortal Truth, the records of Undying Fame,—those whose lives are deemed worthy of such commemoration. When that time shall come,—if it be not here now, —then, Mary Todd Lincoln's part in the life of her illustrious husband will appear in its correct relation to his life, and she will be awarded the recognition her merits have always deserved. Till then she can wait; for, like her husband, she belongs to the ages.

# Abraham Lincoln as Seen in Two Speeches Fifty Years Ago

Sprung from the West,
The strength of virgin forests braced his mind,
The hush of spacious prairies stilled his soul.
Up from the log cabin to the Capitol,
One fire was on his spirit, one resolve—
To send the keen ax to the root of wrong,
Clearing a free way for the feet of God.
And evermore he burned to do his deed
With the fine stroke and gesture of a king;
He built the rail piles as he built the State,
Pouring his splendid strength through every blow,
The conscience of him testing every stroke,
To make his deed the measure of a man.

EDWIN MARKHAM.

# X

## ABRAHAM LINCOLN AS SEEN IN TWO SPEECHES
### FIFTY YEARS AGO

Two speeches delivered by Lincoln, one in 1856 and the other in 1861, impressed those who heard them most profoundly at the time. Five years' space separated them. The first was given at Petersburg, Menard County, in October, 1856, when the presidential election was near at hand. Lincoln's former political associates there, the Whigs, who had sent him to Congress, were now stanch supporters of President Fillmore. The Democrats, of course, supported Buchanan; while Frémont, the standard-bearer of the young Republican Party, had scarcely any following in that county, and polled only six votes at the presidential election of November 6, 1856.

Lincoln's old-time political and personal friends in the county were all supporting Fillmore. With the Democratic party they were united in bitter opposition to the Republican party; and both were specially incensed at Lincoln for the prominent part he had taken in organizing and promoting a new party in the campaign. The Republican State Committee had declined sending any speakers to Menard, that county being considered politically hopeless in that campaign. At length, a few weeks before the election and principally through Lincoln's solicitation, the committee consented to have one meeting there, and sent Lincoln to address it. Mr. Herndon also was sent as late as Saturday, the 3d of November, to speak for Frémont at Athens in eastern Menard, near the Sangamon County boundary.

The Frémont-Buchanan-Fillmore campaign of 1856 was, by far, a more bitterly contested presidential election in central Illinois than any during my past fifty years. The posters and hand-bills announcing the date when Lincoln would speak in Petersburg had been repeatedly torn down and as often put up again. The event and the speaker thus became all the more thoroughly advertised. At length, on a beautiful day in the last of October, 1856, Lincoln arrived in Petersburg by stage-coach, an hour or two after its schedule time. The local committee, tired of waiting, had scattered, when unexpectedly the four-horse coach came dashing up to the Menard House.   Lincoln alighted alone, in one hand his campaign satchel, his  umbrella in the other, wearing the now famous linen duster. In a few minutes the committee met him, and then music by a primitive brass band at the courthouse platform, opposite the Menard House, began to attract the crowd thitherward with popular tunes.   Around the platform, louder and louder, arose hurrahs for Buchanan and for Fillmore. No voice for Frémont rang out through the crisp air to cheer the coming orator.   Lincoln could hardly have had less political sympathy that day if he had entered Charleston or Richmond for that purpose.

The committee, a corporal's guard in number (Republicans), immediately after a hurried lunch for Lincoln, started from the hotel to the courthouse yard and to the platform erected there. They surrounded Lincoln as they marched along, his great height towering head and shoulders above them all as they went. Before reaching the platform they unfurled the campaign banner of Frémont, bearing a life-sized portrait of the Pathfinder in glaring colours, and above this the American Flag, and a long white streamer with black lettering bearing the campaign legend:

## "FREE SPEECH, FREE SOIL, FREE KANSAS AND FRÉMONT."

That streamer affected the crowd very much as
a red rag would a herd of Texan cattle in those
days. For a time it looked as if the meeting
would be delayed or broken up. Rude fellows
of the rowdy sort had boasted, "No d—d abolition
speeches could be made in Menard County this
campaign." Had any other Republican than
Lincoln stood before those Menard people, he
would not have been heard. Several rushes toward
the colours and banners were made, with the evident purpose of tearing them down. Cat-calls,
whistles, and tin horns added to the din. Shouts of
"Abolitionist," "Nigger equality," with snatches
of obscene ballads and campaign songs, made a
bedlam of the court-house yard and the surrounding public square. At intervals, and shrill above
all such sounds, came the conflicting huzzahs for
Buchanan and equally loud shouts for Fillmore.
No slogans for the Republican standard-bearer,
Frémont, came from the excited crowd of voters.

At length, after no little jostle and buffeting,
the committee (half a dozen or so), bearing the
flag and streamer, appeared and mounted the
platform with Lincoln's tall form towering as

before a head and shoulders above the throng that
pressed him.   He handed his hat to Dr. Stevenson
(who later organized the order of the Grand Army
of the Republic), moved leisurely to the front of the
platform, and stood there silent, rigid as a statue,
calmly surveying the turbulent mass of humanity
before him.   The shouts for Buchanan, alternating
with those for Fillmore, and the general din of
dissent and opposition to Lincoln, surged for
awhile with more vehemence than ever.   The
political atmosphere was decidedly warm in
Petersburg that day.   Political differences were
then far more bitter and personal than now.

The orator surveyed the scene in silence.   Nearly
half an hour passed.   He stood there all that
while motionless as a statue.   The only change I
noticed was that at times he folded both arms
across his chest, then releasing them, one hand
clasped the lapel of his coat and the other arm
hung by his side, the hand of that opening and
then clutching in, apparently, unconscious aggressiveness.   These were the only movements of
Lincoln visible to those who stood close by him.
Then a partial lull came, and he began in his low-
est out-door voice to address the assembly which
he thoroughly understood.   Gradually the tumult
near him grew less, then a desire to know what

14

he was saying changed to shouts of "Louder, louder." He paused a brief moment—turned from right to left in a masterful glance over the excited people around the platform,—and then raised his long left arm above his head, moving slowly his large hand up and down, as if for the first time asking silence. He had won a possible chance to be heard. Could he maintain it? He resumed speaking. Gradually came a silence of all voices but the speaker's, and that arose clear and resonant, easily heard throughout the court-house square. That voice and masterful presence demanded, even commanded, the hearing that awaited him. In less than half an hour he was master, and for more than two hours he held the mastery over what had been the most turbulent of audiences. Under his peculiar control, he had held his hearers silent. There was no applause, not even a sign of approval or disapproval throughout his entire speech. The few Frémont men were prudent enough to keep still, thus helping to preserve order.

Several weeks after the election of November 6, 1856, while in a conversation with Mr. Herndon at the law-office in Springfield about this Petersburg speech, which I heard, and the Lincoln

speech at Bloomington, May 29, 1856, before the
first Republican State Convention, which he had
heard, Lincoln came in.  Finding us comparing
these two speeches, he stretched himself on the
office lounge and after a while, becoming interested
in the comparison we were trying to make, he
came to our assistance.  He said that the speeches
were, in essential matters, nearly the same; that
the Petersburg speech was longer in delivery,
because his audience required many things set
forth in detail, which was not necessary before
the more select Bloomington convention.  He di-
gressed to say what a peculiar preparation he had
for the severe ordeal he met when he first arrived
in Petersburg, by telling us of his stage-ride from
Springfield; of the beautiful October morning
and the familiar landscapes bordering the road;
how all these appeared to recall old associations
and memories.  The road on which he came
skirted the Sangamon River past Salem and into
Petersburg.  He arrived thoroughly unprepared,
he said, for the fierce conditions he met, but he
quickly realized the job he had before him and
pulled himself out of the thoughts and memories
suggested by his drive.  He never felt more
thoroughly keyed up to talk to any people than
he did by the time he reached the platform, and

had to stand silent before them so long to get a quiet hearing. He knew they were not the material a mob could be made of; he peppered them first with his silence; he knew all the middle-aged and older people present and many of the younger ones, and he was sure of a hearing by waiting.

"Billy," he said to Herndon as he rose to leave the office, "I never felt so full of just what a crowd ought to hear, and never had a crowd more competent, from the common-sense standpoint, than the Menard County one was to hear a fair and candid statement of facts, if I could just get them still for half an hour as an entering wedge. This I did, and I gave them my best. After I was well under way it was the most enjoyable of all the speeches I made through the entire campaign. The returns show I did a poor day's business down there for the State Committee so far as votes count. But I dropped some things among voters that day in Menard that will stay until the next election. I soaked that crowd full of political facts they can't get away from."

No notes of the speech were taken at the time. It was not even reported in the local papers; neither the *Petersburg Democrat* (Buchanan) nor the *Menard Index* (Fillmore) mentioned the event. It was the campaign tactics of the opposition that year to "damn Frémont by silence," wherever possible. Only a memory of the main division of the speech remains with me. But there are some sentences, as I write, that come back to me clearly, as spoken on that afternoon, fifty-nine years ago, and I repeat them here:

"It is singular that the Courts would hold," said he, referring to slavery, "that a man never lost his property that had been stolen from him, but could claim it anywhere, and in whatever hands found, but that he *instantly* and *forever* lost his right to *himself if he was stolen!*"

The clergy of Petersburg and vicinity were nearly all from the South, and at that time strong advocates of the alleged Biblical authority for slavery. Lincoln had met most of them before while living in Salem, or in his recent attendance at court terms at Petersburg, and knew their attitude on the "peculiar institution," as they termed slavery. They were all present that day, and in the latter part of his speech, following the paragraph first quoted, Lincoln addressed his remarks directly to them, in colloquial style, on

the moral perplexities of slavery. This portion
of his speech I am able to give in this connection
in full, just as I heard Lincoln repeat it the next
year before another audience, where it was taken
down by a reporter and afterwards published.

"The sum, of pro-slavery theology" said
Lincoln, "seems to be about this: Slavery is not
universally right, or wrong; it is better for some
people to be slaves; and, in such cases, it is the
will of God that they be such.   Certainly," continued Lincoln, in his mildest conversational
voice, "certainly there is no contending against
the will of God; and, still, there is some difficulty
in ascertaining and applying it to a particular
case.   For instance," he continued, "we will
suppose the Rev. Dr. Ross has a slave named
Sambo, and the question is: 'Is it the will of
God that Sambo shall remain a slave, or be set
free?'   The Almighty gives no audible answer to
the question, and His revelation, the Bible, gives
none;—or, at most, none but such as admits of a
squabble as to its meaning.   No one thinks of
asking Sambo's opinion on it.   So at last it comes
to this,—that Dr. Ross is to decide the question;
and while he considers it, he sits in the shade,
with gloves on his hands, and subsists on the

bread that Sambo is earning in the burning sun. If he decides that God wills Sambo to be free, he thereby has to walk out of the shade, throw off his gloves, and delve for his bread. Will Dr. Ross be actuated by the perfect impartiality which has ever been considered most favourable to a correct decision?"

Then on asking that question, abruptly changing from his colloquial tone, to that of a prophet and seer, he exclaimed in his highest voice, with emphasis:

"When I see strong hands sowing, reaping, and threshing wheat and those same hands grinding and making that wheat into bread, I cannot refrain from wishing, and believing, that those hands some way, in God's good time, shall own the mouth they feed!"

In the early part of his speech he brought in the scriptural figure that "a house divided against itself cannot stand," in a way similar to that of May 29, 1856, at the State Republican Convention in Bloomington. In deference to friends he had consented not to press this figure, nor the correlated political inferences he had assembled so graphically about it, during that Frémont campaign. But the high tension of that day's surroundings, and his familiarity with the personality of his hearers, overcame the orator too thoroughly for him to avoid giving full utterance to the truth as he saw and felt it.

Nearing the close of his Petersburg speech he also uttered this sentence, twice repeated by him in later speeches, but here delivered for the first time. The words were accompanied by one of his own most characteristic gestures; at first slightly stooping, leaning forward, with hands crossed in front until half through the sentence, then gradually unfolding his stalwart frame and gently rising with each closing word until, standing severely erect, with head thrown back and arms extended, palms outward at its closing, spoke these prophetic words:

"The result is not doubtful—if we stand firm we cannot fail, we *shall* not fail. Wise counsels may accelerate, or mistakes delay, but, sooner or later, *the victory is sure to come.*"

# The Second Speech: Farewell Address

Washington came up from Virginia, Lincoln came down from Illinois; both came in one spotless honour, in one self-denial, in one patience and labour, in one love of man; both came in the name of one simple Christianity; both came breathing daily prayers to God, as though to prophesy a time when Virginia and Illinois, all the South and all the North, would be alike in love, in works, in religion, and in national fame. "The flag is still there," more glorious over the schoolhouse, the church, the home, and the farm, than over a red field of war.

DAVID SWING.

# XI

## THE SECOND SPEECH—FAREWELL ADDRESS
### FEBRUARY 11, 1861

AFTER more than four eventful years, he delivered the other notable address to which I have referred. It was his farewell to the citizens of Springfield, and in both substance and manner of delivery it was a strong, clear expression of his remarkable personality. Its delivery brought out in strongest relief the elements of his innermost character as some great artist might portray his features on canvas.

Lincoln was now President in all save the last formalities which were to take place a few days later at the Capitol in Washington. From his election, November 6, 1860, to February 11, 1861, his life had been the most unusual ever experienced by any President-elect awaiting the ceremony of inauguration. No sketch of the various public and private interests and persons that thronged around him during his last three months

in Springfield, will here be attempted. Some of
these visitors came by his invitation—others from
patriotic motives—but most were self-seekers for
office under the new administration. Thus early
he began to find these the annoying time-con-
sumers of his years in the White House. He
passed those trying first months after his election
with rare wisdom, patience, and tact. Where he
could not agree, or wished to parry questions
which no foresight could then safely solve, he
became the questioner himself, or sent his caller
away with an apt story. No ill-considered promise, no committal on policies to guide his administration, escaped his lips to compromise or tie up
his future usefulness. There were no such indis-
cretions, through inexperience, during these first
months when he appeared in national view as the
President elect.

On the evening of February 10, 1861, he spent
his last hours with his partner in the old office
of Lincoln and Herndon. They conferred for the
last time on a few unfinished legal affairs, and
arranged minor business matters. They remained alone until late, passed down the stairway
together and along the streets, until near Lincoln's
home, where they parted for the last time in
Springfield.

The morning of the next day dawned over Springfield through leaden skies in a cold grey misty air.
Many citizens and visitors gathered at the Wabash
station to witness Lincoln's departure.  He and his
family arrived timely and entered the car reserved
for them, not stopping in the waiting-room.  One
after another of the party who were to accompany
them to Washington, or only part of the way—as
several purposed to do—came, before or after, and
entered the same coach.  Those were tense moments for the people who waited without.  Schedule time for starting was near.  Impatient reporters
were anxious lest they might miss a chance to wire
the last words of the President-elect from Springfield.  Some unfriendly and critical partisan neighbours, lookers on, ventured to say he would leave
without any parting words.  The expectation had
become current that he would have something to
disclose that morning concerning his purposes and
policy, to allay the national anxiety existing at
that hour in regard to his position on slavery and
secession.  There was not the slightest foundation for this in anything Lincoln had intimated;
nevertheless it was the general expectation.

At the very last moment Lincoln appeared at
the rear door of the car.  He paused, as if sur-

prised at the sudden burst of applause occasioned
by his appearance, and removing his hat, stepped
out on the platform, bowing right and left and
remaining silent until the salute ceased. His
short address was a great surprise to reporters
and politicians. In it there was nothing that
satisfied their excited expectations. In its delivery
there were no gestures. His manner was calm
and self-contained, yet his voice was tremulous
with suppressed emotions, while strong emphasis
marked many words and sentences. The last
sentence was spoken in lower tones, with a yearning tenderness in his voice, most unusual to him;
and, with its closing words, he bowed low, and
with firmly compressed lips whose silence meant so
much to those who knew him best, turned from
his position on the platform and stood at the open
door, while the train, just starting, moved slowly
bearing him away from us through that cold grey
misty haze of rain. Little we then knew how he
would return! Thank God for the shortness of
human vision; that he who went, and we who remained, could not then discern the appalling future
that so darkly hung above and before us all!

This was the last view of Lincoln by his home
people. He stood on the platform at the door of

his car, with bared head, looking back on the town
whose citizens he had just reminded so touchingly,
in farewell words, of his love and grateful obligations for all they had been to him and done for
him.   This was the last view of Springfield by
Abraham Lincoln.   These were his farewell words:

MY FRIENDS:—No one not in my situation can
appreciate my feelings of sadness at this parting.
To this place and the kindness of this people I owe
everything.   Here I have lived a quarter of a century,
and have passed from a young to an old man.   Here
my children were born and one lies buried.

I now leave, not knowing when, or whether ever,
I may return, with a task before me greater than
that which rested on the shoulders of Washington.

Without the aid of that Divine Being who ever
aided him, who controls mine and all destinies, I
cannot succeed.   With that assistance I cannot fail.

Trusting in Him who can go with me and remain
with you, and be everywhere for good, let us confidently hope that all will be well.

To His care commending you, as I hope in your
prayers you will commend me, I bid you, friends and
neighbours, an affectionate farewell.

This farewell address received at the time of
its delivery nothing like the attention and com-

ment given to the shorter speeches that Lincoln made at stopping points on his leisurely trip east. The few who heard this address—and they did not exceed two hundred—and the larger public reached by the daily press the next morning, were in no mood to receive enthusiastically so short and serious a farewell address from the President-elect. They were even more indifferent at that time to appreciate his personal and local references; and but few were touched by his familiar recognition of the Divine Being to whose care he commended them and asked them in their prayers to commend him. Springfield and the country, both the North and the South, were in no reminiscent or prayerful mood, that sombre morning of February 11, 1861.

This address and the one he delivered at Gettysburg were at the time of their delivery the most disappointing to the audiences that heard them of any of Lincoln's speeches. They are now appreciated as having had more care in their preparation than any equal number of sentences he ever composed. If at the time of delivery they passed over the heads of those who heard them, time has since borne them into the classical immortality their merits deserve.

The excitement incident to the national turmoil at the time was so distracting that public attention centered on the more practical speeches made by Lincoln from place to place along his route. The last was at Philadelphia, and was followed by a hurried night's trip through Baltimore and an early morning arrival in Washington. When the startling cause for such haste became known it completely diverted public attention from all else and even the beauty and significance of this Farewell Address at Springfield was forgotten. Not until his lifeless form was returned to Springfield did his home people and the public generally recall the beauty and power of Lincoln's farewell "to friends and neighbours."

There has never been any question of difference of opinion about the words or phrasing of Lincoln's Gettysburg speech. That was recorded by skilled reporters and all the copies agree. Very different was the reporting of the Springfield address. The reporters' short-hand notes I saw—and I believe I had access to all of them—showed an incomplete record of Lincoln's words. At that time I had only made sufficient progress in stenography to read copy, but had never "taken down" a public speaker. Only a few catch words were recorded by reporters in their note books until Lincoln began the fourth sentence; from the fifth they followed him closer, and after that on to the close, I was able to reconstruct confidently all his sentences. This text so collated was submitted for careful comparison by several of the friends of Lincoln who were present and this resulted in an agreement on the copy here reproduced. As a result of the partial stenographic notes which were taken and the writing out of some versions entirely from memory, no address Lincoln ever delivered has given rise to so wide a difference of opinion as to what were his exact words.

In this address Lincoln made four marked pauses which are indicated by the spacing between paragraphs in this copy. His pauses between sentences were longer than are usually given to a period. The last two sentences were less audible and his emotions while he delivered them almost controlled his voice. Dr. Bateman who stood nearer him says, "his pale face was literally wet with tears"; I did not observe any.

Were these farewell sentences improvised at the time of delivery? I do not think so. They are unlike Lincoln's words in impromptu speech. I asked Mr. Herndon a few days afterward if he

knew of Lincoln's intention to speak at all, or that
he would be so personal and brief, not dealing
with the political and National situation, as most
people anticipated he would. He replied that
Lincoln in their last interview at the office the
night before his departure said nothing about it;
but that just as he bade him good-bye, he asked
if he expected to give any last words at the Wabash
depot the next morning. Lincoln replied that
he did not suppose there would be occasion for
any, as only those going would be there; and
Herndon's reply was that he thought there would
be many others, and believed there was a general
expectation that he would say something about
the distracted condition of the country. To this
he said Lincoln made no reply. It was Herndon's
opinion that on leaving him he gave his mind up
to meditation on a farewell speech, and that the
thoughts he delivered became shaped before he
slept that night; though neither he nor any one
else could be sure of this.

These few sentences were the fruitage of one of
Lincoln's brooding, concentrated moods. It was
no sudden, impromptu impulse that gave his
friends and neighbours such heartfelt and prophetic
sentences at parting. It did not require Presidential experience to qualify Lincoln to express

as no one else has done, in language of such
pathos and power, the choicest human sentiments and feelings, embodied in plainest English
words.

In the Lincoln National Memorial to be erected
in the city of Washington it is proposed that the
Gettysburg speech, and portions from Lincoln's
two inaugural addresses, be placed on appropriate
tablets.  It is proper and wise patriotism, for
Lincoln's thoughts and spirit thus to find place
in the monumental recognition of a nation's
gratitude and love for its prophet-President,
in the words he spoke on those historic occasions.
Though dead, his character still lives to admonish
and inspire.  But these selections would be incomplete if limited to the ones mentioned.  I
believe we all have reason to anticipate that those
in charge of the erection of this great national
tribute,—as well as those in charge of erecting
the statue of Lincoln on the grounds of the Capitol
of Illinois,—will both appreciate and recognize
this Farewell Address at Springfield as deserving
precedence among the tablets of the one, and at
the base of the other, as a most important part of
Lincoln's eloquent life to be cast in bronze and
carved in granite.  These Farewell words express,

in fullest measure, the spirit and purpose of him
for whom that State Statue and the National
Monument shall arise.   They were his first words
spoken on the threshold of his appearance in
executive view as the Nation's Chief.   They
who knew the man and walked and talked with
him in his daily life before the nation called him
for her executive head, see in this address the
maturity, the goodness, and the greatness of
Lincoln.   In these words he voices his gratitude
for the past; he looks modestly forward to the
stupendous task before him; he pledges his
faith so firmly; he appeals so inspiringly with
hope in, and for, his Country's darkest hour,—
all, inclusive, telling the character of this First
American, and how clearly he discerned even
at that early date the magnitude of the problems before him for solution in our distracted
country.

Carve these words of farewell to Springfield
friends in enduring bronze and granite, for they
embody, as we now see, a Nation's prelude, by
its Chief, to the historic tragedy then ushering
in, whose years of terrific strain and strife should
at last end in the closer union of these reunited
States; and by both this Statue and National
Monument our country shall henceforth forever

commemorate his memory in fraternal unity. These words are no longer for the few he addressed, but—alike with him who spoke them—they belong to the Ages!

# Between the Two Speeches of National Importance

There have been orators whose speeches we may read for the beauty of their language, with little regard to the circumstances of time and place that led to their being delivered. Lincoln is not one of these. His speeches need to be studied in close relation to the occasions which called them forth. They are not brilliant displays of rhetoric. They are a part of his life. They are serious, practical, grave. We feel that the man does not care to play over the surface of his subject, or to use it as a way of displaying his cleverness. He is trying to get right down to the very foundation of the matter and tell us what his real thoughts about it are. There is no superfluous ornament in his orations, nothing tawdry, nothing otiose. He addresses the reason of his hearers, and when he does appeal to emotion, he does it quietly, even solemnly. Alike in thought and language he is simple, plain, direct. But he states certain truths in phrases so aptly chosen and so forcible, that one feels that those truths could have been conveyed in no other words. Few characters stand out so clearly revealed in their words, whether spoken or written, as his does.

JAMES BRYCE.

# XII

## BETWEEN THE TWO SPEECHES OF NATIONAL IMPORTANCE

THE progress of events, after what was claimed to be the final settlement in 1850 by the compromise measures then enacted, went forward rapidly and unexpectedly, North as well as South, East as well as West. In all these conflicts of opinion Lincoln became more and more an earnest active student of the principles, ethical and political, that separated the contending sections. He found himself drifting—but with reluctance—into the practical concession that slavery must, for a while, be a national issue; and its ultimate solution to be worked out in policies of the Federal Government for the new Territories, then rapidly settling up with citizens from both North and South, and soon to be organized as States.

Coals of fire from the altar of Liberty had burned into the soul of Lincoln until a flame of steadfast purpose was kindled, that those new States should never be the home of slaves; that their soil was too sacred to be trod by other than free men. In this resolve, once formed, he never faltered; the Kansas-Nebraska bill of Douglas at once aroused all the active or dormant energies within him who was destined, from 1856 to 1860, to be the leader of a new era in this nation, and thereafter its patient and far-seeing executive head to establish the Union of all the States and secure them from the anarchy of secession.

During this crisis Lincoln did not "lose his head," as did so many North and South. While there was no faltering in his devotion to the principles of Freedom, the political turbulence of the hour brought into view what he considered the most serious peril by which this nation could be confronted, viz., the right of a State to secede at pleasure from the National Union. The two issues in view of national politics had been carefully, even warmly, discussed between Lincoln and Herndon, especially after the national agitations of 1848 and 1850. Mr. Herndon maintained that slavery was the first and paramount—indeed the only—issue; and the union of the States secondary. Lincoln urged, with even greater firmness, that slavery was temporary and would, of necessity, under the influence and pressure of modern financial and social life, cease and pass away because of its inherent weakness and its vicious character. He held that, if slavery alone embodied our national difficulties, then there was no imminent danger; that time and patience would adjust all differences; but that if secession was to be a part of the plan for slavery's preservation, then to permit it was national suicide, never to be allowed. The more violent the attitude of extremists in the North and South on the slavery question became from 1854 to 1860, the more thoroughly convinced and emphatic became Lincoln, in his private talks with his partner, that the secession of the Southern States, on the plea of State rights, was the greater impending calamity that confronted the country. He said this clearly from the beginning.

It was at the climax of these discussions in 1856 that he prepared his speech on "a house divided against itself." He used a portion of the first draft of this in a speech at Bloomington in May of that year. Several political friends, Judge Dickey and Hon. E. B. Washburne among them, strongly urged him not to deliver this speech again. To their earnest plea he reluctantly promised not to press this in the campaign of 1856, but he would not pledge himself never to

repeat it; "For it is God's truth," said he, "and
I am sure we will all come to see it and be willing
to say so before long." Once, in October of that
year, in Petersburg, he felt it necessary to use the
simile with its broadest application among his
former friends and neighbours.

The first draft of this Bloomington and Petersburg speech as delivered in 1856, was written on
odd sheets of paper, old envelopes, or whatever
came handy at the time. Those he filed away
for the present after the Bloomington Convention.
Nearly two years had passed. He had, meanwhile, carefully considered the whole subject anew.
The time for the Republican Convention at
Springfield in June, 1858, was at hand. To Mr.
Herndon he said he had waited long enough. He
would live or die, politically, by the "God's
truth" that speech would declare. He took up
the memoranda prepared so long before and
again carefully wrote out that speech. It was
noticeable to those in his office that he gave more
attention than was his habit while preparing
an important speech to fitting sentences and
historical data, from paragraph to paragraph.
This was personally gratifying to Mr. Herndon,
who had gone almost to the verge of offending
Lincoln to prevail on him to cut out his story-

telling style in speeches. Herndon was the first to discern and appreciate the singular facility of Lincoln for combining a sustained diction of logic with pathos and dignity; and he insisted that here lay his best opportunity and power as a public speaker.

Another aid to this end—though the manner and time when it came made it unfriendly and cruel—was the part taken by *The Springfield Enterprise*, a new and vigorously independent daily paper whose editor, Washington Wright, severely criticized the new party for its choice of Lincoln to contest with Senator Douglas as its candidate for Senator. Wright's criticisms appeared nearly every day for a couple of months before the Springfield Convention of June, 1858. By keenest satire, in both prose and poetry, he kept the political foes, and even some of Lincoln's lukewarm friends, in broad grins of enjoyment at Lincoln's expense. This cut Lincoln deeply, as Editor Wright intended it should, but it had no influence to change the party's choice. Coming at the time when Lincoln was carefully preparing the "house divided against itself" speech, it undoubtedly had some influence with him while writing out what proved to be the most striking speech made by him up to that time.

As the date came near for the Convention of

June, 1858, Lincoln had finished his last draft of
this speech. He proposed to deliver it, should
he be nominated—as was then generally expected,
—as the key-note of his campaign as candidate
for United States Senator. He read it first in the
office to Mr. Herndon and two young friends
familiar with its preparation. Herndon, while
agreeing with all that the speech expressed, was
yet, as he told Lincoln, fearful lest the public was
not yet ready to hear statements so radical. He
conceded that it would be a brave thing, after so
long holding back the speech, to deliver it; saying,
"If you are ready to face the fight on this high
plane, certainly I will stand by you. So should all
true friends of the Republican party." Lincoln was
more than willing to take this lead; he had been
awaiting an opportunity, and gladly accepted the
date of this convention as the time for its delivery.

The next day he invited a number of select
political friends to meet him in the State Library,
to whom he read the speech, or rather, sitting in
his chair, talked it to them, as the pages were
so familiar that he only occasionally turned the
sheets, or followed the paragraphs with an occasional glance. All present listened closely, for it
was understood that his speech would commit
the party in Illinois to its principles in the coming

campaign. It was soon evident that portions of the speech were not approved. After the reading, he called upon one after another for his opinion. Most disapproved and none except Mr. Herndon favoured his delivering it at that time, unless he should leave out the section on the "house divided against itself." Mr. Herndon related to me on the following day what transpired in the conference. He said that Lincoln was courteous and even conciliatory in the discussions, but was firmly determined not to change the speech. It was not changed, but on the evening of the 16th of June, 1858, after his nomination as candidate for United States Senator, he delivered it in the Representatives Hall of the State House to one of the largest audiences ever assembled there. Its main parts were immediately published in all the principal papers North and South.

During the delivery of this speech the orator carried his audience with him surprisingly well. He was at his best throughout, and was loudly cheered. It was a happy ending to the suspense of many of his friends. The speech, as a whole, placed Lincoln in his home city far above the position he had occupied before as a thinker and a speaker. It ended Editor Wright's satire. Thenceforward none of his friends doubted his ability to meet Douglas in the campaign, for which this was the opening challenge.

Within a few days the office began to receive letters deploring the advanced position taken so early in the campaign, and prophecies of disaster followed if Lincoln should prosecute the campaign on "this abolition basis." Had this reactionary wave come two years earlier it would have distressed Lincoln. Not so now. Mature study had established him too firmly to be shaken. The criticisms became less frequent. Portions of this speech, published all over the Union, were the first political introduction of Lincoln to the national public.

It was a remarkable position to be taken at that time. It touched the national conscience, North and South, both for and against its principles. It sized up the political problems before the country in such a practical way as neither Seward's *Irrepressible Conflict* nor Helper's book on the *Impending Crisis* had done. It hastened in all sections public recognition of the exact political issues before the country, and made possible in a practical way, after 1858, that intelligent discussion which ripened public sentiment for the nomination of Lincoln in the campaign of 1860.

# The Cooper Institute Speech

I chanced to open the other day his Cooper Institute speech. This was one of the few printed speeches that I did not hear him deliver in person. As I read the concluding pages of that speech, the conflict of opinion that preceded the conflict of arms then sweeping upon the country like an approaching solar eclipse seemed prefigured like a chapter of the Book of Fate. Here again he was the Old Testament prophet, before whom Horace Greeley bowed his head, saying that he had never listened to a greater speech, although he had heard several of Webster's best.

HORACE WHITE.

# XIII

## THE COOPER INSTITUTE SPEECH

LINCOLN lost the senatorship, but he won a larger victory. He became recognized as the most practical and clear-thinking representative of the free-soil sentiment in the entire nation. To the public Lincoln showed no disappointment under his defeat. Within himself he felt no sting; but from this time forth he manifested an unrest, and was less the office lawyer than ever before. All through the next winter in an unusual degree, he was unsettled as to how he should find an outlet or field for his mental activity. The practice of law had lost its charms for him. He tried the lecture field a few times, with indifferent success, returning home more discouraged and despondent than I had ever seen him.

In October, 1859, he had an invitation from New York to deliver a lecture in the Cooper Institute, the subject to be of his own selection. He assented, and named February, 1860, as the time; his subject to be a political one. He had misgivings, at first, as to his ability to interest an Eastern metropolitan audience in the subject which he had chosen. However, his old campaign interest and energy came back to him the more he became absorbed in the collection of data upon which to build his speech. He had repeated interviews and discussions at the office with Mr. Herndon, going over their stores of campaign literature to block out the matter available for use in preparing this political lecture for what he expected to be a most critical audience. He was at length fully satisfied in his selection of his material and how much he should use in writing out the speech. His first and second drafts were cast aside, and the entire field traversed anew. Mr. Herndon remarked to me that Lincoln had gone into his subjects far too deeply for him to follow. He only offered suggestions on the rearrangement of some sentences and paragraphs in the last copy.

It may be of interest to add some mention of the laborious care Lincoln took in preparation for his debate with Douglas by studious application from June until the debates began. It was a summer in which that mood, spoken of before, of intense application to the work before him shut out everything else.   He was in the State Library nearly every day, searching old volumes of the *Congressional Globe*, and other original sources of information.   He went through the clippings he and Mr. Herndon had made since 1848 from the *Charleston Mercury, Richmond Enquirer, Louisville Journal*, and other Southern papers; and with especial care he again went through the back numbers of the *Southern Literary Messenger*, re-reading articles by the best Southern writers on the policies that divided public opinion on the question of slavery and States' rights.

His campaign note-books, when finished, could not have been more complete to meet the expected and unexpected questions liable to be sprung on him during the debate.   He was no longer the Abraham Lincoln with leisure for the interests of all callers.   He lived through laborious days and often late into studious nights; and when he went forth into that debate it was with a firm foundation of well-settled principles, and fully equipped with all historical and collateral data possible to be acquired by him on the live political issues of the day.   Best of all was the complete confidence he had acquired in himself of his ability to meet Senator Douglas, or any other publicist North or South, in the discussion of the interests and problems then before the country. This was no self-asserting egotism. He was the freest from that of all men who have ever engaged the attention of the nation.

In the preparation of the Cooper Institute speech Lincoln showed the great grasp he had acquired in the discussion of political events, and his peculiar originality in moulding sentences and paragraphs. The finished speech grew very slowly. Herndon's patience was tried sorely at times to see him loitering and cutting, as he thought, too laboriously; but when the speech was completed, he admitted it was well worth the time devoted to it, and that it would be the crowning effort of Lincoln's life up to that time as it certainly proved to be. It was past the middle of February before the speech was completed and put into the folder ready for Lincoln's departure. And even later, every day until it was placed in his travelling satchel, he took out the sheets and carefully went over the pages, making notations here and there, and even writing whole pages over again.

In his later years in Springfield he became more and more in the habit of revising all he had written down to the latest hour possible before delivery.

I was told by his secretary, Mr. Hay, that such was his habit in Washington while President. He disliked very much to give out the advanced copy so dear to the press agents; and his secretary had no little trouble because of this rule. His mind was ever alert to catch his last moment's thought and intuition before public delivery. After delivery he gave himself no concern to change or preserve for use or revision, anything he had written or spoken. Few public men ever repeated themselves so seldom as did Lincoln.

None of Lincoln's friends went with him to New York, or were present when he delivered the Cooper Institute speech. He left Springfield for the East as quietly as if going out to attend some one of the courts of the Eighth District, the local papers not mentioning his absence from the city.

The opinion and estimate of those who heard this speech in New York is the more convincing criterion of its value than anything Lincoln's Springfield friends might say of it. The consideration these new and more critical friends had of him and his speech before and after its delivery are strikingly contrasting ones. I shall therefore give space here to their estimate. There is no better account of this than that written by Charles

C. Nott which was published in 1909 in George Haven Putnam's *Abraham Lincoln: The People's Leader in the Struggle for National Existence.* It is so illuminating of the circumstances connected with Lincoln's appearance before an Eastern audience that I include it here in preference to any other.

The Cooper Institute address [says Mr. Nott], is one of the most important addresses ever delivered in the life of this nation, for at an eventful time it changed the course of history. When Mr. Lincoln rose to speak on the evening of February 27, 1860, he had held no administrative office; he had endeavoured to be appointed Commissioner of Patents, and had failed; he had sought to be elected United States Senator, and had been defeated; he had been a member of Congress, yet it was not even remembered; he was a lawyer in humble circumstances, persuasive of juries, but had not reached the front rank of the Illinois Bar. The record which Mr. Lincoln himself placed in the Congressional Directory in 1847 might still be taken as the record of his public and official life:

"Born February 12, 1809, in Hardin County, Kentucky.

Education defective.

Profession a lawyer.

Have been a captain of volunteers in the Black Hawk War.

Postmaster in a very small office.

Four times a member of the Illinois Legislature and was a member of the lower house of Congress."

Was this the record of a man who should be made the head of a nation in troubled times? In the estimation of thoughtful Americans east of the Alleghanies all that they knew of Mr. Lincoln justified them in regarding him as only "a Western stump orator"—successful, distinguished, but nothing higher than that— a Western stump orator, who had dared to brave one of the strongest men in the Western States, and who had done so with wonderful ability and moral success. When Mr. Lincoln closed his address he had risen to the rank of statesman, and had stamped himself a statesman peculiarly fitted for the exigency of the hour.

Mr. William Cullen Bryant presided at the meeting; and a number of the first and ablest citizens of New York were present, among them Horace Greeley. Mr. Greeley was pronounced in his appreciation of the address; it was the ablest, the greatest, the wisest speech that had yet been made; it would reassure the conservative Northerner; it was just what was wanted to conciliate the excited Southerner; it was conclusive in its argument, and would assure the overthrow of Douglas. Mr. Horace White has recently written: "I chanced to open the other day his Cooper Institute speech. This is one of the few printed speeches that I did not hear him deliver

in person. As I read the concluding pages of that
speech, the conflict of opinion that preceded the
conflict of arms then sweeping upon the country like
an approaching solar eclipse seemed prefigured like a
chapter of the Book of Fate. Here again he was
the Old Testament prophet, before whom Horace
Greeley bowed his head, saying that he had never
listened to a greater speech, although he had heard
several of Webster's best." Later, Mr. Greeley
became the leader of the Republican forces opposed
to the nomination of Mr. Seward and was instrumental in concentrating those forces upon Mr. Lincoln.
Furthermore, the great New York press on the following morning carried the address to the country, and
before Mr. Lincoln left New York he was telegraphed
from Connecticut to come and aid in the campaign
of the approaching spring election. He went, and
when the fateful moment came in the Convention,
Connecticut was one of the Eastern States which
first broke away from the Seward column and went
over to Mr. Lincoln. When Connecticut did this,
the die was cast.

It is difficult for younger generations of Americans
to believe that three months before Mr. Lincoln was
nominated for the Presidency he was neither appreciated nor known in New York. That fact can be
better established by a single incident than by the
opinions and assurances of a dozen men.

After the address had been delivered, Mr. Lincoln was taken by two members of the Young Men's Central Republican Union—Mr. Hiram Barney, afterward Collector of the Port of New York, and Mr. Nott, one of the subsequent editors of the address—to their club, the Athenæum, where a very simple supper was ordered, and five or six Republican members of the club who chanced to be in the building were invited in. The supper was informal—as informal as anything could be; the conversation was easy and familiar; the prospects of the Republican party in the coming struggle were talked over, and so little was it supposed by the gentlemen who had not heard the address that Mr. Lincoln could possibly be the candidate that one of them, Mr. Charles W. Eliott, asked, artlessly: "Mr. Lincoln, what candidate do you really think would be most likely to carry Illinois?" Mr. Lincoln answered by illustration: "Illinois is a peculiar State, in three parts. In northern Illinois, Mr. Seward would have a larger majority than I could get. In middle Illinois, I think I could call out a larger vote than Mr. Seward. In southern Illinois, it would make no difference who was the candidate." This answer was taken to be merely illustrative by everybody except, perhaps, Mr. Barney and Mr. Nott, each of whom, it subsequently appeared, had particularly noted Mr. Lincoln's reply.

The little party broke up.    Mr. Lincoln had been cordially received, but certainly had not been flattered.

The others shook him by the hand and, as they put on their overcoats, said: "Mr. Nott is going down town and he will show you the way to the Astor House." Mr. Lincoln and Mr. Nott started on foot, but the latter observing that Mr. Lincoln was apparently walking with some difficulty said, "Are you lame, Mr. Lincoln?" He replied that he had on new boots and they hurt him. The two gentlemen then boarded a street car. When they reached the place where Mr. Nott would leave the car on his way home, he shook Mr. Lincoln by the hand and, bidding him good-bye, told him that this car would carry him to the side door of the Astor House. Mr. Lincoln went on alone, the only occupant of the car. The next time he came to New York, he rode down Broadway to the Astor House standing erect in an open barouche drawn by four white horses. He bowed to the patriotic thousands in the street, on the sidewalks, in the windows. on the house-tops, and they cheered him as the lawfully elected President of the United States and bade him go on and, with God's help, save the Union.

His companion in the street car has often wondered since then what Mr. Lincoln thought about during the remainder of his ride that night to the Astor House. The Cooper Institute had, owing to a snow-storm, not been full, and its intelligent, respectable, nonpartisan audience had not rung out enthusiastic applause like a concourse of Western auditors magnet-

ized by their own enthusiasm.   Had the address—
the most carefully prepared, the most elaborately
investigated and demonstrated and verified of all
the work of his life—been a failure?   But in the
matter of quality and ability, if not of quantity and
enthusiasm, he had never addressed such an audience;
and some of the ablest men in the Northern States
had expressed their opinion of the address in terms
which left no doubt of the highest appreciation.   Did
Mr. Lincoln regard the address which he had just delivered to a small and critical audience as a success?
Did he have the faintest glimmer of the brilliant effect
which was to follow?   Did he feel the loneliness of
the situation—the want of his loyal Illinois adherents?
Did his sinking heart infer that he was but a speck
of humanity to which the great city would never
again give a thought?   He was a plain man, an
ungainly man; unadorned, apparently uncultivated,
showing the awkwardness of self-conscious rusticity.
His dress that night before a New York audience was
the most unbecoming that a fiend's ingenuity could
have devised for a tall, gaunt man—a black frock
coat, ill-setting and too short for him in the body,
skirt, and arms—a rolling collar, low-down, dis-
closing his long thin, shrivelled throat uncovered
and exposed.   No man in all New York appeared that
night more simple, more unassuming, more modest,
more unpretentious, more conscious of his own
defects than Abraham Lincoln; and yet we now know

that within his soul there burned the fires of an
unbounded ambition, sustained by a self-reliance
and self-esteem that bade him fix his gaze upon the
very pinnacle of American fame and aspire to it in a
time so troubled that its dangers appalled the soul
of every American.  What were this man's thoughts
when he was left alone?  Did a faint shadow of the
future rest upon his soul?  Did he feel in some
mysterious way that on that night he had crossed
the Rubicon of his life-march—that care and trouble
and political discord, and slander and misrepresentation and ridicule and public responsibilities, such as
hardly ever before burdened a conscientious soul,
coupled with war and defeat and disaster, were to be
thenceforth his portion nearly to his life's end, and
that his end was to be a bloody act which would
appall the world and send a thrill of horror through the
hearts of friends and enemies alike, so that when the
woeful tidings came the bravest of the Southern
brave should burst into tears and cry aloud, "Oh!
the unhappy South, the unhappy South!"

The impression left on his companion's mind as he
gave a last glance at him in the street car was that he
seemed sad and lonely; and when it was too late,
when the car was beyond call, he blamed himself
for not accompanying Mr. Lincoln to the Astor
House—not because he was a distinguished stranger,
but because he seemed a sad and lonely
man.

Following this retrospect of Mr. Nott's of the events and scenes of February 27, 1860, written by him in 1908, I wish to go back to events that occurred in the spring of 1860. The most comprehensive and appreciative presentation of facts regarding this Cooper Institute speech ever published, was that issued by the "Young Men's Republican Union," of New York City, in September, 1860. This organization in May of that year had decided to publish a revised edition for general campaign distribution, preceding the presidential election. They wished this reprint to have such historical and analytical notes as would authenticate the statements and principles Lincoln had presented in the speech.

With this in view they wrote Lincoln for the notes and references he had collated in its preparation. Lincoln replied he had not preserved such memoranda as he had used at the time, and that he was then too busy to re-examine the authorities again. The facts connected with this correspondence can be best understood and appreciated by giving the following letters that were exchanged between Mr. Charles C. Nott and Lincoln dated May 23, 31, 1860, respectively.

These letters show the appreciation of this speech by Eastern Republicans so soon after its delivery. Lincoln's reply is even more interesting, for it indicates the maturity and independence of his thoughts on the political issues then distracting the country. It shows at that early date that he had a masterful self-confidence in his political opinions and his own method of expressing them. He was unwilling to have any corrections, from even his scholarly Eastern friends, "that would change the sense, or modify to a hair's breadth," what he had said before them that night of February 27, 1860. It will be recalled that Lincoln wrote this reply to the New York Republican Club only seventeen days before the National Republican Convention met in Chicago that nominated him as their candidate for President. These letters are as follows:

69 WALL ST., NEW YORK,
May 23, 1860.

DEAR SIR:

I enclose a copy of your address in New York.

We (the Young Men's Rep. Union) design to publish a new edition in larger type and better form, with such notes and references as will best attract readers seeking information. Have you any memoranda of your investigations which you would approve of inserting?

You and your Western friends, I think, underrate this speech. It has produced a greater effect here than any other single speech.  It is the real platform in the Eastern States, and must carry the conservative element in New York, New Jersey, and Pennsylvania.

Therefore I desire that it should be as nearly perfect as may be.  Most of the emendations are trivial and do not affect the substance—all are merely suggested for your judgment.

I cannot help adding that this speech is an extraordinary example of condensed English.  After some experience in criticising for Reviews, I find hardly anything to touch and nothing to omit.  It is the only one I know of which I cannot *shorten* and—like a good arch —moving one word tumbles a whole sentence down.

Finally—it being a bad and foolish thing for a candidate to write letters, and you having doubtless more to do of that than is pleasant or profitable, we will not add to your burden in that regard, but if you will let any friend who has nothing to do, advise us as to your wishes, in this or any other matter, we will try to carry them out.

Respectfully,<br>CHARLES C. NOTT.

To HON. ABRAHAM LINCOLN.


SPRINGFIELD, ILLS., May 31, 1860.

Charles C. Nott, Esq.

MY DEAR SIR:

Yours of the 23d, accompanied by a copy of the speech delivered by me at the Cooper Institute, and

17

upon which you have made some notes for emendations, was received some days ago— Of course I would
not object to, but would be pleased rather, with a more
perfect edition of that speech.

I did not preserve memoranda of my investigations;
and I could not now re-examine, and make notes,
without an expenditure of time which I cannot bestow
upon it—some of your notes I do not understand.

So far as it is intended merely to improve in grammar, and elegance of composition, I am quite agreed;
but I do not wish the sense changed, or modified,
to a hair's breadth— And you, not having studied
the particular points so closely as I have, can not be
quite sure that you do not change the sense when you
do not intend it— For instance, in a note at bottom
of first page, you propose to substitute "Democrats"
for "Douglas"— But what I am saying there is *true*
of Douglas, and is not true of "Democrats" generally;
so that the proposed substitution would be a very
considerable blunder— Your proposed insertion of
"residences" though it would do little or no harm,
is not at all necessary to the sense I was trying to
convey— On page 5 your proposed grammatical
change would certainly do no harm— The "*impudently
absurd*" I stick to— The striking out "*he*" and inserting "*we*" turns the sense exactly wrong— The striking
out "*upon it*" leaves the sense too general and incomplete— The sense is "act as they acted *upon that
question*"—not as they acted generally.

After considering your proposed changes on page 7, I do not think them material, but I am willing to defer to you in relation to them.

On page 9, striking out "*to us*" is probably right— The word "*lawyer's*" I wish retained. The word "*Courts*" struck out twice, I wish reduced to "Court" and retained—"Court" as a collection more properly governs the plural "have" as I understand— "The" preceding "Court," in the latter case, must also be retained— The words "quite," "as," and "or" on the same page, I wish retained. The italicising, and quotation marking, I have no objection to.

As to the note at bottom, I do not think any too much is admitted— What you propose on page 11 is right— I return your copy of the speech, together with one printed here, under my own hasty supervising. That at New York was printed without any supervision by me— If you conclude to publish a new edition, allow me to see the proof-sheets.

And now thanking you for your very complimentary letter, and your interest for me generally, I subscribe myself.

Your friend and servant.<br>A LINCOLN.

Nothing discouraged by failing to get Lincoln's notes for the reprint, Messrs. Charles C. Nott and Cephas Brainerd undertook and prepared an appendix consisting of thirty-eight historical

and analytical notes.  These were so full that
they covered nearly as many pages as the reprinted speech.  The labour incident to this
corroborates the mention I have made of the
time and care Lincoln bestowed in collating
the facts and historical data he elaborated his
speech from.  As late as August 18, 1909, Mr.
Cephas Brainerd, who assisted Mr. Nott in making
the reference notes, writes that in doing this,
they "ransacked all the materials available in
the libraries of New York, and also, had interviews
with Mr. Bancroft and Mr. Hildreth and Mr.
Goodell, who was in those times a famous anti-
slavery man."  This reprint edition with their
notes appeared in September, 1860, and the
committee sent Lincoln two hundred and fifty
copies, promising to send him as many more as
he might wish.  The preface to this annotated
edition by the eminent and scholarly gentlemen
who edited it, is worth reproducing here as an
expression of their estimate of the labour Lincoln
had bestowed in its preparation and the masterful
assemblage his logical argument had given to his
historical citations.  Their preface was as follows:

This edition of Mr. Lincoln's address has been prepared and published by the Young Men's Republican
Union of New York, to exemplify its wisdom, truth-

fulness, and learning. No one who has not actually attempted to verify its details can understand the patient research and historical labour which it embodies. The history of our earlier politics is scattered through numerous journals, statutes, pamphlets, and letters; and these are defective in completeness and accuracy of statement, and in indices and tables of contents. Neither can any one who has not travelled over this precise ground appreciate the accuracy of every trivial detail, or the self-denying impartiality with which Mr. Lincoln has turned from the testimony of "the Fathers," on the general question of slavery, to present the single question which he discusses. From the first line to the last—from his premises to his conclusion, he travels with swift, unerring directness which no logician ever excelled—an argument complete and full, without the affectation of learning, and without the stiffness which usually accompanies dates and details. A single, easy, simple sentence of plain Anglo-Saxon words contains a chapter of history that, in some instances, has taken days of labour to verify and which must have cost the author months of investigation to acquire. And, though the public should justly estimate the labour bestowed on the facts which are stated, they cannot estimate the greater labour involved on those which are omitted— how many pages have been read—how many works examined—what numerous statutes, resolutions, speeches, letters, and biographies have been looked through.   Commencing with this address as a political pamphlet, the reader will leave it as an historical work—brief, complete, profound, impartial, truthful —which will survive the time and the occasion that called it forth, and be esteemed hereafter, no less for its intrinsic worth than its unpretending modesty.

NEW YORK, September, 1860.

Lincoln's temperament was a placid one, free from extreme tendencies.  His associates and his education at Salem, and also with both Stuart and Logan, had been of the most conservative character.  He was in those earlier years a well-established Henry Clay Whig of the olden school. The radical abolition and free-soil literature, which Mr. Herndon had supplied so liberally, brought for the first time strongly before Lincoln that side of the slavery question.   It illustrates the unusual fairness of his mind that he was not satisfied with these views alone, but consulted those of Southern authors as well, that he might thus pass both sides in review while studying the whole country's political differences.   This thorough study by Lincoln is revealed in the Cooper Institute speech and therein was its convincing strength.

It was only through such processes of thought about the peculiar events rapidly transpiring that he arrived at his later conviction that there was a Southern slave-holding oligarchy with its views so intimately woven into the texture of Calhoun's doctrine of State rights, that both together must be throttled, or the Union of the States would be broken up. The Southern people, through their own political literature, were Lincoln's instructors as to their policies and how they expected to carry them out. By their own political leaders and representative men and women, so far as their views were publicly expressed in their home papers after 1850, he had been keeping constantly informed.

Besides all this, Lincoln while in Congress, had made the acquaintance with, and had great confidence in and affection for, many Border State men and several from the Gulf States, long before the strife of the Civil War sundered his life work from theirs. Nor did he, after this period, fail to estimate fairly the whole Southern people and their view-point of national affairs, whether before, during, or after the fierce conflict had reached its exhausting end. His first inaugural voiced those broad national conceptions of policy; though North and South could not then read and interpret or appreciate its plain utterances aright, much less see the latent intensity of feeling and love that in later years are now discovered between the lines of that remarkable address.

The Southern people had not in all the world a friend whose life was worth so much to them as was Abraham Lincoln's the night that misguided partisan sent the fatal bullet which stilled forever his just and generous heart.

# What Religion Meant to Abraham Lincoln

"I have never united myself to any church, because I have found difficulty in giving my assent, without mental reservation, to the long, complicated statements of Christian doctrine which characterize their Articles of Belief and Confession of Faith. When any church will inscribe over its altar, as its sole qualification for membership, the Saviour's condensed statement of the substance of the Gospel, 'Thou shalt love the Lord thy God with all thy heart, and with all thy soul, and with all thy mind, and thy neighbour as thyself,' that church will I join with all my heart and all my soul."

*The Inner Life of Lincoln*, 1868, by F. B. CARPENTER.

## XIV

### WHAT RELIGION MEANT TO ABRAHAM LINCOLN

OF all things in and around New Salem, from its earliest to its latest days, there was nothing about the little village that existed in forms and opinions more crude and vague than its religion. For the most part its inhabitants had no religion to speak of, in the conventional sense of the word. In the case of any who had held church membership elsewhere, the relation had lapsed with their removal to a community that had no church. Yet perhaps no other hamlet so small and short-lived as New Salem has ever had a citizen whose religion has been more discussed.

The people of New Salem and its vicinity were a plain and industrious folk. Their material needs were indeed few as compared with ours; yet they required a diligence in their daily labours to provide for these necessities that absorbed their time and interest to such an extent as only those can appreciate who know the hardship, toil, and exposure endured by the early settlers and their families.

Hither came Abraham Lincoln, April 19, 1831. Here he spent most of his next seven years amid various surroundings and associations which became formative and controlling influences in his life. It is important to estimate correctly and to recognize the work he did there; the men with whom he there measured muscle and mind; the women whom he respected and those he admired, and one he loved. Those were important years that he spent there with his interests centred in and about this primitive little hamlet. Important they were to him, as we have seen; important also to New Salem, for with his departure its glory also departed.

Salem soon ceased to be a neighbourhood centre, and its people were scattered. One by one the buildings were moved away, leaving nothing familiar but the blue sky above and the hill on which the houses had stood, washed then as now by the sluggish Sangamon. Gone, too, at length, are the old mill-dam that obstructed the current of the river, and the old mill that still stood on the bank for many years after the village had vanished, and the rumbling of whose whirring stone burrs, grinding grain for later settlers, might be heard a mile or more up and down the river's timbered bluffs. How distinct those echoes come back

in memory as I write, recalling many delightful
Saturday afternoons spent there ofttimes alone
with rod and line! How exultantly the barefoot
boy trudged home after sunset with his "catch,"
to meet therefor the welcome and the praise of a
then unbroken family circle, of which now I alone
remain!

In a chapter intended to tell something about
what religion meant to Abraham Lincoln, the
influences of New Salem should always be given
a prominent place. For fifty years the chroniclers
have been busy recording a mass of fact and
fiction relating to Lincoln's seven years' residence
there; and in no other direction is the mingling
of fact and fiction more in evidence than in
relation to his religious faith during those seven
years. Much of this record has come to us at
second or third hand, distorted by the lapse of
time and repeated narration, and even the worse
confusion of preconceived notions and biased
opinions of some of the writers.

The charge of infidelity was originated and circulated by Lincoln's political foes. It has come
down to us in the record of that intensely hot
Congressional campaign of 1846 in which Lincoln's
opponent was the famous though eccentric

Methodist pioneer preacher, Peter Cartwright. It was one of the personalities that arose out of an unusually bitter and personal political campaign. The circumstances upon which the charge was based dated back fifteen years before the campaign in which it was used to discredit and defeat him. In order to determine the measure of credence that this story deserves, it is necessary to consider the characteristics of several residents of New Salem and vicinity who were familiar with the events of those seven years. More especially is it important to inquire into the burning, by Samuel Hill, of a mysterious manuscript said to have been an infidel production written by Abraham Lincoln.

These charges, which I shall attempt to sift for the few grains of truth that they may contain, were trivial matters at the time. It was never supposed that they would be exploited as historic evidence to the discredit of Lincoln. Had the political enemies who first circulated this charge in 1846 anticipated that the campaign canard, "The Infidelity of Lincoln," would attain a world-wide currency to the damage of his reputation, they would never have set it afloat. This admission I had from Cartwright himself as late as 1862, when he described the incident at a dinner party given him by James Harper that year in New

York City. Cartwright's statement regarding this matter will appear a little farther on.

Reverting to the seven years of Abraham Lincoln's life spent at New Salem, we find them full of contradictory view-points from which he observed his fellow men. In his discussions on various subjects with all classes of people, he showed a respect for their peculiar views and often adjusted himself with much skill to meet their arguments, as the trend of the discussion might require. For this reason it would be extremely difficult by traversing all his expressions of opinion to trace out and define in a consistent manner Lincoln's religious faith, along moral, spiritual, or ethical lines, in harmony with conventional forms or sectarian dogmas.

There is no small element of human personality and of our human nature mixed up with the religious opinions of most of us. This may be observed even among Christ's twelve chosen disciples, though dwelling in the celestial light of the Master's own teaching. Lincoln was no exception in this respect; and the Salem atmosphere was one not especially filled with celestial light. The essentials of his religious belief, that so largely formed and controlled his ideals and actions, were

modified far more than is usually the case by the
sympathy of his nature and by the experiences
and responsibilities of his life through which he
passed from time to time. The assumption
that Lincoln's opinion on any subject at any
particular time was thenceforth fixed and un-
changeable is contrary to recognized facts of
history. It must be evident that with such de-
liberate habits of thought and painstaking care
in reaching conclusions, no radical departure
from the fundamental beliefs amid which Lincoln
had lived from his youth up to his twenty-third
year could have occurred so rapidly as some claim
that he experienced at Salem. To render such a
claim deserving of acceptance, it must be supported
by convincing proof. This is certainly lacking
so far as the evidence from his life at Salem is
concerned.

After his removal to Springfield, and finally
to Washington, on until the mortal part of our
First American was brought home to Springfield
and laid in its last resting-place among us, his
addresses and state papers bear on their pages
such direct evidence of what religion meant to
Abraham Lincoln that to deny its presence and
significance there, and in the soul of him who
delivered them, would be as unreasonable as to

deny the existence of a sun in the heavens at noonday.

After the Congressional campaign of 1846, when this charge of infidelity was first made, nothing more was heard of it again until 1870,—five years after Lincoln's death. For nineteen years after this charge was first made, Lincoln had been a most prominent figure in political life. He had been subjected to all sorts of criticisms, political and personal, in public addresses, in newspaper articles and caricatures, beyond any other man of his time. His entire record was scrutinized, and every act or opinion of his past life that could be used against him with any semblance of truth was used by his vindictive foes to discredit him before the country.

When Douglas, in the Senatorial campaign, of 1858, in one of his speeches referred to Lincoln's past and his occupation, when he first met him, as being "a grocery keeper dispensing drinks," had it been possible for him to have added the slur of "infidel" he certainly would have done so. Douglas was thoroughly familiar with his habits and opinions at Salem and Springfield up to the time of those debates. He omitted nothing that he could then urge against Lincoln to impair his reputation before the public. The epithet

18

"infidel" if successfully applied to a candidate aspiring to Senatorial honours in Illinois in 1858 would have been as demoralizing to his supporters as the cry of "Fire!" at the midnight hour. Douglas never once, in public or private, referred to this political canard of the Congressional campaign of 1846. Long before that remote date, it had failed because it was unsupported by facts. It had gone down under the defeat of Cartwright in that election by the largest majority ever recorded in that Congressional district for a Whig candidate.

I am able to add Cartwright's own later testimony as to the falsity of this charge of infidelity. In the winter of 1862 Cartwright visited the East, addressing large audiences in many of the large cities. After his return he spent several days with my parents, and I shall repeat here the account he then gave us of a dinner party given in his honour by James Harper, the senior member of the Harper publishing firm in New York. While the time of this visit was considerably later than the Salem incident of which this chapter treats, it is yet so pertinent to the charge of "infidelity" made in 1846 that I introduce it here in connection with that earlier date.

Cartwright said that for some reason which he never could understand, the Eastern people of the business and literary classes were always anxious to meet him. This company at the Harper reception and dinner party was composed, he said, of representative merchants, bankers, lawyers, and a few ministers. The ministers seemed less desirous of meeting him than were the others. He said that they met at an hour earlier than usual for such functions because he had previously made an engagement with a Brooklyn pastor to address a meeting for him at 8:30 the same evening, and he had accepted Mr. Harper's invitation subject to this earlier engagement. Cartwright said that he "felt like a cat in a strange garret" on meeting so many celebrated men for the first time. When he was introduced by Mr. Harper to the guests he said he was "all doubled up," but (using a favourite expression when endeavouring to be cautious and conventional) that he "poised himself" so as not to reflect discredit upon his backwoods raising. How poorly he kept his "poise" will shortly appear.

He said he had hoped to play the inconspicuous part of a quiet listener among these eminent men whom he regarded as vastly his superiors. Instead, for an hour or more, he was forced to take the most prominent part, answering their questions concerning frontier life, his experiences as a preacher at camp meeting, and on other occasions among the rough characters of the Far West. At length he succeeded, he said, in directing the conversation to the sad condition of national affairs. Having then succeeded in diverting attention from himself, he lapsed into silence in order that he might learn the attitude of such a representative company of New York men toward Abraham Lincoln and his efforts along civil and military lines to crush the rebellion. He knew how seriously the loss of Southern trade had affected the business of some of the guests; and he expected to find their sympathies were influenced by this condition of their pocket-books. But he did not expect to find anyone there whose sympathies were strongly with the Southern Confederacy.

To Cartwright's great surprise he heard nothing but criticisms of President Lincoln's course since his inauguration, and the Northern policy of prosecuting the war for preserving the integrity of the Union by force of arms. The opinions expressed by the gentlemen present reflected either their entire approval of Jefferson Davis and the action of the Confederate States in seceding from the Union, and glorifying their military prowess; or the milder view of "anything for peace," and a compromise guaranteeing whatever conditions the South might demand. "The consciences of the entire crowd," said Cartwright— to use his exact words—"were choked with cotton and cankered with gold." He said that he had never felt his blood so hot with indignation as it was while sitting there as the guest of honour and listening to such conversation. He waited in vain to hear some one speak in defence of the use of force for preserving the Union of the States, or in appreciation of the stupendous efforts then being made by President Lincoln and the Congress at Washington to enable the army and navy to crush out the rebellion.

Looking at his watch he saw that it was nearly time for him to be on his way to Brooklyn. Still holding his watch in his hand, he addressed Mr. Harper, asking to be excused, since, making allowance for delays in transit, he had only sufficient time to meet his appointment in Brooklyn. Mr. Harper protested: "No, no, Father Cartwright, not until after the next course, which is the best and rarest to be served, and it was procured specially to give you a surprise and to honour your presence with us tonight." Cartwright enquired what it was; and when told by Mr. Harper that it was prairie chicken from the prairies of Iowa, the doughty divine, with a disdainful wave of the hand, replied that he had had such a plenty of prairie chickens at home that he was cloyed with them long ago, and did not need to come to New York to feast on them. Mr. Harper replied: "Well, if you must leave so soon, remain a little longer at any rate and see the relish your Eastern brothers have for your Western game bird; and to assure your getting to the Brooklyn appointment in time, I have had my carriage ordered and it will be ready to take you promptly across; so sit down, sit down, Father Cartwright."

Cartwright replied: "That is very kind and considerate, Brother Harper, very kind indeed, and I thank you for your forethought. But instead of sharing the next course with you, I beg your attention before I leave to hear from me a few parting words of admonition and counsel." The request was granted, and I repeat what he said as nearly as I can recall his report of the startling words with which he addressed them:

"I am an old man; the sands in the hour-glass of my life have nearly finished their flow. What I can say and what I can do in this world, if accomplished at all, must be done promptly. So I wish to speak very plainly to you tonight the last words I may ever address to you. If I had known I would meet such a nest of tories and traitors here, I would never have put my legs under your boards, nor sat down and broken bread with you at this table."

The reader can readily imagine the consternation that opening sentence brought to the guests. I shall not attempt to record Cartwright's description of the scene, but among other things he said that "every mother's son of them straightened their backs bolt upright and looked as though their hearts had ceased to beat, while they glared on me, waiting for what would come next. I saw that I was going to have attention from that table full of the solid men of New York and I never had more attentive listeners."

"My father," resumed Cartwright, "was a Revolutionary patriot. He gave the best years of his life to this country as a soldier in wresting from the British Crown the independence of the Colonies and winning the West for these United States. Since then as boy and man, first in 'the dark and bloody battle ground' of Kentucky's Indian strife, and later as a pioneer in the frontier settlements of Illinois, I have kept most sacred, by personal service in an humble way, my faith and loyal devotion to the priceless legacy of these

United States, left me by my patriot-father. I know what this united country is worth to us now. I have seen and rejoiced in its growth, I have lived its glorious life. I have been baptized with the blood that won, and have had a part in the labours that cemented together, these United States. These States now span the land from ocean to ocean with more happy and prosperous homes than God's sun ever shone on before.

"As I near the sunset days of my life I behold, with none of your dollar-blurred vision, what is to be our country's future if we hold these States united as our fathers bequeathed them to us. At the same time I see in anticipation and horror fully as clearly, through what would be my blinding tears of wrath and dismay, the huge hell of jealousy and discord that can be opened up within our country's boundaries if the secessionists succeed in rending the Union of our States. You, their sympathizers on this side of the Mason and Dixon line, are accomplishing here today more for those secessionists against maintaining the Union of the States, by your criticisms and lack of sympathy for President Lincoln's noble labours for the Union than you could do were you down South this hour and enrolled in the ranks of Jeff Davis's Confederacy.

"As I have personalized the rebellion in its president's name, and have tonight listened to such unpatriotic censures by you of the President of the United States, allow me to express to you from first-hand knowledge my opinion of the personal capacity and patriotism of President Lincoln. As the crow flies, I have lived within a score of miles of Abraham Lincoln for a third of a century. Until shortly before he took the oath of office as President of the United States, we had trained in different political camps, he a Whig and I a Democrat. I remained a Democrat until the firing on Fort Sumter. Since then I know no party save that of my undivided country and Abraham Lincoln its President.

"Once we were opposing candidates for a seat in Congress, and, measured up in the ballot-box, I went down in defeat. But it was defeat by a gentleman and a patriot. I stand here tonight to commend to you the Christian character, sterling integrity, and far-seeing sagacity of the President of the United States, whose official acts you have, in your blind money-madness, so critically assailed tonight. I am confident that he is the man to meet and go forward in this crisis to lead his countrymen amid and through the terrible strife in which we are now engaged.

He has a cool-headed, God-fearing, and unselfish love of his country, and knows from top to bottom the life and spirit of men both North and South.

"When you go from here to your homes tonight I want you to bear with you the assurances of his neighbour and once-political opponent that the country will be safe in his hands. I wish to have you understand that back of him will stand an unflinching host of Western men, who have no financial ghosts that terrify them and who are destined to rescue this nation from the perils now before us. We have got the men who have got the right kind of grit in them out West. Why stand ye here idle critics? May God send patriotic light into your stingy souls!

"I am through. I may have said too much, and said it too harshly, for I am not a man of smooth, soft words. I was born in a cane-brake, where my mother was hastily hurried and secreted to escape the tomahawks of savage Indians; I was rocked in a bee-gum for my cradle; and my graduation degrees were taken from, and in, life's thunderstorms. I may be considered by you a very rude guest; but in such national distress, when I feel so intensely my country's perils, I could not speak less strongly than I have spoken. I could not withdraw in silence and go sneaking away from this company and this table without feeling that I had been a coward and false to my country. I can be neither, now nor ever, as God is my witness,—so help me God!

"In a last word and as my farewell, I shall give you a toast: In this glass of Heaven-brewed 'Adam's Ale,' I proclaim and admonish you with the sentiments uttered by the great Webster in the United States Senate, and its patriotic companion-piece announced by Senator Douglas the last time he stood before an Illinois audience."

Cartwright said that as he spoke this last sentence he reached before him for the glass of water by his plate and, holding it high above him, repeated the words of the two illustrious senators: "Liberty and Union, now and forever, one and inseparable!" "There are now but two parties,— Patriots and Traitors!"

Nothing more vivid rises up out of my memories of more than half a century past than these earnest words as he repeated them to us with that intensity and emotion so characteristic of that veteran hero of Western Methodism, that life-long Jacksonian Democrat of the stalwart, old-school type of partisanship.

This conversation occurred in the latter part of 1862, ten years after Cartwright's autobiography had been published. In that book he had made no mention of his candidacy for Congress with Lincoln as his opponent, though that campaign was made ten years before his autobiography appeared. This omission seemed to me at the time peculiar; and I was all the more at a loss to account for it on hearing him speak so favourably of President Lincoln. So I ventured to mention this omission and to ask him whether there had not been some very interesting matters connected with the Congressional campaign of 1846 between himself and Lincoln well worth the telling in his autobiography.

Cartwright replied that I should remember that when he published his autobiography in 1856 Lincoln had not attained national prominence. But he said that the principal reason for this omission was that he thought his own political ventures the most unsatisfactory part of his life to him and to many of his friends. He said that this was a portion of his past that he referred to in the closing page of his book where he asked forgiveness for all the shortcomings and imperfections without number in his eventful life. He added: "That 1846 campaign cured me of all

political hankerings for office, and I hope the good
Lord will forever save me from getting any more
political bees in my bonnet."

It was at this point in the conversation that
my mother referred to the campaign story of 1846
in regard to Lincoln's being an avowed infidel
when at Salem.  She put the direct question to
him whether he was not now convinced that the
charge was false; and that the story circulated at
that time, that Lincoln wrote a book at Salem
attacking the Bible,—which manuscript was
burned by Samuel Hill,—was not a gross fabrica-
tion based upon the burning of another paper
having no relation to the Bible, or any religious
subject.

Cartwright replied that he had learned as much
as that from an intimate conversation he had
with Menter Graham some years after that
campaign.  From him he learned the facts concerning that unfortunate story.  He found that
he had been woefully misinformed and misled
by the account he had received, believed, and
circulated, about the infidel book said to have been
burnt by Hill.  He said that he was so chagrined
and abashed by the discovery of the political
purpose in that story that it was one of the

inducements that caused him to ignore in his book everything connected with his candidacy against Lincoln in 1846.

"I did not wish," he said, "to embalm in my history a story that nobody since has ever referred to. It was dead. It was very silly in me not to have verified the whole story at the time and found how false it was. A short time after Lincoln's nomination for the presidency by the Republican party in 1860," he went on to say, "I found more substantial reasons than any I ever had before, to assure me that Lincoln was not what my party friends and I, relying upon them, had charged him with being in 1846. This came from my meeting Dr. Smith, the pastor of the First Presbyterian Church of Springfield, and spending an evening in his company at the home of a mutual friend in Springfield. I found him a pleasant Christian gentleman and the evening in his society was a profitable one. He was a college man, but I found he had roughed it on the frontier as well, and got the college starch out of him. Dr. Smith told me that Lincoln and his family were regular attendants at his church, and that at some time he expected Lincoln to unite with his church, as Mrs. Lincoln had done. Dr. Smith said that Mrs. Lincoln had been brought up as an

Episcopalian and previous to their marriage had attended that church; but that in deference to Lincoln's strong Baptist views against so many formalities in church worship, she had joined the Presbyterian Church as a compromise, expecting Lincoln at some future time to come into that church." In line with his strong sectarian bias that remained even in his old age in spite of all the enlightening influences surrounding him, Cartwright went on to say: "I have no sympathy or use for Presbyterian Calvinism myself, but nevertheless it is probably a saving doctrine. I have known too many devout men and women in the Presbyterian Church to quarrel with them as much as I did in my earlier days. Jacquess also assured me that during the year he was stationed in Springfield he had spent many hours with Lincoln in the State Library, and by their conversations, was well satisfied that Lincoln's attitude toward religion was not that of an infidel."

Cartwright said that his being a member of the State legislature had put such political ambitions into his head that it was not hard for his friends to get him into the canvass for Congress in 1846. That hereafter, if the Lord and the good people would forgive him for the political campaigning of his life in the past, he felt proof against being tempted into any political strife again in his few remaining days. He believed that Lincoln was fitted for political life and knew how to keep his eye on the laurel while he played the game; but for himself he had tried and most ingloriously failed in it, and knew that for Peter Cartwright, hereafter, it would be better to stick to Methodism and fighting the devil and his imps, and when no longer able for that work he should settle down on his farm at Pleasant Plains until God should call him home.

From these digressions, in which later incidents in Lincoln's life have been considered, we now return to the earlier period presented in the opening pages of this chapter. For a score of years, beginning about 1870, the matter of Lincoln's religious belief while at Salem became a question of great interest and inquiry. In the lectures that were delivered and the books published on this subject at that time, extreme statements were made on both sides of the question. I shall not undertake to review all, or even a considerable part, of the assertions and evidence in their support set forth during those years, much less to share in the partisan spirit that marked those discussions by extremists on both sides.

The statement of a few facts will be sufficient to explain and entirely eliminate the basis of the charge that Lincoln wrote a book or essay attacking the Christian religion in general, and the Bible in particular, and that this manuscript was consigned to the flames by Samuel Hill. This charge is quite on a par with the story of the patient to whom his physician administered an emetic with the result that the sick man threw up something of a very dark colour. As the story was repeated in the neighbourhood gossip it grew in colouring and detail, each narrator generously contributing his share toward the building up of a story of cumulative interest in which the effect of the emetic was successively said to be the vomiting of something "very dark,"—"as black as a crow," —"a crow," "two crows!" So the man who took the emetic was known thereafter as "the man who threw up two crows." The story of Lincoln's infidel book being burnt by Samuel Hill grew farther beyond the simple original facts than the story of the emetic and its startling effect on the poor patient with the black crow record.

Mr. Hill was a very efficient merchant of Salem. He was the first to place on his shelves for the accommodation of the early settlers a wide variety of goods embracing a full assortment of the necessities and some of the luxuries of life, similar to the department stores of the present day. He made a financial success, measured by the standards and within the limits of mercantile affairs of that time. When this has been said all has been said in his favour that is possible upon the theory that business versatility develops a well-rounded character. Did it not take us too far afield from the subject of this chapter, many amusing incidents might be related illustrating Mr. Hill's peculiar and not always amiable weaknesses when acting outside of the strictly mercantile lines of his affairs. Some of his peculiarities, as described by his nephew, will be mentioned later.

For my account of some things leading up to the story of the burning of the manuscript, I rely upon my mother's memory. She had her information from Ann Rutledge, who in turn had the story from McNeil before he started on his journey to visit his parents in the East.

Æsop was not more popular among Greek boys than was Abraham Lincoln with the boys and girls, big and little, older or younger, in and around Salem. He wrote their letters, read the

answers for those who could not read, and was
a general factotum for the village and its neighbourhood. One day a fat letter, or roll of manuscript, was found on the road by some one who
could not read and it was quite naturally taken
to Lincoln to decipher. It proved to be a letter
addressed to McNeil by Hill enclosing invoices
of goods. It was, besides, a letter which should
have been guarded with special care; for upon
reading it Lincoln found the explanation for the
sudden dissolution of the firm of Hill & McNeil,
which had occurred some time before when Hill
had purchased his partner's interest in the business.
The reasons for this abrupt ending of the partnership were given in unmistakable terms by Hill
in the letter. He made a violent personal attack
upon McNeil for disloyalty to his senior partner
by becoming the accepted suitor of Miss Ann
Rutledge, and thus destroying Hill's hopes of se-
curing her hand at some future time for himself.
It is certainly not unreasonable to assume that
Lincoln was intensely interested and amused as he
read the letter. Hill's age was nearly twice Miss
Rutledge's, and she said when communicating the
incident to my mother that from their occasional
meetings at the store or at her father's home she
had never gained the slightest idea that Hill had

any warmer interest in her than that of a merchant desirous of her father's trade. McNeil was also in blissful ignorance of his partner's secret adoration of Miss Rutledge; and it is quite natural to suppose that he was greatly surprised on receipt of the letter, if one of his cool temperament was capable of surprise. Hill's letter demanded the closing out of the partnership and McNeil's retirement at once, and offered a handsome sum in consideration of his share in the store and the outstanding accounts.

McNeil being a man of quick judgment and few words in matters of business, curtly accepted Hill's offer. It was amid the disorder attending the rapid closing up of his business affairs at Salem outside the store, preliminary to his trip east to visit his parents, that McNeil lost Hill's letter which was found and taken to Lincoln. He was not at all interested in the bulky sheets of invoices with their mazes of figures, but the subject-matter of the letter and the direct personal attack upon McNeil aroused Lincoln's sense of humour immensely; and without considering how sensitive Hill might be concerning the very private nature of his business relations with his partner and the more delicate matter of Hill's affection for Miss Rutledge, Lincoln at once,

in his most humorous mood, took the letter to
Hill. The result was startling. Hill flew into a
towering rage over the disclosure of his private
business affairs; but the publicity given to his
grievance against McNeil because of his attention
to Miss Rutledge was doubtless the more serious
occasion of his wrath. Lincoln stood near him
with the unfolded letter in his hands. It con-
sisted of many long pages containing invoices and
lists of merchandise, as well as the more personal
pages so painfully embarrassing to Hill and so
amusing to Lincoln. It was more than Hill could
endure. He went all to pieces. In his wrath he
snatched the package from Lincoln and thrust it
into the fire.

That was the manuscript of such historic
notoriety that was burned by Hill. From its
ashes came forth the story charging Lincoln with
the authorship of an infidel attack on the Bible
and the Christian religion. This story was used
against him in the Congressional campaign of 1846,
and resurrected in the biographies written years
after Lincoln's death. Why it was not exposed at
the time may be readily seen. At the time of the
Congressional campaign of 1846, Hill, McNeil (now
McNamar), and Lincoln all had been married;

Hill for eleven years, McNamar nine years, and Lincoln four years. At that time, and in the midst of a warm political campaign, it would have been a very difficult matter to explain and publish the actual facts regarding the manuscript that had been burned, without involving several families in serious embarrassment by the explanation. Hill was then a violent Democratic partisan and was quite willing that Cartwright's candidacy should be helped by his silence to say nothing of his reluctance to renew his own chagrin and embarrass his family by a statement of the facts. Moreover, Lincoln was the soul of honour and would suffer misrepresentation in silence rather than embarrass a lady by giving the facts. And this Hill knew full well.

Samuel Hill's action in snatching these sheets from Lincoln and burning them and the false assertions circulated by others concerning their contents, have brought Hill's name into such peculiar prominence as to suggest further consideration of his personality, to discover whether his characteristics may throw light upon his actions in this matter. With this in view I wrote Hon. A. G. Nance of Petersburg, asking for such recollections of Hill's peculiarities as he could furnish. Mr. Nance was a nephew of Mrs. Hill; and I will give his own words in reply to my request:

My grandparents moved from Kentucky to Illinois in the Fall of 1832 and settled on a farm three miles south of Salem. They brought with them a large family, the youngest of whom was Parthena, a girl of sixteen. Hill was twice as old as my aunt, but he became infatuated with her at once, and after a courtship lasting until July 28, 1835, he was married to my aunt at my grandfather's. I own the farm now, it never having passed out of the Nance family.

Hill was a successful merchant but had a peculiar temper. It was such that he could not drive the team when he took his wife out for a drive. His wife sat on the front seat and drove the horses while Hill sat on the back seat. Mrs. Hill was a balanced woman; she had common sense;—I mean she had good sense about ordinary things. She was tactful; she could manage the team and her husband, and would not get into trouble with either.

Mr. Hill appreciated her splendid qualities and if anyone dropped a remark about a place or thing that could be construed into a criticism of his wife he would fight his weight in wild cats about it. Hill would get offended sometimes when no offence was intended. Major Thos. L. Harris when in company with Uncle Samuel Hill one day, made the remark about Green

County, Kentucky, not being the best county in Kentucky (which was true); but it being the county Mrs. Hill emigrated from when she came to Illinois, Hill took exceptions to the remark and became dangerously angry and abused Major Harris until the bystanders were amazed and wondered how Harris could take it. Herndon in his book says that this difficulty was between Lincoln and Hill. Herndon is mistaken, I am quite sure. My aunt regretted it and never believed for a moment that Major Harris thought of her when he made the remark, and at the time and always afterwards was a warm friend of Major Harris and his wife.

My aunt, Mrs. Parthena Hill, was a remarkable woman. She was not fickle-minded. Her love was uniform and could be depended upon. The man who sawed her wood did this job for more than thirty years without a change. She loved all who came in contact with her and all loved her.

This letter of Hon. A. G. Nance illustrates the personality of Mr. Samuel Hill very well. It shows his susceptibility to the charms of youth while at New Salem and his hot temper at all times when any one offended him or crossed his purposes; and the fidelity and love with which he clung to and defended his most excellent wife. To the reader it may suffice to explain the reasonableness of this most unreasonable incident of his snatching from Lincoln's hand the harmless papers and consigning them to the flames. It also makes it easier for us to understand why Hill never explained to any one the facts that would have vindicated Lincoln from the unfortunate story that at last passed with such false interpretation into an exciting Congressional campaign, and with sensational trimmings into some of his biographies after his death.

In connection with this report that I received from my mother and she from a person who was present when the letter and invoices were burnt, I would call the reader's attention to a reference in the letter of Menter Graham dated March 17, 1874, to Mr. B. F. Irwin which appears in this chapter. This substantially refers to and verifies the facts concerning the papers that were burned, as shown in the more detailed account which has been already given here by me.

Under date of April 20, 1874, Mr. B. F. Irwin of Pleasant Plains, Sangamon County, Illinois, sent to the *Illinois State Journal* a lengthy communication entitled, "Lincoln's Religious Belief." The occasion for the article, Mr. Irwin said, was his reading of a lecture by the Hon. William H. Herndon, delivered in the court house in Springfield some months before. In the opening paragraph he states that he was urgently requested to review Mr. Herndon's lecture and that he at that time promised to do so at the proper time. This article, published so soon after Herndon's lecture and in reply to it, with its strong clearcut sentences, and including letters received by Mr. Irwin from several gentlemen on the subject-matter of his article, was never, so far as I have been able to learn, contradicted or answered in the papers of Springfield or elsewhere by either Mr. Herndon or anyone else.

I knew Mr. B. F. Irwin quite well during the years preceding the Civil War and after, meeting him occasionally up to a short time before his death. I had been present on several occasions when he visited the law office of Lincoln & Herndon, before as well as after Lincoln's election to the presidency. I know that both members of the firm had a high respect for Mr. Irwin and at various times consulted with him in confidential political conferences in the office, and treated him and his opinions with marked deference and respect.

I shall endeavour to give in this connection the material part of Mr. Irwin's article, together with the full text of several letters and the substance

of certain interviews reported in the article. I
can assure the reader that entire confidence may
be placed in Mr. Irwin's statement of facts as he
understood them, and that the letters as published in his article, and here reproduced, are
authentic copies of the genuine originals all of
whose authors were living when the article was
published. Mr. Irwin begins his article by saying
that the time to reply to some points in Mr.
Herndon's lecture has arrived:

I propose noticing a few points in the address of Mr.
Herndon, and I think I will be able to show that Mr.
Herndon himself never knew nor understood really
what the faith or religious belief of Lincoln was. I
wish it now and here understood that Mr. Herndon's
candour, or veracity, I do not call in question, nor will
I designedly say anything to offend him. He and I
have been for twenty-five years good friends, and I
hope that friendship may continue. Mr. Herndon
has a right to prove Lincoln an infidel, if he can. I
claim the same right to prove that Lincoln was not
an infidel, if I can. If Mr. Lincoln was an infidel, as
Herndon says, it is proper for the world to know it.
If he was not an infidel, the charge is wrong and a
slander, for infidelity in the nineteenth century is no
honour to any man, dead or alive.

Mr. Herndon in his speech uses this language:

"One side of this question can be proved. It is admitted on all hands that Lincoln once was an infidel; that he wrote a small book or essay, or pamphlet against Christianity, and that he [Lincoln] continued an unbeliever until late in life." Herndon further says: "It is a rule of law as well as a rule of common sense, that when a certain state or condition of affairs is once proved to exist, the presumption is that it still exists until the contrary is proved; this rule to have full force until the contrary is proved."

Now I stand by that proposition as a true one. Will Mr. Herndon do so? But he is woefully mistaken in his statement that "all admit that Lincoln was once an infidel." I have never yet heard one single man express the belief that Lincoln was an infidel, either early or later in life, while I am confident I have heard one hundred different persons express astonishment at Mr. Herndon's writing and publishing Lincoln to the world an infidel. Mr. Herndon, it is true, did have opportunity and advantages over others in knowing Lincoln's religious opinions. But other men had some opportunities as well as Mr. Herndon, and to them I shall have to appeal, for I do not claim personally to know anything about Lincoln's religious faith. Though personally acquainted with Lincoln for twenty-five years, and often in his office, I never heard him say a word on the subject of Christianity or religious belief. Hence, my own opinion of Lincoln's faith or belief is based on the

testimony of those who do know, who had it from Lincoln himself; and I believe them; for the weight of testimony is certainly against Mr. Herndon. The Scriptures of Truth lay it down as a Divine rule that the evidence of two or three witnesses is better than one. Common law lays down the same rule, borrowed from Divine authority, and our courts are governed by it in their decisions.

Mr. Herndon, in his reply to Mr. Reed, says he is talking to establish the truth of a controversy between those who hold that Lincoln was a disbeliever, and those who hold that he died a Christian (a believer in Christ); and then says: "If I fail to establish my point, it will be because of the manner and method of presenting the facts." I have read that lecture over carefully, and I fail to find any proof of Herndon's proposition that Lincoln ever was an infidel or an unbeliever. The nearest I see to it is the statement of Col. J. H. Matheny. He uses this language substantially: Mr. Lincoln's earlier life is his whole life and history in Illinois up to the time he left for Washington City. He [Lincoln] was, as I understand it, a confirmed infidel.

Now Matheny fails to tell us how he got that understanding. Did he get it from Lincoln? He doesn't say so, and the reason he doesn't say so is he got it from some other source, probably from Herndon. But clearly, to be of any weight as evidence he must have got that understanding from Mr. Lincoln himself. Mr. Matheny may sometime in life have heard Lincoln use some of the arguments of Tom Paine or advance infidel ideas, and still not be an infidel. I have heard an official member of the Methodist Church in this town advance as strong infidel sentiments as Tom Paine ever did, and you would insult the man to say he was an infidel. So any Christian may use the language or advance some of the sentiments of Tom Paine, and be far from an infidel. Lincoln may have done all that, and still not be an infidel.

I do not believe Lincoln ever was an infidel, and I can state truly and say just what Matheny said. I understood Lincoln was an infidel, but I never believed the statement true. Matheny understood it; in other words, he had heard it, but knew nothing about the facts in the case. I have seen Mr. Matheny since, and he states that he never had it from Lincoln that he was an infidel, and never believed it. If Mr. Herndon is in possession of the evidence in writing or otherwise to prove that Lincoln was an infidel, either earlier or later in life, he ought to bring forth the proof to sustain his proposition; for he has long since learned that the statement alone fails to satisfy the public mind that Lincoln ever was an infidel. Mr. Herndon, in his Abbott letter, truly says the charge of infidelity was made against Lincoln when he was a candidate for Congress in 1846; and then adds: "Mr. Lincoln did not deny the charge, because it was true." The charge of infidelity was made against Lincoln at that time, and I suppose Lincoln made no public denial of the charge for the reason the canvass was being made on political grounds and not on religious faith or belief. This much was said at the time, as I well remember to be the facts in the case.

About the time of building the flat-boat on the Sangamon River in 1830 when Lincoln was quite a young man, a religious controversy was the topic in which Lincoln took a part. [This was in a neighbourhood debating club that met twice a month, all sorts of questions being discussed. The two chief disputants were appointed by the chairman, without regard to their opinions on the subject to be debated, and they chose from the members of the club their respective colleagues without regard to their opinions. In these debates some startling things were often said.] And in the argument, Lincoln used the language that, according to the history of the case in the New Testament, Christ was a bastard and his mother a base woman. This he may have used at the time, as young men sometimes do use vain language, and seventeen years afterwards, when he was a candidate for Congress against Peter Cartwright, a Methodist preacher, that vain remark was remembered and, Tom Paine having used similar language, Lincoln was published in some of the papers as an infidel. The above was the explanation published at the time, and the charge of infidelity did no harm.  Had Lincoln been known as an infidel or believed to be one at that time, I am certain he would have been beaten badly by Cartwright in the canvass.

Again, Mr. Herndon, in his Abbott letter, says: "It is not to be found in print that Lincoln ever used the word Christ." In fact, Herndon says, he never did use it, only to deny Christ as the son of God. Now that statement may be true, that he did not use the term Christ, but if Mr. Herndon will examine the speeches of the public men of this nation I believe I am safe in saying that Lincoln used and quoted more Scripture than any man in the nation; and that he quoted the parables and language of Christ oftener than any public man living. Not only did Lincoln quote Scripture, but he used it as being of Divine authority, and applicable to the affairs of earth.

Mr. Herndon gives us to understand that Lincoln did not believe the New Testament Scriptures to be any more inspired than Homer's songs, Milton's *Paradise Lost*, or Shakespeare. If Herndon is correct, it seems strange Lincoln made no use of those books. On the 16th of June, 1858, as a foundation for an argument, he used the language of Christ, "A house divided against itself cannot stand," in reply to Douglas. In the same campaign he four times used the parables of Christ; in his second inaugural address, "woe unto the world because of its offences," Christ's language again.

But I need not multiply quotations. His speeches, proclamations, and messages are so full of quotations of Scripture, and always the language of Christ himself. He could not have been an infidel without being a base hypocrite; and I don't believe a more honest man lived on earth.

Mr. Herndon has said that in Lincoln's early life he wrote a pamphlet, book, or manuscript, against Christianity. I propose to show that the manuscript written by Lincoln was in favour of Christianity; to do so, I will offer the evidence of Mr. Graham, who knew Lincoln when he was a boy in Kentucky, and with whom Lincoln boarded for some two years; and if any man on earth ought to know Lincoln's religious faith or belief that man is Menter Graham who was intimate with Lincoln from the time he came to Illinois to the time he left for Washington City. I will give the letter in full:

*Statement of Mr. Menter Graham*

"Petersburg, Ill., March 17, 1874.
"B. F. Irwin:

"Sir:—In reply to your inquiries:—Abraham Lincoln was living at my house in New Salem, going to school, studying English grammar and surveying, in the year 1833. One morning he said to me: 'Graham, what do you think about the anger of the Lord?' I replied: 'I believe the Lord never was angry, or

20

mad, and never would be; that "His loving kindness
endureth forever"; that He never changes.' Said
Lincoln: 'I have a little manuscript written, which
I will show you'; and he stated that he thought
of having it published.   Offering it to me, he said he
had never showed it to any one, and still thought
of having it published.   The size of the manuscript
was about one-half quire of foolscap, written in a very
plain hand, on the subject of Christianity and a
defence of universal salvation.   The commencement
of it was something respecting the God of the universe
ever being excited, mad, or angry.   I had the manuscript in my possession some week or ten days.   I
have read many books on the subject of theology and
I don't think that in point of perspicuity and plainness
of reasoning I ever read one to surpass it.   I remember
well his argument.   He took the passage, 'As in
Adam all die, even so in Christ shall all be made alive,'
and followed up with the proposition that whatever
the breach or injury of Adam's transgression to the
human race was, which no doubt was very great, it
was made just and right by the atonement of Christ.
As to Major Hill burning the manuscript, I don't
believe he did, nor do I think he would have done such
a thing. . . .

"About the burning of a paper by Hill.   I have some
recollection of his snatching a letter from Lincoln
and putting it into the fire.   It was a letter written by

Hill to McNeil. His real name was McNamar. Some of the school children had picked up the letter, and handed it to Lincoln. Hill and Lincoln were talking about it when Hill snatched the letter from Lincoln and put it in the fire. The letter was respecting a young lady, Miss Ann Rutledge, for whom all three of these gentlemen seemed to have respect.[1]

"Yours truly,
"MENTER GRAHAM."

Now the next point I wish to notice is Mr. Herndon's statement, in his Abbott letter, that Lincoln, in 1846, was charged with being an infidel. Herndon says he [Lincoln] did not deny the charge, because it was true. As I before stated, I admit the charge was made, and I think at the time there was no public denial by Lincoln, for the reason that the canvass was made on political grounds, and not religious faith or belief. Nevertheless, the charge was denied, as the following letter will show:

### Statement of Thomas Mostiller

"PLEASANT PLAINS, Ill., April 28, 1874.
"B. F. IRWIN:
"SIR:—In regard to your inquiry just received, of

[1] The old-time use of "respect" means in later years "in love."—H. B. R.

what I heard Lincoln say about a charge of infidelity made against him when a candidate for Congress in 1846 or '47, it was this: I was present and heard Josiah Grady ask Lincoln a question or two regarding a charge made against Lincoln of being an infidel, and Lincoln unqualifiedly denied the charge of infidelity, and said, in addition, his parents were Baptists and brought him up in the belief of the Christian religion; and that he believed in the Christian religion as much as any one, but was sorry to say he had no pretensions to religion himself. I can't give his exact words but would make oath anywhere that he positively denied the charge made against him of infidelity. That was the first time I had ever heard of the charge of infidelity against Lincoln. Grady did not say that he would not vote for Lincoln if he was an infidel, but my understanding from Grady was that he would not vote for Lincoln if he was an infidel, and Grady did, as I suppose, vote for him. I understood him that he should.

> "Respectfully,
> "THOMAS MOSTILLER,
> "Menard Co., Ill."

The next evidence I shall offer, is that of Isaac Codgal, an intimate friend of Lincoln's from the time Lincoln came to Salem, Menard County, to the time he left for Washington City, and I will let Codgal speak for himself:

*Statement of Isaac Codgal*

"April 10, 1874.

"B. F. IRWIN:

"Yours received, making inquiries about what I heard Lincoln say about his religious belief. It is this, as near as I can tell it and recollect: I think it was in 1859 that I was in Lincoln's office in Springfield, and I had a curiosity to know his opinions or belief religiously; and I called on him for his faith in the presence of W. H. Herndon. At least Herndon was in the office at the time. Lincoln expressed himself in about these words: He did not nor could not believe in the endless punishment of any one of the human race. He understood punishment for sin to be a Bible doctrine; but that the punishment was parental in its object, aim, and design and intended for the good of the offender; hence it must cease when justice is satisfied. He added all that was lost by the transgression of Adam was made good by the atonement, all that was lost by the fall was made good by the sacrifice. And he added this remark, that punishment being a provision of the gospel system, he was not sure but the world would be better off if a little more punishment was preached by our ministers, and not so much pardon for sin. I then in reply told Mr. Lincoln he was a sound Universalist and would advise him to say but little about his belief, as it was an unpopular doctrine, though I fully agreed

with him in sentiment. Lincoln replied that he
never took any part in the argument or discussion
of theological questions.  Much more was said, but
the above are the ideas as advanced by Lincoln there.

"Respectfully yours,

"ISAAC CODGAL."

The next witness I shall offer on the subject is
Jonathan Harnett, of Pleasant Plains.  Mr. Harnett
is here.  I shall now furnish a statement over his
signature, as he is present and dictates as I write.
(Note.—I understood, as was often the case with
many very intelligent among the pioneer settlers, Mr.
Harnett could not write.)

Mr. Harnett says:

That in 1858, a short time after he came to Illinois,
he had a curiosity to see Lincoln, and went into his
office.   There were several others in the office that he
did not know and religious faith seemed to be the subject of conversation.   After some time was spent in
the controversy, it seemed to be Lincoln's time, and
in a few words he heard Lincoln condense in a small
space greater thoughts and larger ideas and sounder
logic than he ever heard brought into so small a space.
Lincoln, he says, covered more ground in a few
words, than he could in a week, and closed up with the
restitution of all things to God as the doctrine taught
in the Scriptures.   If any one was in doubt in regard

to Lincoln's belief in the atonement of Christ and the final salvation of all men, he removed those doubts in a few questions he answered and propounded to others. After expressing himself, some one or two took exceptions to his position, and he asked a few questions that cornered his interrogators and left no room to doubt or question his soundness on the atonement of Christ, and salvation finally of all men. He did not pretend to know just when that event would be consummated, but that it would be the ultimate result that Christ must reign supreme, high over all, the saviour of all; and the Supreme Ruler, he could not be satisfied with one out of the fold; all must come in, was his understanding of the doctrine taught in the Scriptures. [The above statement, since writing it, has been read to Mr. Harnett and endorsed by him.]

The next evidence I shall offer is Erasmus Manford, of Chicago. About 1850, he had a debate in Springfield, Ill., with Mr. Lewis. In his book, *Twenty-five Years in the West*, page 219, he says: "I remember well seeing Mr. Lincoln then punctually every day and every night. He often nodded his head to me when I made a strong point." Does that look as though Lincoln was an infidel? Manford was discussing the proposition of the restitution of all things to God which is manifested in Jesus Christ our Lord. Manford gives the quotation, chapter and verse, and

Lincoln nods assent to the position. That nodding
assent to the restitution agrees precisely with Mr.
Harnett's statement of Lincoln's position in his presence, seven or eight years afterward. Everyone
understands that nodding assent to the argument of a
speaker is an endorsement of what is said, and about
the equivalent to speaking it yourself. Manford so
understood it; and so anyone would understand it.

What has been recorded already in this chapter
concerning what religion meant to Abraham
Lincoln is justly liable to criticism as being
desultory and fragmentary. It is, however, entirely consistent with the statement made at the
very outset that it was not my purpose in recording
these recollections of Lincoln to write a connected
history of any portion of his life, or a systematic
analysis of his opinions or principles. It was
proposed merely to put on record some material
facts furnished by these flashlights of my memory,
that might assist the future historian to gain
a clearer vision of Lincoln's life during the
period covered by my own personal acquaintance and that of the friends from whom I
quote, whose statements about him and past
events and persons were not drafts on their
imagination for the facts and incidents presented
by me.

There were times in the privacy of the home
life or in an interview with a friend in the office,
when Lincoln spoke freely of what religion meant
to him. Such times, however, were not frequent.
They were rare occasions. He did not wear his
religion as a personal exhibit on his sleeve, as some
have done. He lived his religion. It was a
constant, pervasive part of the man, but he was
averse to advertising it and never used it for
purposes of display. Mrs. Lincoln said: "Mr.
Lincoln's religion was poetry!" She was probably
correct. If so, it was of an idealism akin to those
who "do always behold the face of my Father in
Heaven."

The religion of Lincoln was so intermingled and
incorporated with the other elements of his unique
personality as to defy complete analysis, or
description. No stranger touch, outside himself,
can reveal his religion in other than a fragmentary
and desultory manner. Its evidence was dis-
tributed throughout all his life, and was disclosed
in a manner so intermittent and recurrent as to
render orderly delineation of it impossible. The
most that can be undertaken in this chapter is to
present the religious features of his life in their
every-day settings, as the writer and some others
knew them from time to time; and to do this with-

out any attempt to systematize, interpret, or colour them, through a memory lens, into any systematic connection with each other or to bring them into harmony with any personal shades of opinion or belief on these subjects of my own.

It is with regret and reluctance that I find it necessary to present so many statements that depend upon my own testimony and that of my family, not only for the facts but for the words in which they are repeated. This has been unavoidable hitherto, and will be even more necessary in the private interviews about to be narrated. On the occasions when Lincoln expressed so freely his religious beliefs it was never intended or expected by him, or those present, that they would pass beyond the circle within which the conversations took place. But since then Lincoln's life and character have loomed so large upon the field of our country's life and history, as to render whatever he said or did, even in privacy, a matter of such public interest and importance as to overrule the courtesy of that silence which was his due while living.

In recent years it has become recognized as the patriotic duty of those who knew him to reveal all that their memory may retain regarding his personality and life, for the use of the future historian. History awaits and recognizes every assistance that can come from those whose opportunities and privilege it was to know Lincoln with any degree of intimacy, and this revealing of him is cordially welcomed and highly prized by a nation of his admirers. This should be contributed freely and fully, and without the hesitation or restraint that should ordinarily be observed in private life in respect to intimate and confidential interchange of religious beliefs and ideals. With this explanation I shall venture to set forth some of the more private episodes of Lincoln's life, more personal and intimate than any related before, dealing with what religion meant to him.

Abraham Lincoln when nine years old met his first great grief in the death of his mother. Her illness was a brief one, compared with most others who suffered with the disease with which she is said to have been afflicted. The rude cabin home where she spent these last days was thirty-five miles from the nearest doctor, and it is said that no medical aid was given during the seven days of her illness other than the friendly nursing of the doctor-woman, who, in those primitive times, was found in nearly every neighbourhood.

Of what passed between mother and son during the few years preceding her decease there is little known. The few references to them made by Lincoln in private conversation with friends at different periods in his life give all that we have. We learn from his words how vividly he recognized, and recalled with generous tenderness, the deep and lasting impressions those nine years of mother-love had made on him. From more than one friend I have heard of Lincoln's remarking that he owed all he was, or ever would be, to the inspiration so early instilled into his mind by his mother. The isolation of their home made their companionship in every way closer than is usual between mother and son. Her memory should ever be held in sacred reverence for the influence she had on the life she gave our country, even though, as her son said after he attained national prominence, those years had for their only record, "the plain and simple annals of the poor."

In my boyhood days, I was present once when Lincoln spoke of his mother with a strong affection which I have always remembered. At that time I was little more than the age of Lincoln when his mother died. I recall the time and circumstances of that evening's visit at our home,

the peculiarity of his manner as well, but could not have been able to mention the substance of what he said there, as I now do, had it not been through my mother's memory of it, and her statements to me of what was said. This conversation was related to me in the summer of 1889, while my mother was reading the Herndon–Weik *Life of Lincoln*, then just published, in connection with her second reading, for comparison, of the *Life of Lincoln*, by Lamon, published in 1874. My mother possessed a very tenacious verbal memory. Her ability to recall accurately the events, conversations, and personalities of her past life was remarkable. She was intensely interested at that time in her reading of those two lives of Lincoln, but was both surprised and indignant over certain parts of them.

Without here entering into the details of her criticisms of their inaccuracy, or as she said, "the imaginary history of some imaginary events and persons" in those books, I shall relate her account of one particularly interesting conversation that took place at our home in Petersburg, and which reveals how absurd is the word "infidel" when applied to Lincoln. This was the occasion to which I have referred before as making such a lasting impression on me. This was because of

Lincoln's emotional manner at the time, a manner which I had never before seen him manifest. I was so impressed by my recollection of this, and by the conversation as she repeated it to me, that at the time I wrote down from her rehearsal the substance of what she recalled of Lincoln's words, and I record them here together with the circumstances that called them forth.

Lincoln was attending the circuit court in Petersburg at the time referred to. Mother thought it was in June, 1846, for it was soon after his nomination, by the Whigs in May of 1846, as their candidate for Congress. Lincoln was at my parents' home spending the evening. The Rev. J. F. Jacquess was also present. He was the Methodist minister on the Petersburg circuit that year, and made his home at my father's when not out of town on the circuit. Jacquess came of a vigorous frontier ancestry. His youth and early manhood were full of strenuous toil. He was ten years younger than Lincoln; a graduate of the Indiana University, and of the Transylvania University College of Law of Lexington, Kentucky. A warm personal friendship had been growing up between Lincoln and Jacquess ever since the latter had come to Illinois. This continued during Lincoln's life, and while he was President, Jacquess

was intrusted by him with a confidential mission
to Richmond which proved of great importance
at the time. The circumstances that made this
mission desirable and the results of the conference
have been told fully by writers on both the Federal
and Confederate sides since the close of the war,
making unnecessary any extended mention here of
that remarkable visit, or of its failure to accomplish
the results Jacquess so fondly expected it would.

The week before this meeting at my father's
home there had been held in Petersburg a convention of Sunday-school workers,—the first ever
held in that portion of Illinois. Strange as it may
appear now, many good people then contended
that there should be no infant class below six or
eight years of age in a Sunday-school. One of
the subjects under lively discussion before the
convention was the fixing of the age limit for
"moral accountability" of scholars which would
determine when they should enter the Sunday
school. In the convention Jacquess and my
father had contended that there should be no
limit in age, or even in ability to read; that oral
teaching could and should meet the needs of all
who would come into these schools. Out of the
warmth of such recent discussions, the evening

conversation for a while had centered upon the same question.

Lincoln's opinion was asked for by my mother. He replied that he was not an authority in such matters; that there were no such schools in his childhood, and that he had never attended a Sunday-school except by request to make a short address. But the age limit, he thought, should find no place in any Sunday-school. He might illustrate this, he said, by mention of his own boyhood and the influence that biblical and moral instruction given in early years could, and did, have in his life. He said he was nine years old when his mother died; that his instruction by her in letters and morals, and especially the Bible stories, and the interest and love he acquired in reading the Bible through this teaching of his mother, had been the strongest and most influential experience in his life. He referred with evident sadness to the lonely months after his mother's death, and said that the Bible she had read, and had taught him to read, was the greatest comfort he and his sister had after their mother was gone. It was from this Bible of her's, he said, that he had asked Rev. David Elkin to read when he came into their home to preach the funeral sermon of his mother several months after her death.

Lincoln continued speaking of the vividness of childhood's impressions and how potent they were to influence and control mature years. He recalled how his mother had interested him in Bible stories before he had learned to read. He said that for years afterwards, and even yet, when he read certain verses which he had in early boyhood committed to memory by hearing her repeat them as she went about her household tasks, the tones of his mother's voice would come to him and he would seem to hear her speak those verses again.

My mother said that this unusual freedom with which he had referred to his early years, and the emotion he had manifested as he dwelt on them, caused her to refer to his life at Salem. This conversation, as I have said, was in the summer of 1846, when Lincoln and Peter Cartwright were candidates of opposing parties for Congress, and when Cartwright's friends, with his approval, had made the charge that Lincoln was an infidel. This assertion, and the bitter partisan energy with which the report was circulated at the time, had greatly disturbed my mother who through many years had entertained a warm friendship for both of them. This regard was, from long

21

acquaintance and friendship, one of personal esteem and not a political preference for either. She was aware how false this unqualified charge against Lincoln was, and she grieved because Cartwright had yielded to political influences and motives in making so false an assertion.

She therefore felt at liberty to inquire of Lincoln how much his opinions on religious subjects had been influenced by his sceptical associates at Salem, and by the books they had supplied him with while there. She introduced her inquiry by referring to several discussions that had taken place years before at her father's home between Lincoln and her brothers in connection with his frequent visits. She made a more especial reference to the conversation that took place one evening when Lincoln, Dr. Gershom Jayne, of Springfield, and Rev. John Berry were storm-bound one wintry day and remained overnight at the Rogers home.

My mother said that Lincoln listened very attentively while she was making reference to these visits and to his past life at Salem; and when—in connection with such references to the past—she noticed that he was deeply moved by her inquiry, at the moment she almost regretted asking him the questions. . . . He rose from his

chair where he had been sitting and walked slowly
across the room and stood at one end of the
hearth, at the side of the chimney breast before
the old-fashioned fire-place. He rested an elbow
on the wide mantel, leaning his head on his hand,
with the long fingers thrust through his hair.
Although so young at the time, I clearly recall
the peculiarity of his manner and the pose of his
body, as he stood there, facing those in the room
in silence for a few moments. Then he began to
speak quite slowly, and with a most impressive
emphasis. My mother reports his words as
follows:

Mrs. Rankin, you have asked me a question opening
up a subject that is being thrust into this Congressional
campaign and which I have resolved to ignore. It is
one having no proper place, or call for an answer by
me, in the political present or future before us. I
will not discuss the character and religion of Jesus
Christ on the stump! That is no place for it, though
my opponent, a minister of His gospel, thinks it is.
But in this private circle of friends, with the inquiry
coming from you, Mrs. Rankin, who have known me
as long as any of my Salem friends, and in some
respects more intimately than any of them, I will
frankly answer your question. I do not wish what
I may say here now to be quoted in this Congressional

canvass to any one, and I am sure that I can depend that every one of you will respect my wishes.   [This they did.]

At the time you refer to [continued Mr. Lincoln], I was having serious questionings about some portions of my former implicit faith in the Bible. The influence that drew me into such doubts were strong ones,—men having the widest culture and strongest minds of any I had known up to that time. In the midst of those shadows and questionings, before I could see my way clear to decide on them, there came into my life sad events and a loss that you were close to and you knew a great deal about how hard they were for me, for you were, at the time, a mutual friend.   Those days of trouble found me tossed amidst a sea of questionings.   They piled big upon me, experiences that brought with them great strains upon my emotional and mental life.   Through all I groped my way until I found a stronger and higher grasp of thought, one that reached beyond this life with a clearness and satisfaction I had never known before.   The Scriptures unfolded before me with a deeper and more logical appeal, through these new experiences, than anything else I could find to turn to, or ever before had found in them.

I do not claim that all my doubts were removed then, or since that time have been swept away.   They are not.   Probably it is to be my lot to go on in a twilight, feeling and reasoning my way through life, as questioning, doubting Thomas did. But in my poor maimed, withered way, I bear with me as I go on a seeking spirit of desire for a faith that was with him of the olden time, who, in his need, as I in mine, exclaimed: "Help thou my unbelief."

I do not see [he went on to say, after leaving his position on the hearth and resuming his former seat], I do not see that I am more astray—though perhaps in a different direction—than many others whose points of view differ widely from each other in the sectarian denominations. They all claim to be Christian, and interpret their several creeds as infallible ones. Yet they differ and discuss these questionable subjects without settling them with any mutual satisfaction among themselves.

I doubt the possibility, or propriety, of settling the religion of Jesus Christ in the models of man-made creeds and dogmas. It was a spirit in the life that He laid stress on and taught, if I read aright. I know I see it to be so with me.

The fundamental truths reported in the four gospels as from the lips of Jesus Christ, and that I first heard from the lips of my mother, are settled and fixed moral precepts with me. I have concluded to dismiss from my mind the debatable wrangles that once perplexed me with distractions that stirred up, but never absolutely settled anything. I have tossed

them aside with the doubtful differences which divide
denominations,—sweeping them all out of my mind
among the non-essentials.  I have ceased to follow
such discussions or be interested in them.

I cannot without mental reservations assent to
long and complicated creeds and catechisms.  If the
church would ask simply for assent to the Saviour's
statement of the substance of the law: "Thou shalt
love the Lord thy God with all thy heart, and with
all thy soul, and with all thy mind, and thy neighbour
as thyself,"—that church would I gladly unite with.

The conversation passed on to other matters,
and it was late when Lincoln left to return to the
hotel.  Mr. Jacquess went with him.  It was not
until the small hours of the morning, my mother
said, that Jacquess returned.  At breakfast next
morning, when I was present, I recall Jacquess
saying he had never had so interesting an interview as that with Lincoln the evening before; that
Lincoln had insisted on his going in with him to
the hotel, where they had spent a couple of hours
talking on national and social affairs.  He said
the acquaintance he had formed with Lincoln
had been a most profitable one to him and that he
wished to see more of him whenever possible and
get his practical vision of life.  He said Lincoln
had an insight into the common people's life and

needs, and how to meet them, which as a minister he must get hold of.

My mother asked if there had been any reference to the religious views spoken of by Lincoln the evening before. Jacquess replied, "None at all," and he went on to say that he could see nothing in Lincoln's views on religious subjects more sceptical than any active inquiring mind would be apt to have and that would be helpful in passing through life, and he felt sure that Lincoln would safely do so. He said that "Uncle Peter" (Cartwright) was making no less a political than theological mistake in putting up against such a man as Lincoln the issue of "infidel" in a political canvass having no religious issues connected with it to advance or assail. "He cannot make it stick, and it will react against him, and be his sure defeat if he persists in it." And so it was.

This private conversation of Lincoln's, as here given, is not claimed to be in the exact words. But these words give the substance of what he said, as literally as my mother's excellent memory had retained them in 1889, when I wrote them down from her dictation; and she carefully revised them afterwards. I believe the discerning student of Lincolnian sentences will find these to have some of the private and peculiar stamp of Lincoln's style which no stranger pen could imitate,—and certainly, this mother or her son would not undertake, knowingly, such counterfeiting or simulation.

To test the accuracy of this report of Lincoln's sentences, I submitted them to Colonel Jacquess the next time we met. We had not seen each other since 1862, when he resigned his presidency of a college to accept a commission as colonel of the 73d Regiment of Illinois Volunteers from Governor Yates, who made this appointment on the special request of President Lincoln. This meeting was in June, 1897, and proved to be our last, for he died at St. Paul, Minnesota, June 17, 1898. He carefully read the manuscript here reproduced,— some parts of it several times. He said that he could neither add to nor take anything from it; that her account was correct, and that reading it recalled most vividly to his mind those first meetings with Lincoln. He further said that his acquaintance and the various interesting conversations with Lincoln were the most remarkable and helpful influences that had come into his life. He spoke of how the meeting, of which I have given this account, was supplemented by many others he had with Lincoln the next year, when he was stationed at Springfield as pastor of the First Methodist Church.

# The Real Lincoln in Portraits and Photographs

# TO  A  PORTRAIT  OF  ABRAHAM  LINCOLN

Thy rugged features more heroic are
  Than chiselled outlines of some godlike Greek;
  Thy steadfast lips more eloquent did speak
Than lips of orators renowned afar;
While gentle wit and tolerance of folly,
  And human sympathies and love of right
  Shone never more kind and steady light
Than from the cavern of thy melancholy.
O prophet sorrowful, did thy deep eyes
Foresee and sweep thy country's agonies?
  And did thy lonely heart foreread thy doom
  To give thy brow such majesty of gloom?
Ah, hadst thou seen the end, thou still hadst led
Thy people with the same unwavering tread!

EDITH COLBY BANFIELD.

# XV

## THE REAL LINCOLN IN PORTRAITS AND PHOTOGRAPHS

MUCH difference of opinion is current regarding the accuracy of photographs and portraits of Lincoln. These are to be henceforth the only record preserved of the lineaments of his expressive, but most changeful, countenance. To me this does not seem difficult to account for. He was not less like other men in his physical build, or the expression of the fixed features of his face, when that was at repose, than in the strange illumination that lit up the whole outer man when his mental and spiritual manhood was aroused to action.

He was the most unlike all men of his time—or even of all times—in the transformation at such moments when aroused by the intense thoughts and feelings that seized and controlled his whole personality. In the words of Herndon: "He was odd, but when that grey eye and that face and those features were lit up by the inward soul in fires of emotion, then it was that all the apparent ugly features sprang into organs of beauty, or

331

disappeared in the sea of inspiration that flooded
his face. Sometimes it appeared as if Lincoln
was fresh from the hands of his Creator."

I shall endeavour here to represent the personality of Lincoln as shown by his appearance
when in full mental and emotional activity, in the
delivery of two speeches, so as to explain, in a
degree, what appears to account for the unsatisfactory impression the various photographs and
portraits make on many who never met him, and
even on those who were passingly familiar with
his private and public appearance while a resident
of Springfield.

All his photographs are unsatisfactory, or only
partially successful as portraits of the real Lincoln,
to those who knew him as he appeared in his most
earnestly delivered speeches, or in intense, almost
inspired moments of private conversation. He
had at such times an indefinable distinction of
character entirely his own. This peculiarity of
personality has been shown only within restricted
limitation by any, or all, of his photographs.
They are only shadowy presentments of the outer
man. You see the outline in them as you see
our battleships at rest, and from the outside.
The man, the inner Abraham Lincoln in action

behind the guns, is not revealed in any photograph. On occasion he arose from *within himself*, and through his seamed and battle-scarred visage something from his inner life, and more than any of these prints or portraits show, lit up the outer visage of the man, startling the beholder as prophetic in its intensity, when his inner power and grandeur revealed itself. There was a deep conviction among many of his friends, at such times, which singled him out as destined for some great purpose, hidden alike from him and from them.

Lincoln, while living, was a favourite subject for cartoonists in a large variety of distorted caricatures. Photographers were equally active to preserve his shadow by their art. To the latter, Lincoln was a most unsatisfactory subject. He was never at his ease before the camera. He remarked this on several occasions when proofs were sent to the office for approval. Lincoln himself never would make any choice from these. The office critics at his suggestion were directed to select the ones "least objectionable."

The photographic art previous to 1861 was not one of "snap shots," but required "counting time" by the operator, who waited watch in hand, to fix the shadow. Under such circumstances Lin-

coln was always a poor "sitter." So patent was
this, that I recall that Mrs. Lincoln, when on a
hurried call at the office once, where some matter
was put to Lincoln that puzzled him in a way to
control temporarily the usual expression on his
face, said sharply, "Mr. Lincoln, you look like you
were having your picture taken." He joined
in the laugh that followed as heartily as any of us.
Artists should not depend on photographs of
Lincoln as being anything more than suggestive
shadows of him in outline. They are entirely
wanting in Lincoln's forceful expressiveness of
countenance.

Passing to descriptive writings about Lincoln's
appearance and peculiarities, published since his
death, they will be found to give views of him
equally misleading. Writers of sensational biography and fiction, in their many pages, have done
their worst and exhausted the resources of historic
fiction to write him down to their level, and to the
level of persons and associates among whom he
lived, but to whom he never belonged,—never was
one of them in active sympathy.

No wonder artists who sincerely wish to preserve by life-revealing statuary the strong personality and peculiar pose of this great man find

themselves in the midst of peculiar difficulties. Nor is the effort of the portrait painter less difficult and perplexing to portray his strong individuality on canvas. Inquiry has often come to me, from artists who never saw Lincoln, regarding the pose of his large body and the expression on his change-ful features that would present him most naturally and life-like. I have usually replied by asking for the picture of him that had historically be-come impressed upon their minds. The composite reply of many artists could be summarized as an unfortunate committal to the view that Lincoln was a man of shambling gait, a body loosely hung together, uncertain how to place his feet and legs, and holding his hands and arms so as to appear at reposeful ease; that he had constantly an apologetic stoop of his shoulders, an ill-fitting neck that seemed embarrassed how to incline so as to best fit on his chest, or carry his woe-begone face and head with its crown of bushy hair.

The facial appearance which they seemed to have decided upon for him, as they described it to me, could be represented by some half a dozen photo-graphs;—all of them, at best, shadowy outlines, dull, leaden, blank, silent faces,—expressionless of this man whose features when in mental activity were, of all things about him, his crowning strength, and the most life-revealing part of him, even more so than the words he spoke. There is a large opportunity for such artists to do some honest and thorough forgetting and sponging out of their artistic imaginations much in their visions of the personal appearance of Abraham Lincoln. They need to get nearer Lincoln and with an open mind make a broad and loving study of his real life. After all this has been done, still his peculiar personality will require of the artist the gift of genius, as well as thorough technical skill, to produce truthful results.

There is as distinctive and royal a personality of Lincoln for artists to reveal in their sphere and by their art, as there has been revealed by Lincoln himself through his letters, speeches, and state papers of his literary personality through those strong sentences he produced in such vigour of thought and simplicity and clearness of style as to be so intelligible to all. These masterpieces from his pen have been accorded an abiding place among the models of purest English.

There is certainly a great reward awaiting the artist who can so study Lincoln as to reproduce, and permanently preserve for all future time, his commanding presence in the dignity and compos-

ure manifested by him on public occasions. The
severe and honest study of Lincoln from the many-
sided angles his life presented,—mental and
emotional,—as well as of his tall, muscular, well-
knit body,—all these elements, blending as they
did so peculiarly in his personality, are necessary to be kept in view by them to enable
them to reproduce, in any statue or portrait,
results that would adequately represent him.
The artist who does this must have loved him and
lived through laborious days in close and sympathetic study of his inner personal life, and of the
public affairs that engrossed the attention and
absorbed the steadfast purposefulness of Abraham
Lincoln throughout his eventful life.

The statue or portrait of Abraham Lincoln that
will truly express his unique personality, however, cannot be one showing restfulness or repose.
He was not such a man. Every part of Lincoln's
body betokened readiness,—a man of action,—an
alert, a living, watchful, sensitive, seeing personality ready for service. There was in his whole presence, when he arose from within to active mental
and emotional occasions, an alertness, a poise of the
entire man, as if every part of his being contributed
to act harmoniously, and was springing up and
forward into the thoughts and purposes of those

22

present moments then and there engaging him. This was his appearance when mentally or emotionally in full activity in all three of his moods.

At such times, if engaged in public speaking, he did not have the forward droop his inclining shoulders seemed to suggest. They were thrown slightly backward. The head rested squarely and erect, supported on the sturdy muscles of his strong, sinewy, well-rounded neck, and these became, after speaking a few minutes, tense enough almost to give a trace of defiance and aggression. It was defiance and aggression, at these times—exactly this; but his facial lines and their muscles, as he continued speaking, became softened, and the flush of colour, and the hard curves on his face, became relieved; and those far-visioned eyes lit up with an animation that, taken all together, freed his countenance from any severity of outline it often had when in repose, and which is, unfortunately, so strongly marked upon it in his photographs.

It was this facial expressiveness in public speaking and animated conversation,—its lines, curves, and colour tints coming and passing, only to return in changeful successions,—to which Herndon referred when he said, "Lincoln appeared at times like he was fresh from the hand of his Creator."

Herein lies the challenge and the hope—almost the despair—of any artist's technic, be he a Raphael or an Angelo, to represent Lincoln on canvas or in marble as he appeared in times of highest mental activity. Such was Lincoln's expressive personality when animated by strong emotional or mental stimulus. It was the same, be it in his home, in his office, or in the courts, whenever his interest or sympathy was thoroughly aroused. There was nothing in all this like posing for special public functions. When he entered the strong periods of political discussions in their storm-centres, from 1856 to 1861, this deep undercurrent of vigour and aggressiveness in his public appearance became stronger, rendering him all the more effective. He had found himself. The hour for which he had been so unconsciously in training had arrived, and he arose awake and fully prepared for the task before him. I think it was at this period he had become conscious of his own awakening and thereafter better understood and depended more exclusively on himself.

But in the aggressive energy of these occasions he did not lose the charming gentleness of his quieter days. Beneath the defiant vigour of his speeches in which he appealed so strongly for truth and justice, for liberty and union, he still possessed a gentle, kindly charity that remained with him to the end, enabling him to bear, believe, hope, and endure all things during his Presidential years. This gentle quality was the source of the vigour and the strength with which he met difficulties and won the confidence of the nation. His was a patience that endureth all things; a fidelity that hopeth all things, and never failed to be an active part in the vigour and aggressiveness with which he met and accomplished results in the common duties and greater emergencies that he had to meet in his life. This complexity of character is the distinctive quality in Abraham Lincoln that posterity will recognize, when put in statue and portrait as representing to the eye the same great man who is revealed, so interpretively, by what history records of him in his letters and speeches. Behold the man!

A Greek poet tells us that Grief walks the earth and sits at the feet of each by turns. She certainly lingered along the path of Abraham Lincoln's life, casting her shadows about him with unusual persistency. It was a strange, sad school through which he passed during all his years, his graduation at last in death; a tragedy. The turning points of his life scarce passed beyond one and through another of Grief's shadows before other events sprang into it to stir and vibrate his every hour, until, in his later years, there were piled big, in and around his life, the denser shadows of a whole nation's griefs. These finally filled the whole heavens with the black war clouds of a nation's conflict and peril, lightened and intensified only by the lurid gleam and thunderous crash of battles. His response was equal to their every demand. Yet his stalwart body bore record of the heavy load under which it had been bent but never broken.

There is, in the deepened furrows and increasing seriousness of his sad face, to be read the record of his mental struggles, the strain of his emotions and the draft upon his vital sympathies. His was a face marred by toils and anguish, such as seldom come to the sons of men, for the face to bear a record of! This is the face and this the body, bearing in form and feature such records of experiences as may yet find worthy expression in statue or portrait by the skill of some master artist, whose genius and technic may yet bring before us again the personality and power we once beheld in Abraham Lincoln. Less than this result will be such a failure as history will neither condone nor have any saving grace to cover or forgive.

If I were to undertake to paint in words a portrait of Abraham Lincoln that would express his peculiar possession of this hidden power as observed in him before becoming President, as well as after, I should present two views of him as he appeared on two widely different occasions. Then, blending these together in the stereoscope of memory, the result would be a faithful composite picture of the inner, the greater, the real, Abraham Lincoln.

These two views represent him in the delivery of two speeches, and are offered here as furnishing character outlines for critics of his portraits and photographs who profess to see in none of them an adequate presentation of this man's superiority. They are presented as snapshots, as it were,— flash-light views,—revealing character by catching the expression of the features and pose of the stalwart body of Abraham Lincoln, when his inner soul lit up the outer man and revealed that forceful personality with which he was endowed by his Creator for the vast task before him. Out of these personal memories of Lincoln's private and public life, recalling so vividly the exaltation brought into his countenance by the great soul within, I see before me as I write the revealing portrait and statue of the First American.

I see him first as he stood at bay that October day, 1856, at Petersburg, silently waiting for a hearing by old friends, now his fierce political foes. In his face, in his strong towering form was revealed all that was brave and heroic in a man of undaunted dignity and determination. The countenance, the muscular vigour, the splendid self-control, showed the well balanced, resolute soul within, and a will that could, would, and did, when necessary, hold the plain people of the nation steadily against tide and storm for five fearful, fateful years of battle's shock and even more serious dissensions, legislative, diplomatic, and internal. They stood steadfastly with him, and he with them; through all, abiding in increasing mutual faith until the end. All this—far more than any words can express—awaits an artist's skill to put on canvas for a life-size portrait of that Abraham Lincoln, as he stood in silence a long half-hour on that beautiful autumn day before that turbulent though familiar throng.

The second speech delivered from the rear platform of the train as he was leaving Springfield for Washington, revealed his strong character from a different angle. It was here he gave his last word to neighbours and friends, old and new; and to some

there present who were then far from friendly.
As he delivered this farewell orison, all there was
of tenderness and love in Abraham Lincoln came
out in the pathos wrung from his great soul at
that parting moment.  The home ties of his past
life rushed in and tightened about his heart, as he
had never felt them before, while he gave utterance
to these last tender and prophetic words.  At the
same time, and far more expressive than his words,
there came out into the face of the departing
President-elect, as he spoke, the spirit of the inner
life of Abraham Lincoln: so yearning, so sorrowful,
so solicitous to retain the good will and to share
in the prayers of all good people to help nerve and
fit him for the fateful months he fully realized
were before him; so lingeringly drawn back by old
ties and old friends, but so hopefully brave—
a prophet and a seer—in looking forward to dare
and to do for the right, with the clearest political
vision of any American of his time.  He stood
there already firmly fixed and settled on the great
central truths, and in the policies and principles
that he should pursue; but the consummation of
which he expected to reach only through the help
of that Infinite One his spirit had just called
on to aid him, and all others, in the problems before
the country; problems harder than any since that

Infinite One had sustained Washington for eight
long years before victory and peace were achieved.

These two speeches,—exceptionally strong as
presentations of Lincoln's personality and so revealing of his characteristics,—of course, passed
with the critical moments that called them forth.
Of those there present, who now bear in memory
the hour and the man, few remain who can give
in word-tracings any account of the physical,
mental, and moral inspiration that these, and
many other occasions, revealed of Lincoln's
masterful manhood. None can be more conscious than myself, as I write this sketch in pen-
portraiture, that the genius, the virility, the
inner personal character of Abraham Lincoln
transcended occasions, and permeated, more or
less, all the words and deeds of his eventful life.
His best portraits are those traced on the pages
of his country's history, and equally in the hearts
of his reunited countrymen. These, when combined, assemble the best tonings and tracings of
Abraham Lincoln's portraiture; mirrored in the
one, and in the other wrought into the nation's
character, by the power of his unique personality
and lofty ideals.

Seek you the picture of this man to pass on

to future ages? Look around you. Behold its portrayal in the united fraternity of these States, in a government of the people, by the people, for the people, with malice towards none and charity for all. He still lives in the new national spirit vibrating in unison among a hundred million citizens, now fused into one people, as his first inaugural foretold they should—and would be—when touched by the warmth of our better nature. His faith never faltered!

Out of such memories, personal and historic, emerge outline tracings for a possible composite portrait, or life-revealing statue, of Abraham Lincoln in the epic dignity and prophecy of his life. Who could, who can, who will present it? The pen is powerless to accomplish it in words, and no artist's skill appears likely ever adequately to place him on canvas, or in enduring marble and bronze, since the great Masters of Art passed away long before this Master of Men stepped upon the scene.

With this criticism of the unsatisfactory photographs and portraits of Lincoln, and as a further explanation, I will avail myself of the privilege of reminiscence, granted to the elderly, to mention some of the strange changes of positions and principles which come alike to individual lives and the public opinion of nations in very brief periods. Sometimes, as was the case with Lincoln in these momentous years, the scroll of personal history unfolds rapidly. It was as if the Unseen One—to quote his own words—"who controls mine and all destinies," had led him quietly thus far, but now touched his life anew. The period of his mission had now arrived; his hour of destiny had struck. The Yesterdays and Todays in Lincoln's life now followed each other in quick succession, each one freighted with events of greatest moment. One who was near him in those affairs, who would outline some of those changes, finds the canvas crowded and asks the reader's patience in following the sketchy transitions they present.

Looking back to that day, in 1856, at Petersburg, I remark that it was here in this little town, which his compass and chain had measured out and platted for record; it was among this people with whom he had lived for several years, and at whose firesides he had been a welcome visitor; before whom on scores of occasions he had been the most heartily welcomed speaker;—it was here

that Lincoln met the first fierce strokes of dissent
and hostility that were to usher him into the awful
arena of that civil war between the States, of
which he was later to be the front and centre.
Thenceforward there was to be in his life only
restless strife and turmoil.

Equally remarkable, on the people's side, was
the change in political view that came to nearly all
of those citizens before whom he delivered his
speech.  Of those who met him with noisy dissent, and who so reluctantly gave him a hearing,
at least one third of their number afterwards
became enthusiastic soldiers in the Grand Army
of the Republic, and at his second Presidential
election all who had the opportunity voted the
way they shot.  Little did these sturdy yeomen
on that day expect to respond to the call for volunteers by this orator as their Commander-in-Chief,
or that the time was so near when, as well drilled
veterans, they would march under his orders across
many a crimson battle-field amid the shadows of
Death at Donelson, Vicksburg, Shiloh, Gettysburg,
and many other fields of conflict; until at length,
passing around Atlanta, they would go "Marching
through Georgia" to the sea; to Washington; and to
the fraternal peace and Union between the States.

No prophetic vision brought to these future veteran soldiers the forecast of the last time they would see this speaker; that this would be on their returning victorious through the national capital, there to pass in grand veteran review before their Commander-in-Chief, this same orator—then the twice-elected President of the United States. None of this Menard County throng, friend or foe, on that day saw any prophet or seer in the tall familiar form of the earnest orator before them—his long dark hair tossed to and fro by the October wind, while he proclaimed anew that, "A house divided against itself cannot stand," and his thrilling prophetic words declaring that "Sooner or later, the victory is sure to come." That day it once again was true, as of old, that a prophet was without honour in his own country.

We did not then see the Abraham Lincoln of four years later—a victorious Presidential leader for the nation's new birth of freedom and a more perfect Union of the States.  Our vision could not penetrate the future nor foresee the tense and terrible hours that all our people, South as well as North, at their homes or away amid the armed citizen soldiery of both sides, would all have to pass through, day by day, night by night, until time's heart-beats counted off the days and nights of the five longest, darkest, saddest years in American history.

Then later—so sad and cruel alike to both South and North, now a united country—we all knew the great services of Abraham Lincoln who had passed away from his countrymen all too soon; yet a joy and honour to us all that he would be for ever on the scroll of our country's history, canonized as our First American, who, in the sad lament of his War Secretary over his lifeless form, "belonged to the Ages!"

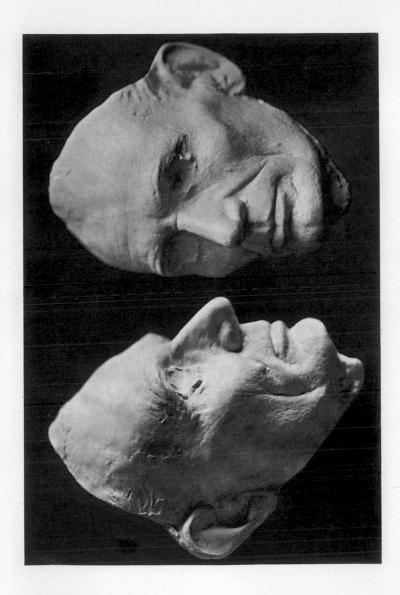

# The Lincoln Life-Mask

This mask doth keep the very form and mold
   Of our great martyr's face.  Yes, this is he:
   That brow all wisdom, all benignity;
That human, humorous mouth; those cheeks that hold
Like some harsh landscape all the summer's gold;
   That spirit fit for sorrow, as the sea
   For storms to beat on; the lone agony
Those silent, patient lips too well foretold.
Yes, this is he who ruled a world of men
   As might some prophet of the elder day—
   Brooding above the tempest and the fray
With deep-eyed thought and more than mortal ken.
   A power was his beyond the touch of art
   Or armed strength—his pure and mighty heart.

RICHARD WATSON GILDER.

# XVI

## THE LINCOLN LIFE-MASK

So interesting had the study of Lincoln's photographs and portraits become as long ago as December, 1881, that the appearance at that time of an article by Leonard Volk describing the first time he met Abraham Lincoln in 1858, and the subsequent sittings of Lincoln for his life mask, made by that sculptor, attracted then and has since received, no little attention from those interested in Lincoln's characteristics.

But this contribution of Mr. Volk's, written more than twenty years after the events narrated, with all the merit it contains, nevertheless should not go into history without some explanations that explain and some corrections that will clarify certain statements that he has made. The attention Mr. Volk's article has received from artists and writers of prominence makes more necessary the corrections and comments here submitted.

The article of Mr. Volk is here printed in full

in order that such comments and corrections as are made may be more intelligible to my readers.

The world is so greatly indebted to Leonard Volk for this life-mask of Lincoln that it is not personally pleasant to introduce his article here with adverse comments. Mr. Volk made this life-mask at a time when no other sculptor had been attracted by the personality of Lincoln in a way that had induced them to wish to represent him by their art. Therefore all artists, all admirers of our First American, now recognize the debt of gratitude the present and future generations owe to Leonard Volk for this life-mask. Lincoln's greatness had not then been recognized outside of a limited few. In 1860 the capacity of this remarkable man was neither realized nor anticipated by his State or Nation, much less by any other artist or sculptor.

I bespeak for certain parts of Mr. Volk's article the kindly charity of my readers not to allow the few lapses in memory the sculptor betrays in his article, to render them less grateful for this contribution, or less appreciative of the glimpses the article affords of Lincoln's personality herein preserved for us by the great sculptor.

## THE LINCOLN LIFE-MASK AND HOW IT WAS MADE

### BY LEONARD W. VOLK

REPRINTED FROM THE CENTURY MAGAZINE FOR DECEMBER, 1881.—BY PERMISSION OF THE CENTURY COMPANY

My first meeting with Abraham Lincoln was in 1858, when the celebrated senatorial contest opened in Chicago between him and Stephen A. Douglas. I was invited by the latter to accompany him and his party by a special train to Springfield, to which train was attached a platform-car having on board a cannon, which made considerable noise on the journey. At Bloomington we all stopped overnight, as Douglas had a speech to make there in the evening. The party went to the Landon House, the only hotel, I believe, in the place at the time.

While we were sitting in the hotel office after supper, Mr. Lincoln entered, carrying an old carpet-bag in his hand, and wearing a weather-beaten silk hat,—too large, apparently, for his head,—a long loosely fitting frock-coat of black alpaca, and vest and trousers of the same material. He walked up to the counter, and, saluting the clerk pleasantly, passed the bag over to him, and inquired if he was too late for supper. The clerk replied that supper was over, but thought enough could be "scraped up" for him.

"All right," said Mr. Lincoln, "I don't want much."

Meanwhile, he said he would wash the dust off; he was certainly very dusty, for it was the month of June and quite warm. While he was so engaged several old friends, who had learned of his arrival, rushed in to see him, some of them shouting out, "How are you, Old Abe?" Mr. Lincoln grasped them by the hand in his cordial manner, with the broadest and pleasantest smile on his rugged face. This was the first good view I had of the "coming man," though I had seen him at a distance, and passed him on the sidewalk in Chicago a few days before.

Mr. Lincoln was on the platform in front of the court-house when Mr. Douglas spoke, and replied to the Senator when he had finished. I regretted to hear some hard words which passed between them while Mr. Douglas was speaking.

The next day we all stopped at the town of Lincoln, where short speeches were made by the contestants, and dinner was served at the hotel, after which and as Mr. Lincoln came out on the plank walk in front, I was formally presented to him. He saluted me with his natural cordiality, grasping my hand in both his large hands with a vise-like grip and looking down into my face with his beaming dark, dull eyes, said:

"How do you do? I am glad to meet you. I have read of you in the papers; you are making a statue of Judge Douglas for Governor Matteson's new house?"

"Yes, sir," I answered; "and sometime, when you are in Chicago and can spare the time, I would like to have you sit to me for your bust."

"Yes, I will, Mr. Volk—shall be glad to, the first opportunity I have."

All were soon on board the long train, crowded with people going to hear the speeches at Springfield. The train stopped on the track, near Edwards' Grove, in the northern outskirts of the town, where staging was erected and a vast crowd waiting under the shade of the trees. On leaving the train, most of the passengers climbed over the fences and crossed the stubble-field, taking a short-cut to the grove, among them Mr. Lincoln who stalked forward alone, taking immense strides, the before-mentioned carpet-bag and an umbrella in his hands and his coat-skirts flying in the breeze. I managed to keep pretty close in the rear of the tall, gaunt figure, with the head craned forward, apparently much over the balance, like the Leaning Tower of Pisa that was moving something like a hurricane across that rough stubble-field. He approached the rail fence, sprang over it as nimbly as a boy of eighteen, and disappeared from my sight. Soon after, and while Douglas was speaking, Mr. Lincoln suddenly reappeared in the crowd, mounted upon a fine, spirited horse.

In the evening I went to hear him speak in the Hall of Representatives of the old State House. He spoke with much deliberation and earnestness and I thought there was sadness in his tone of voice; he reminded his friends of the difficulty of carrying the State for himself, owing to the way in which it was districted at the time, and cautioned them not to be over-sanguine—to be prepared for defeat; if they wished for victory, no stone must be left unturned.

I did not see him again for nearly two years. I spent most of the winter of 1860 in Washington, publishing a statuette of Senator Douglas, and just before leaving, in the month of March, I called upon Mr. Douglas' colleague in the Senate from Illinois and asked him if he had an idea as to who would be the probable nominee of the Republican party for President, that I might model a bust of him in advance. He replied that he did not have the least particle of an idea who he would be, only that it would not be Judge Douglas.

I returned to Chicago, and got my studio in the "Portland Block" in order and ready for work, and began to consider whose bust I should first begin in the clay, when I noticed in a morning paper that Abraham Lincoln was in town—retained as one of the counsel in a "sand-bar" trial in which the Michigan Central Railroad was either plaintiff or defendant. I at once decided to remind him of his promise to sit to me, made two years before. I found him in the United States District Court-room (in a building known at the time as the "Larmon Block") his feet on the edge of a table, one of his fingers thrust into his mouth, and his long, dark hair standing out at every imaginable angle, apparently uncombed for a week. He was surrounded by a group of lawyers, such as James F. Joy, Isaac N. Arnold, Thomas Hoyne, and others. Mr. Arnold obtained his attention in my behalf, when he instantly arose and met me outside the rail recognizing me at once with his usual grip of both hands. He remembered his promise and said in answer to my question, that he expected to be detained by the case for a week. He added:

"I shall be glad to give you the sittings. When shall I come and how long will you need me each time?"

Just after breakfast, every morning, would, he said suit him the best, and he could remain till court opened, at ten o'clock. I answered that I would be ready for him the next morning, Thursday. This was in the early part of April, 1860.

"Very well, Mr. Volk, I will be there, and I'll go to a barber and have my hair cut before I come."

I requested him not to let the barber cut it too short, and said I would rather he would leave it as it was; but to this he would not consent. Then, all of a sudden, he ran his fingers through his hair and said:

"No, I cannot come tomorrow, as I have an engagement with Mr. W—— to go to Evanston tomorrow and attend an entertainment; but I'd rather come and sit to you for the bust than go there and meet a lot of college professors and others, all strangers to me. And I will be obliged if you will go to Mr. W——'s office

now and get me released from the engagement. I
will wait here till you come back."

So off I posted, but Mr. W—— would not release
him, because he said it would be a great disappointment to the people he had invited. Mr. Lincoln
looked quite sorry when I reported to him the failure
of my mission.

"Well," he said, "I suppose I must go, but I will
come to you Friday morning."

He was there promptly—indeed, he never failed to
be on time. My studio was in the fifth story and
there were no elevators in those days, and I soon
learned to distinguish his steps on the stairs, and am
sure he frequently came up two if not three steps at a
stride. When he sat down the first time in that hard,
wooden, low-armed chair which I still possess, and
which has been occupied by Douglas, Seward, and
Generals Grant and Dix, he said:

"Mr. Volk, I have never sat before to sculptor or
painter—only for daguerreotypes and photographs.
What shall I do?" I told him I would only take the
measurement of his head and shoulders that time,
and next morning, Saturday, I would make a cast of
his face, which would save him a number of sittings.
He stood up against the wall and I made a mark above
his head, and then measured up to it from the floor
and said:

"You are just twelve inches taller than Judge
Douglas, that is six feet one inch."

Before commencing the cast next morning and knowing Mr. Lincoln's fondness for a story, I told him one in order to remove what I thought an apprehensive expression—as though he feared the operation might be dangerous, and this is the story:

I occasionally employed a little black-eyed, black-haired, and dark-skinned Italian as a *formatore* in plaster work, who had related to me a short time before that himself and a comrade image-vendor were "doing" Switzerland by hawking their images. One day a Swiss gentleman asked him if he could make his likeness in plaster. "Oh, yes, signor; I am a sculptor!" So Matteo Mattei—such was the name of the pretender—got some plaster, laid the big Swiss gentleman on his back, stuck a quill in either nostril for him to breathe through, and requested him to close his eyes. Then "Mat" as I called him, poured the soft plaster all over his face and forehead; then he paused for reflection; as the plaster was beginning to set he became frightened, as he had never before undertaken such a job, and had neglected to prepare the face properly, especially the gentleman's huge beard, moustache, and the hair about the temples and forehead, through which, of course, the plaster had run and become solid. "Mat" made an excuse to go outside the door—"then," said he, "I run like——."

I saw Mr. Lincoln's eyes twinkle with mirth.

"How did he get it off?" said he.

I answered that probably, after reasonable waiting

for the sculptor, he had to break it off, and cut and pull out all the hair which the tenacious plaster touched, the best way he could. "Mat" said he took special pains to avoid that particular part of Switzerland after that artistic experience. But his companion, who somewhat resembled him, not knowing anything of his partner's performance, was soon afterwards overhauled by the gentleman and nearly cudgeled to death.

Upon hearing this, the tears actually trickled down Mr. Lincoln's bronzed cheeks, and he was at once in the best of humours. He sat naturally in the chair when I made the cast and saw every move I made in a mirror opposite, as I put the plaster on without interference with his eyesight or his free breathing through the nostrils. It was about an hour before the mold was ready to be removed, and being all in one piece, with both ears perfectly taken, it clung pretty hard, as the cheek-bones were higher than the jaws at the lobe of the ear. He bent his head low and took hold of the mold and gradually worked it off without breaking or injury. It hurt a little, as a few hairs of the tender temples pulled out with the plaster and made his eyes water; but the remembrance of the poor Swiss gentleman evidently kept him in good mood.

He entered my studio on Sunday morning, remarking that a friend at the hotel (Tremont House) had invited him to attend church; "but," said Mr. Lincoln, "I thought I'd rather come and sit for the

bust. The fact is," he continued, "I don't like to hear cut-and-dried sermons. No—when I hear a man preach, I like to see him act as if he were fighting bees!" And he extended his long arms, at the same time suiting the action to the words. He gave me on this day a long sitting of more than four hours, and when it was concluded, went to our family apartment on the corner of the building across the corridor from the studio, to look at a collection of photographs which I had made in 1855–6–7, in Rome and Florence. While sitting in the rocking-chair, he took my little son on his lap and spoke kindly to him, asking his name, age, etc. I held the photographs up and explained them to him, but I noticed a growing weariness and his eyelids closed occasionally as if he were sleepy, or were thinking of something besides Grecian and Roman statuary and architecture. Finally, he said: "These things must be very interesting to you, Mr. Volk, but the truth is I don't know much of history, and all I do know of it I have learned from lawbooks."

The sittings were continued daily until the Thursday following, and during their continuance he would talk almost unceasingly, telling some of the funniest and most laughable of stories, but he talked little of politics or religion during those sittings. He said: "I am bored nearly every time I sit down to a public dining-table by some one pitching into me on politics." Upon one occasion he spoke most enthusiastically of

his profound admiration of Henry Clay, saying that he "almost worshipped him."

I remember also, that he paid a high compliment to the late Gen. William A. Richardson, and said: "I regard him as one of the truest men that ever lived; he sticks to Judge Douglas through thick and thin—never deserted him and never will. I admire such a man! By the by, Mr. Volk, he is now in town, and stopping at the Tremont. May I bring him with me tomorrow to see the bust?" Accordingly he brought him and two other old friends, ex-Lieut.-Gov. McMurtry of Illinois and Ebenezer Peck, all of whom looked a moment at the clay model, saying it was "just like him!" Then they began to tell stories and rehearse reminiscences, one after another. I can imagine I now hear their hearty laughs, just as I can see, as if photographed, the tall figure of Lincoln striding across that stubble-field.

Many people, presumably political aspirants with an eye to future prospects, besieged my door for interviews, but I made it a rule to keep it locked, and I think Mr. Lincoln appreciated the precaution.

The last sitting was given Thursday morning and I noticed that Mr. Lincoln was in something of a hurry. I had finished the head but desired to represent his breast and brawny shoulders as nature presented them; so he stripped off his coat, waistcoat, shirt, cravat, and collar, threw them on a chair, pulled his undershirt down a short distance, tying the sleeves

behind him, and stood up without a murmur for an hour or so. I then said that I was done and was a thousand times obliged to him for his promptness and patience, and offered to assist him to re-dress but he said: "No, I can do it better alone." I kept at my work without looking toward him, wishing to catch the form as accurately as possible while it was fresh in my memory. Mr. Lincoln left hurriedly, saying he had an engagement, and with a cordial "Good-bye! I will see you again soon," passed out. A few moments after, I recognized his steps rapidly returning. The door opened, and in he came, exclaiming: "Hello, Mr. Volk! I got down on the sidewalk and found I had forgotten to put on my undershirt, and thought it wouldn't do to go through the streets this way." Sure enough, there were the sleeves of that garment dangling below the skirt of his broadcloth frock-coat! I went at once to his assistance, and helped him to undress and re-dress all right, and out he went, with a hearty laugh at the absurdity of the thing.

On Thursday, May 18th, following, Mr. Lincoln received the nomination on the third ballot for President of the United States. And it happened that on the same day I was on the cars, nearing Springfield. About midday we reached Bloomington, and there learned of his nomination. At three or four o'clock we arrived at our destination. The afternoon was lovely—bright and sunny, neither too warm nor too cool; the grass, trees, and the hosts of blooming roses, so profuse in Springfield, appeared to be vying with the ringing bells and the waving flags.

As soon as I had brushed off the dust and registered at the old Chenery House, I went straight to Mr. Lincoln's unpretentious little two-story house. He saw me from his door or window coming down the street, and as I entered the gate, he was on the platform in front of the door, and quite alone. His face looked radiant. I exclaimed: "I am the first man from Chicago, I believe, who has the honour of congratulating you on your nomination for President." Then those two great hands took both of mine with a grasp never to be forgotten. And while shaking, I said: "Now, that you will doubtless be the next President of the United States I want to make a statue of you, and shall do my best to do you justice." Said he: "I don't doubt it, for I have come to the conclusion that you are an honest man," and with that greeting I thought my hands were in a fair way of being crushed. I was invited into the parlour and soon Mrs. Lincoln entered holding a rose bouquet in her hand, which she presented to me after the introduction; and in return I gave her a cabinet size bust of her husband, which I had modelled from the large one, and happened to have with me. Before leaving the house it was arranged that Mr. Lincoln would give Saturday forenoon to obtaining full-length photographs to serve me for the proposed statue.

On Saturday evening the committee appointed by the convention to notify Mr. Lincoln formally of his nomination, headed by Mr. Ashmun of Massachusetts, reached Springfield by special train, bearing a large number of people, two or three hundred of whom carried rails on their shoulders, marching in military style from the train to the old State House Hall of Representatives, where they stacked them like muskets. The evening was beautiful and clear, and the entire population was astir. The bells pealed, flags waved, and cannon thundered forth the triumphant nomination of Springfield's favourite and distinguished citizen. The bonfires blazed brightly and especially in front of that prim-looking white house on Eighth Street. The committee and the vast crowd following, passed in at the front door and made their exit through the kitchen door in the rear, Mr. Lincoln giving them all a hearty shake of the hand as they passed him in the parlour.

After it was all over and the crowd dispersed, late in the evening I took a stroll and passed the house. A few small boys, only, were in the street, trying to keep up a little blaze among the dying embers of the bonfire. One of them cried out:

"Here, Bill Lincoln—here's a stick."

Another chimed in:

"I've got a good one, Bill"—a picket he had slyly knocked from a door-yard fence.

By previous appointment I was to cast Mr. Lincoln's hands on the Sunday following this memorable Saturday, at nine A.M. I found him ready, but he looked more grave and serious than he had appeared on the previous days. I wished him to hold something in his right hand and he looked for a piece of pasteboard but could find none. I told him a round stick would do as well as anything. Thereupon he went to the woodshed and I heard the saw go, and he soon returned to the dining-room (where I did the work), whittling off the end of a piece of broom-handle. I remarked to him that he need not whittle off the edges.

"Oh, well," said he, "I thought I would like to have it nice."

When I had successfully cast the mold of the right hand, I began the left, pausing a few moments to hear Mr. Lincoln tell me about a scar on the thumb.

"You have heard that they call me a rail-splitter, and you saw them carrying rails in the procession Saturday evening; well, it is true that I did split rails, and one day, while I was sharpening a wedge on a log, the ax glanced and nearly took my thumb off, and there is the scar, you see."

The right hand appeared swollen as compared with the left on account of excessive hand-shaking the evening before; this difference is distinctly shown in the cast.

That Sunday evening I returned to Chicago with the molds of his hands, three photographic negatives

of him, the identical black alpaca campaign-suit of
1858, and a pair of Lynn newly-made pegged boots.
The clothes were all burned up in the great Chicago
fire. The casts of the face and hands I saved by taking
them with me to Rome and they have crossed the sea
four times.

The last time I saw Mr. Lincoln was in January,
1861, at his house in Springfield. His little parlour
was full of friends and politicians. He introduced
me to them all, and remarked to me aside, that since
he had sat to me for his bust, he had lost forty pounds
in weight. This was easily perceptible, for the lines
of his jaws were very sharply defined through the
short beard which he was allowing to grow. Then he
returned to the company and announced in a general
way that I had made a bust of him before his nomination and that he was then giving daily sittings at the
St. Nicholas Hotel to another sculptor; that he had
sat to him for a week or more, but could not see the
likeness, though he might yet bring it out.

"But," continued Mr. Lincoln, "in two or three
days after Mr. Volk commenced my bust, there was
the animal himself."

And this was about the last, if not the last remark
I ever heard him utter, except the good-bye and his
good wishes for my success.

I have omitted to say that when sitting in April for
the model, and speaking of his Cooper Institute speech,

24

delivered in New York a short time before, he said that he had arranged and composed this speech in his mind while going on the cars from Camden to Jersey City. When having his photograph taken at Springfield, he spoke of Colonel Ellsworth, whom he had met a short time before, and whose company of Zouaves he had seen drill. Lincoln said:

"He is the greatest little man I ever met."

### COMMENTS AND CORRECTIONS ON "THE LINCOLN LIFE-MASK AND HOW IT WAS MADE"

The contribution to *The Century Magazine* of December, 1881, by Leonard Volk, giving the circumstances preceding and connected with "The Lincoln Life-Mask and How It Was Made," is a very valuable contribution in many ways.

To the artists and sculptors this mask is of indispensable value, for with them it has settled forever the bony formation and facial outlines of Lincoln's remarkable face and head. In this respect it can never have any adequate comparison. To the student of Lincoln's personal peculiarities, the story Mr. Volk gives of his interviews with Lincoln during the sittings is exceedingly interesting and revealing in many ways and we are grateful for the brief account he has written.

But there are explanations called for by some of

Mr. Volk's descriptions of Lincoln's personality and manners, and corrections required by other statements he makes that he no doubt inadvertently placed in his otherwise most excellent account. The most important correction required is the statement in Mr. Volk's last paragraph where he reports Lincoln saying that the Cooper Institute speech was "composed in his mind while going on the cars from Camden to Jersey City." Because of my own opportunities for observation of Lincoln while near him through several years, I wish to make these comments, correcting some and explaining others of Volk's statements in his *Century Magazine* article.

In his sixth paragraph Mr. Volk says, at his first introduction Lincoln grasped his hand in "both his large hands with a vise-like grip and looked down into my face with his beaming, dark, dull eyes." That Lincoln's eyes had all these shades of expression as well as some others is quite correct; but he never bestowed their variety on a stranger at any one time, as Mr. Volk's pen records their appearance when "beaming" on him at this first introduction. Volk meant no doubt to express by his description of Lincoln's eyes, that they were changeful in their expression far more than the ordinary men he had met in his professional work.

He gives in that sentence an artist's appreciation
of Lincoln's expressive eyes as he recalled seeing
them during the various sittings Lincoln had with
him twenty years before.

As I recall the variations of Lincoln's changeful
features, and more especially his expressive eyes,
they never impressed me as rapidly changeful ones.
Mentally he was slow in his transitions from one of
his moods to another. All his facial muscles of
expression responded more readily to reveal his
thoughts than did his eyes. The eyes were reserved
and lit up later to reveal the inner fires of Lincoln's
feelings and thoughts.

Mr. Volk tells of meeting Lincoln again at
Chicago, "in the United States District Court-
room, his feet on the edge of a table, one of his
fingers thrust in his mouth, and his long, dark
hair standing out at every imaginable angle,
apparently uncombed for a week. He was surrounded by a group of lawyers, such as James F.
Joy, Isaac N. Arnold, Thomas Hoyne, and others."
The position of Lincoln with his feet on the
table and the view of him with his "dark hair in
every imaginable angle," were characteristic ones
of Lincoln in his easy office-negligee manner. The
careless arrangement of his locks was caused by a

habit he had, of which he was unconscious, of frequently thrusting by a quick movement of first one hand and then the other upward from the temple through his hair, past the crown of his head. This left his locks in that careless abandon Volk describes. The manner of his thrusting his fingers through his hair was so frequent and characteristic with Lincoln that Volk made a mistake in consenting to Lincoln's suggestion that he have his hair trimmed before taking his mask. He usually wore his hair longer than Volk's cast shows, and those who recall Lincoln as he appeared in the office life, the court room, or outdoor platform speaking, associate his rugged and expressive face with the crown of abundant locks that he wore and that had been tossed by his long fingers in unstudied abandon at all angles over his head. The short hair in Volk's mask of Lincoln with the ears standing out less at right angles from the head than they did, are the only serious defects noticed by those who saw him daily during his residence in Springfield.

To the additional mention by Volk in the same sentence, that Lincoln had "one of his fingers thrust in his mouth," I must demur and contradict. Lincoln was neat and in all personal ways free from offensive peculiarities. He was never addicted to so crude and unsightly a mannerism as "holding one of his fingers thrust in his mouth." This charge requires a special explanation of another of Lincoln's habits for correctly understanding Mr. Volk's mistake. Lincoln had at times, the peculiarity of supporting his face with his hand, when he was attentively listening to some one, or meditating on a subject that absorbed his thoughts. He was then oblivious to all else and had at such times a habit of placing the thumb of his left hand below his chin with his index finger partly curved and extending to his lips, or sometimes laying across them and along the side of his nose. This was no doubt the position that Volk noticed and tells us about, and mistook as being "the finger thrust in his mouth."

When Lincoln was sitting at his office table writing and had paused, seeming to be meditating of what he should write, he usually placed his left elbow on the table, his chin on his thumb, with the index finger as described above, and the three other fingers closed on the palm of the hand, thus with his thumb partly supporting the chin that rested in his large hand. I have seen him, in the privacy of the office, maintain this position as immovable as a statue for more than half an hour, though generally less time, if not writing, but while he was listening to some one addressing him on a subject he was deeply interested in.

Mr. Volk was correct in saying there was a foot's difference in the height of Senator Douglas and Lincoln. The latter's height was, however, more than six feet one inch, as Volk says. Lincoln was six feet four inches, and Douglas' height was certainly not less than five feet four inches, instead of five feet one inch, as Volk gives it. The "Little Giant" was always sensitive about any reflections regarding his height and Volk's taking three inches from his crown must not remain uncorrected.

To any one familiar with a gentleman's attire it is manifestly absurd that Lincoln discovered after leaving Volk's studio and descending the stairs that the "sleeves of his undershirt were dangling below the skirts of his broadcloth frock-coat," as Volk described them. It is quite evident that in the first event, when the undergarment having been released from his arms and neck and "the sleeves tied behind him," while Volk was taking the cast, that it would have there lain in folds around Lincoln's waist. When the latter put on his outer linen shirt and his vest and then his frock-coat over all, the offending negligee

would only have been visible by the enlarged
waist line revealing it. It was probable, by this
fulness that Lincoln himself recognized he was not
properly "harnessed up for the street," as he
would usually have remarked, as the reason for his
return to the studio to properly arrange this undergarment. Why do reminiscent pens, when writing
about Lincoln, so persistently seek the most gro-
tesque posing of him that they possibly can present,
instead of describing the clean, plain, simple-man-
nered man that he always was? They reflect their
own coarseness and vulgarity, and not Lincoln's.

This latter incident makes opportune the mention here that Mrs. Lincoln was in the habit of
giving her careful attention to the quality and
fitting of all articles connected with her husband's
wardrobe as well as to their proper distribution on
his person when he was dressed and left their home,
or wherever they were together when away from
home. Lincoln had become so accustomed to this
thoughtful oversight by Mrs. Lincoln that when
away from his wife's inspection, he was more
helpless in matters regarding his health, his dress,
and his personal appearance, than most men are.
His mind was always engaged on things he deemed
more important to him than his clothing or his

food, and this little omission in his dressing to leave the studio very well illustrates his inattention to "Those little links which make up the chain of woman's happiness," that Miss Owen, in 1866, mentioned about Lincoln's personal habits, as they appeared to her as early as in 1836 and 1837, when they were friends at Salem. This neglect was apparent through the years I was near him, and if Mrs. Lincoln was away from their home for several days, this absence was more or less recognized at the office, in Lincoln's personal apparel, and the disregard he had of any regular hours for his meal-time.

The most important correction to be made in Mr. Volk's article is the statement he makes in his last paragraph. In that he reports Lincoln saying, "when sitting in April for the model, and speaking of the Cooper Institute speech, delivered in New York a short time before, he [Lincoln] said he 'had arranged and composed this speech in his mind while going from Camden to Jersey City.'" So seriously is Mr. Volk's memory at fault in his quoting Lincoln on this subject, and so very different are the facts, from his statement, that it is important for the truth of history, to mention the facts and relate some incidents connected with the preparation and delivery of that celebrated Cooper Institute speech.

I was in the Lincoln & Herndon law office daily
during the three or four months while Lincoln—
between the intervals of his law business—was
writing and revising this great speech. He spent
most of this time, at first, in the study and arrangement of the historical facts he decided to use.
These he collected or verified at the State Library.
His discussions with Herndon and the Hon. Newton Bateman whose office adjoined theirs, as to
the historical facts and the arrangement of these
in his speech, were frequent and full of interest to
the two young law students who were privileged
to be present at that time.

I have told the story of the preparation, delivery,
and estimate of this Cooper Institute speech by
New York people, in this volume beginning on
page 247 to which I refer my readers. This gives,
with a fulness of detail I will not here repeat, the
circumstances connected with Lincoln's preparation for, and his studious care in, the composition
of the Cooper Institute speech. Without a doubt
he devoted more time to research and gave more
thought to this speech than any he ever delivered.
When he left Springfield for New York for its
delivery, he carried with him the manuscript
finished, just as he delivered it.

# Characteristic Moods of Abraham Lincoln

A blend of mirth and sadness, smiles and tears;
A quaint knight-errant of the pioneers;
A homely hero born of star and sod;
A Peasant-Prince; a Masterpiece of God.

WALTER MALONE.

# XVII

## CHARACTERISTIC MOODS OF ABRAHAM LINCOLN

IN the years when I was intimate with the daily life at the Lincoln and Herndon office, I learned to know and respect the peculiarity of Lincoln's moods. These were interchangeable with each other from time to time, and explain, or interpret, peculiarities of his character which were often greatly misunderstood or misinterpreted by those not intimate with his daily life. These temperamental peculiarities I may describe under general terms as three characteristics, or moods, which I wish to record as I knew them.

The first to be mentioned, and by far the strongest and most difficult to interrupt, or even penetrate, while he was under its control, was his power to concentrate strictly all his mental faculties on the task or purpose immediately before him. In this mood he was absolutely impenetrable to anything else, or by any other person. He was thoroughly oblivious to surroundings. Every faculty of this remarkable man, while in this mood, was focussed upon the fact or problem before him, viewing it from all angles and endeavouring with the keenest logic and most fertile, truth-inspired imagination to solve any problem or settle any question of fact or duty which challenged his attention. No person or influence could distract or hasten any of his peculiar mental processes at such times.

I could cite numerous times and circumstances illustrating this mood of Lincoln that came under my observation in Springfield. Those who knew him in Springfield and were afterwards near him in Washington, with whom I have spoken of this mood, told me that this peculiar characteristic became more and more a fixed habit there under the pressure of his Presidential duties. I will refer to one instance and that on an occasion of much historic importance.

During the last weeks of his residence in Springfield it was difficult for him to find any place where he could be free from the interruption of callers. His home, his office in the State House, or the State Library, afforded him no privacy by day or night. To avoid this, Mr. C. M. Smith—his brother-in-law—fitted up a room in the third story over his store for Lincoln's private use, which could be entered only through the private office of Mr. Smith, in the back part of his large storeroom. This arrangement was known by a limited few, and he was to be seen when there only by persons bringing a line to Mr. Smith by Herndon. It was in that room that he prepared his first inaugural address, and thither I was sent twice by Herndon with books and clippings which the latter, at Lincoln's request, had selected from the State Library, the law office, and Herndon's home library, for study before preparing that remarkable state paper. On my return the last time, Herndon asked me if any word was sent back. I replied that I had no message and was sure Lincoln had not seen me when I came in and placed the packages on the table before him, or when I left the room. To this he replied with a satisfied smile, "That's what I expected; he wishes nothing now so much as to be left alone."

In this mood lay his remarkable capacity for that special study necessary during the first months of his official duties as President, covering as it did so many new executive functions and judicial fields whose problems he must solve for himself. In the later and more momentous years this mood fitted him finally to be the master of all politicians and of most of the military men around him, and the equal of his best generals in outlining the strategy of campaigns during the closing years of the Civil War. This mood was by no means always a happy one to those near him in public or private affairs, and even the domestic life. I suggest that this mood may explain some of the peculiar trials Mrs. Lincoln endured, and to which she could not at all times pleasantly adjust herself.

The second mood was a blank, unapproachable habit of inner meditation; at times a sombre black melancholy. There are depths in every great soul where none should intermeddle or try to fathom. The Lincoln of this mood was a mystery to which even those nearest and dearest to him were as strangers, and they failed to understand. There was to me always an unapproachable grandeur in the man when he was in this mood of inner solitude. I approach this part of my record with awe and not analysis. It was a part of his remarkable make-up that I reverenced then, and in memory I now refrain from any extended mention of this peculiar eclipse while under its power that occasionally shadowed his life. It isolated and—I always thought—exalted him above his ordinary life, or the comprehension and companionship of his associates, most of whom misunderstand and misinterpreted him whenever he was in this mood. History will discern and reverently disclose the strength in Lincoln's character and the executive foresight for which this mood gave him revealings. When in this mood it was best to leave him severely alone. He wished it, and if he had companionship then which was silent also, he plainly manifested his appreciation—I might almost say, his gratitude—for the quiet, silent, friendly fellowship which understood him and granted the sociability of its sympathetic silence. He would express this appreciation by sometimes turning those deep, sad, tender eyes, brimming with the loneliness of dry tears, as he raised them in a blank gaze upon his companion. Herndon's uniform respect and deference for this silent mood in his partner became one of the strong bonds connecting their long and peaceful relation.

How dominant this mood was in some of the darker days of his Presidential years may appear from the following words which I quote from Edward Dicey, the English historian. He was competent to testify of those intense years in

25

Lincoln's life, by frequent observations he had of him in Washington. He writes:

Never in my knowledge have I ever seen a sadder face than that of the late President during some of the times his features were familiar to me. It is so easy to be wise after the event; but it seems to me now that someone ought somehow to have foreseen that the stamp of a sad end was impressed by nature on that rugged haggard face. The exceeding sadness of the eyes and their strange sweetness were the one redeeming feature in a face of unusual plainness, and there was about them that odd, weird look, which some eyes possess, of seeming to see more than the objects in the world around.

This was pre-eminently the mood of Lincoln through much of the appalling summer of 1864. Anxiety, responsibility, care, thought, disaster, defeat, and the unaccountable impending shadows of the dark days before him that no human vision could penetrate, focussed their fiercest into that year of his life. The injustice of friends and the envenomed hate of foes wore into his giant frame. He exclaimed one day: "I feel as though I shall never be glad again!"

The third, and the most usual, mood of Lincoln was that of complete relaxation, of sheer

irresponsibility, of complete withdrawal from all
the affairs that vex or disturb. Happy, indeed,
were the times one met him in this mood. He
was then the most receptive of men, as well as
the most cheerful and bountiful dispenser of all
his rich store of varied experiences, of his quaint,
original stories, and his revealings of his thoughts
and feelings; ready for the widest variety of subjects; easily passing from one interest to another;
enjoying equally any and all things in turn,
the most genial and cheerful of men. All this
happened without a trace of self-consciousness.
This mood was the more habitual, and the one
in which most people remember him, and which
history will cherish most and garner in its memory.
But aside from the pleasure of his companionship,
when in this genial mood, we must remember that
it was from the two former ones that the brooding
and fruitful hours of Lincoln's life came. Through
the depths of such mysterious concentrations and
silences arose our masterful First American.

# Abraham Lincoln's Position in
# History

A mountain is a mystery; such was Lincoln. It is tall, isolated, alone; so was he. It has fissures and crevices that would disfigure the beauty of a hill, but which constitute no blemish on its massive nobility. Amid its crags are sheltered nooks where flowers bloom and streamlets flash in the sunlight. But there are also huge masses of denuded rock which tell of the harsh attrition of earlier times. The clouds that gather about its peak lend it an air of aloofness and melancholy. Mighty storms make war upon it, waging battle with the swift strokes of lightning to the music of deep-toned thunders. But it remains unchanged, unshaken. In all moods, in all mists, its mission is the same. The same God that made the mountain made the man, and His ways are past finding out.

JOSEPH FORT NEWTON.

# XVIII

## ABRAHAM LINCOLN'S POSITION IN HISTORY

IT may be worth while, in closing my pages of personal reminiscences of Lincoln, to glance before and after and pass in hasty review the three men of this continent whose services have so appealed to mankind, and whose history is our most valuable and inspiring American heritage; the better to see the background against which our First American must be studied and the worth of his labours estimated.

History, in the great conception of it, has often been compared to a mountain chain seen afar off in a clear sky, where the peaks seem linked to one another, toward the crest of the group. An ingenious and learned writer has recently amplified this image by speaking of a set of volcanic islands lifting themselves out of the sea, at such angles and distances that only the eye of a bird, and not of a sailor cruising among them, would discover that they are the heights of one and the same submerged range. The sailor is the ordinary student, while the eagle is the historian who takes long views and sees the whole scene in the clearer, juster light of time.

Such a historian surveying the pageant of American history, searching for its epic periods and its epochal men, would discern three periods and three personalities which have left age-lasting impress upon this continent. The differences in the times in which they lived, and the tasks which they accomplished, were not more variant than the differences of the characters and individualities of the master-men who wrought the work appointed them to do. Above all others, by the inspiration of their lives, by the example of their characters, and by the uniqueness of their personalities, stand the names and achievements of Columbus, Washington, and Lincoln.

One believed that this continent existed, and that by sailing westward across the unknown waters a passageway would be found for reaching eastern lands. He went from court to court through Europe, seeking for a hearing and pleading for friends to aid him. Year by year he followed his dream-thought, which yielded him only privation, failure, and ridicule. Yet was he undaunted through all those years by the slow

progress he made. Shattered hopes had no
agony of disappointment that could dismay or
turn him aside. Nothing daunted his purpose,
nothing quenched his ambition. He saw before
him always the lure of new coast-lines and the
peoples to whom his coming would bring the
story of the Cross. To him in every sunset there
were promises of new worlds to the adventurous
keel that would sail westward. He was a great
soul troubled by a dream, aflame with a mission.
Still he plead, he begged, he implored for aid
that he might lead the way into those silences of
western seas which had appalled the centuries.

His church did not believe him; his King did not
believe him; and the learned men of his age had
no faith in him or his dream. All Europe scorned
him. Nevertheless, his intuitions and his reason-
ings convinced him that he was right, and he had
faith. A woman, only, believed in him. She
pledged the jewels of her crown, and bade him go.
He sailed. His crew disbelieved, and mutinied.
Alone he went, a master ploughing the chartless
waters, sustained by his settled conviction;
alone he gazed westward through sleepless nights
of waiting, until, behold! he saw a light—and
there was a New World. Interests and scenes
were revealed by his adventure more vast and

entrancing than any dream-visions of his past
He had drawn aside the sombre curtains that had
shadowed those western waves of doubt and
darkness. He had opened a pathway into a new
continent which was destined to be the nursery
and the home of the future's highest ideals. The
times were ripe and human hearts hungered for
these new lands that could reveal and realize the
possibilities of the last great hopes of humanity.

Years passed, and the New World was peopled
by brave pioneers, lovers of liberty and fugitives
from the injustice and oppression of ages. Where
once the red man had roamed the forests, settlements grew into cities. Then came revolt by
these picked men from all climes against the
King's government; for that government enacted
laws without extending to the Colonies the equal
privileges of representation that freemen demand.
There followed eight long faith-trying years.
Amid a chaos of confusion and strife there stood
up a calm, poised, self-contained man, appointed
of God to establish liberty under the law, leading
his people into the light. His mother-country
counted him a rebel; his fellow-citizens were often
unjust, envious, petty. Discord and dismay
assailed him. He was maligned, defamed, de-

nounced.  Despite all, amidst jealousies and
dissensions of which history has left faint record
for very shame, thirteen Colonies were welded
into a nation destined to be the first and freest
of republics.   But for the character of Washington, who was too great to wear a crown, this
Republic would never have existed.  Against his
massive nobility of manhood the angry storms
of partisan passion beat in vain, leaving him
unmoved, unscarred.  Firm, far-seeing, wise, he
brought forth on this continent a new nation
"dedicated to the proposition that all men are
created equal,"—the Constitutional Nationality
of our United States.

Other years passed, and troublous times came
again—strife of brother against brother, of State
against State—and the work of Washington
seemed about to be undone and the hope of
humanity defeated.  Dark clouds filled the sky,
bursting at last into a storm of bitter hate and
bloody war.  Then, when the hour of need had
struck, from the valley of the Father of Waters
there came a tall, homely, gentle, strong man,
heroic and sad, who took the helm of state in a
time of revolution and guided it through blood
and fire and tears.  Who, by human foresight,

would have chosen such a man to lead the nation out of chaos into orderly liberty and progress? Those who knew him in the quiet life he had lived, or socially as an apt teller of stories, or professionally as a lawyer in country courts, or even politically as a debater, were amazed, almost dismayed, to see the nation placing upon him a task "greater than that which rested upon the shoulders of Washington." They little realized then Who had commissioned him to "go forward with His people," and Who had prepared and would sustain him in that wild and fateful hour, and with him hold the "common people who heard him gladly."

There were occasions when he was, seemingly, all things to all men and drifted with the currents among widely dissimilar classes of people; at such times his life appeared to be almost submerged by the local and circumstantial; yet, with all, through all, more than all others of his time, he arose equal to every opportunity. Taking the reins of power from the trembling hand of a man skilled in all the arts of diplomacy, to which he himself was a stranger, he measured up to his task. When the commander of the army advised that he should say to the seceding States, "Wayward Sisters, go in peace," and a great journalist joined with the

Senator who had proclaimed an "irrepressible conflict" in the cry of "peace at any price," affirming
that a "Union to be fought for was not worth
saving," this quiet, far-seeing man, untrained in
statecraft and with a Quaker's hatred of war, said
to those who would rend the Union: "We will not
go out, *and you shall not!*" Through long years
of battle his endurance, his fertility of resources,
his magnanimity, his patience, were sorely tried,
and never found wanting. Never rash, never vindictive, keeping a kind heart toward friend and
foe, he became more firm under each successive
disaster, whether in legislative halls or in a military
campaign. Standing on the battle-field of Gettysburg, to dedicate a portion of the ground as the
last resting place of those who had fallen there,
his words were few—so few that men were then
disappointed that he said so little—but his words
have become a national Psalm and part of the
sacred writings of this Republic, never to be erased
while men love liberty.

Fourscore and seven years ago our fathers brought
forth upon this continent a new nation, conceived in
liberty and dedicated to the proposition that all men
are created equal.

Now we are engaged in a great civil war, testing
whether that nation, or any nation so conceived and

so dedicated, can long endure. We are met on a great battle-field of that war. We have come to dedicate a portion of that field as a final resting place for those who here gave their lives that that nation might live. It is altogether fitting and proper that we should do this.

But in a larger sense we cannot dedicate, we cannot consecrate, we cannot hallow this ground. The brave men, living and dead, who struggled here, have consecrated it far above our power to add or detract. The world will little note nor long remember what we say here, but it can never forget what they did here.

It is for us, the living, rather, to be dedicated here to the unfinished work which they who fought here have thus far so nobly advanced. It is rather for us to be here dedicated to the great task remaining before us; that from these honoured dead we take increased devotion to that cause for which they gave the last full measure of devotion; that we here highly resolve that these dead shall not have died in vain; that this nation, under God, shall have a new birth of freedom; and that government of the people, by the people, and for the people, shall not perish from the earth.

Looking back across a century of American history, no other personality towers so high in the admiration of mankind, or casts so benign a light upon the character and destiny of our Republic, as that of Abraham Lincoln. He was indeed the

First American.  Greater than was comprehended by those who walked with him, while yet he wrote and wrought for all humanity, he stands today, a century after his birth, the most unique and unforgetable figure in our history and one of the mighty spirits of the race.  He rendered not only unto Cæsar the things that were Cæsar's, to the States the things that were the States'; but he stood above those of his time in waiting patiently, serenely, inflexibly to lead his countrymen to render to God the things His justice required in national life.

Such a man the time and the task demanded, and such a man God in His providence gave to his country and his race.  He was equal to every opportunity, he accomplished his mission, and of his fame there will be no end. [7]

Pass on, thou hast overcome!

Your sorrows, O people, are his peace! Your bells and bands and muffled drums sound triumph in his ear.

Pass on, thou victor!

Four years ago, O Illinois, we took from you an untried man,—and from the people; we return him to you a mighty conqueror. Not thine any more, but the nation's; not ours, but the world's.

Give him place, ye prairies!

Ye winds that move over the mighty places of the West, chant his requiem! Ye people, behold a martyr whose blood, as so many articulate words, pleads for fidelity, for law, for liberty!

HENRY WARD BEECHER.

# INDEX

## A

## B

Ellsworth, Colonel, 370
Emerson's, Ralph Waldo, tribute to Lincoln, 16
Engle, William, 10
English, 39; becoming settler, 39; neighbour tells speculator's plans, 40; land shark, 41; stirrups for shorter legs, 42
*Enterprise, The Springfield,* a cruel aid, 237

**F**

Farewell address, 223
Father of Waters, valley of, 395
Fillmore, Millard, and young voter, 27–29; "Good Man" in canvass, 28; President, 181
First American, 350, 354, 387, 391, 399
First settlers of Salem, 62
First Sunday-school, 78
Fleury, Mrs. Anna M., 88
Francis, Simeon, editor of *State Journal,* 182
Francis, Mrs. Simeon, 169; invited Lincoln to meet Miss Todd, 169
Frémont campaign of 1856, 27; campaign banner of, 207

**G**

Geniality, 134
Gettysburg speech, 397, 398
Gilder, Richard Watson, 352
"God's side," 30
Goodell, Mr., famous anti-slavery man, 260
Graham, Menter, Lincoln's tutor, 65; text-books from Cooperstown, 65; "Hardshell Baptist," 78; introduced to Calhoun, 101; letter to B. F. Irwin, 305–307
Grant, U. S., 360

Greeley, Horace, 249, 250
Greene, Bowling, farmhouse, 49; location, 49; association with Lincoln, 49; entry of farm tracts in 1829 and 1831, 49; Mrs. Greene's spread, 52; Lincoln at funeral, 53–55; granddaughter, 53; illness and death, 53; Justice of Peace, 53; Masonic fraternity, 53; first Mason to die, 53; chaplain, tyler regalia, 53; account given by Greene and Menter Graham, 54; graves of family, 56, 57; Lincoln's rest cure, 82; memories of, 82, 83, 88
Greene, Graham, Hill, Short, and Godbey families, 88

**H**

Harnett, Jonathan, statement of, 310, 311
Harper, James, 270; gives dinner party, 274; senior member of firm, 274
Hay, John, Lincoln's secretary, 247
Height, of Lincoln—of Judge Douglas, 360, 375
Helm, Mrs. Emily Todd, statement of, 167, 168; quoted, 186, 187; paragraphs by, 197, 199
Herndon's stables, 42
Herndon, Wm. H., contrasting with Lincoln, vii.; daughter of, 88; publications of joint authorship, 89; office life of Lincoln and Herndon, 89; temperament, 89; use of morphine, views, theories, etc., 90; letter to, from Henry B. Rankin, 91–95; law partner, 111–153; characteristics contrasted, 111, 141; first met, 112; education, 113; at Illinois College, 113–117; anti-slavery speech, 115; breach with father, 117;

# Lincoln and Episodes of the Civil War

## *By* William E. Doster

### Late Brev. Brig.-General U. S. V., Provost-Marshal of Washington

*12°. $1.50*

The book occupies a distinctive place in the bibliography of Civil War Literature for, though the events of the author's distinguished career are traced with the help of a diary which he had kept, an important part of the volume is devoted to an account of the trials, experience, and observations of the Provost-Marshal of Washington, an office which the author filled during 1862–3. The author likewise had the distinction of being one of the lawyers for the defense in the famous conspiracy trials of 1865, an account which, written with knowledge from the inside, closes the book. Many matters are considered that have been neglected in other records of the Civil War. The initial chapter of the volume consists of an address which the author delivered some years ago before Lehigh University.

---

New York   **G. P. Putnam's Sons**   London

# The Everyday Life of Abraham Lincoln

### By

## Francis F. Browne

**Late editor of *The Dial***
**Compiler of " Bugle Echoes," " Golden poems," etc.**

*12°. With Portraits. $1.75*

The original edition of this book was published about twenty years after Lincoln's death, and has continued to attract attention among the growing circle of Lincoln's admirers.

This book brings Lincoln the man, not Lincoln the tradition, very near to us. It embodies the reminiscences of over five hundred contemporaries and friends of Lincoln—reminiscences which were gathered largely at first hand.

## G. P. Putnam's Sons

New York                              London

# Abraham Lincoln

## The People's Leader in the Struggle for National Existence

### By

## George Haven Putnam, Litt.D.,

### Late Brevet-Major, 176th Regt. N. Y. S. Vols.

*12°. $1.25*

The monograph presents a study of the development of Lincoln's character and of the growth of his powers from boyhood to his work at the Bar, of his work as a leader in the political contests that preceded the war for the Union, and of his final service to the country as War President and as Commander-in-Chief of its forces. Special attention is given to Lincoln's relations with his Cabinet and with the successive Army commanders. The volume includes a reprint of the famous speech given by Lincoln at the Cooper Institute in February, 1860, to the text of which speech have been added an introduction by Charles C. Nott, late Chief Justice of the Court of Claims, and a series of invaluable historic annotations by Judge Nott and by Cephas Brainerd of the New York Bar. This speech is now recognized as constituting one of the historic documents of the Republic.

*New York*  **G. P. Putnam's Sons**  *London*

*A Selection from the*
*Catalogue of*

# G. P. PUTNAM'S SONS

❦

**Complete Catalogues sent
on application**